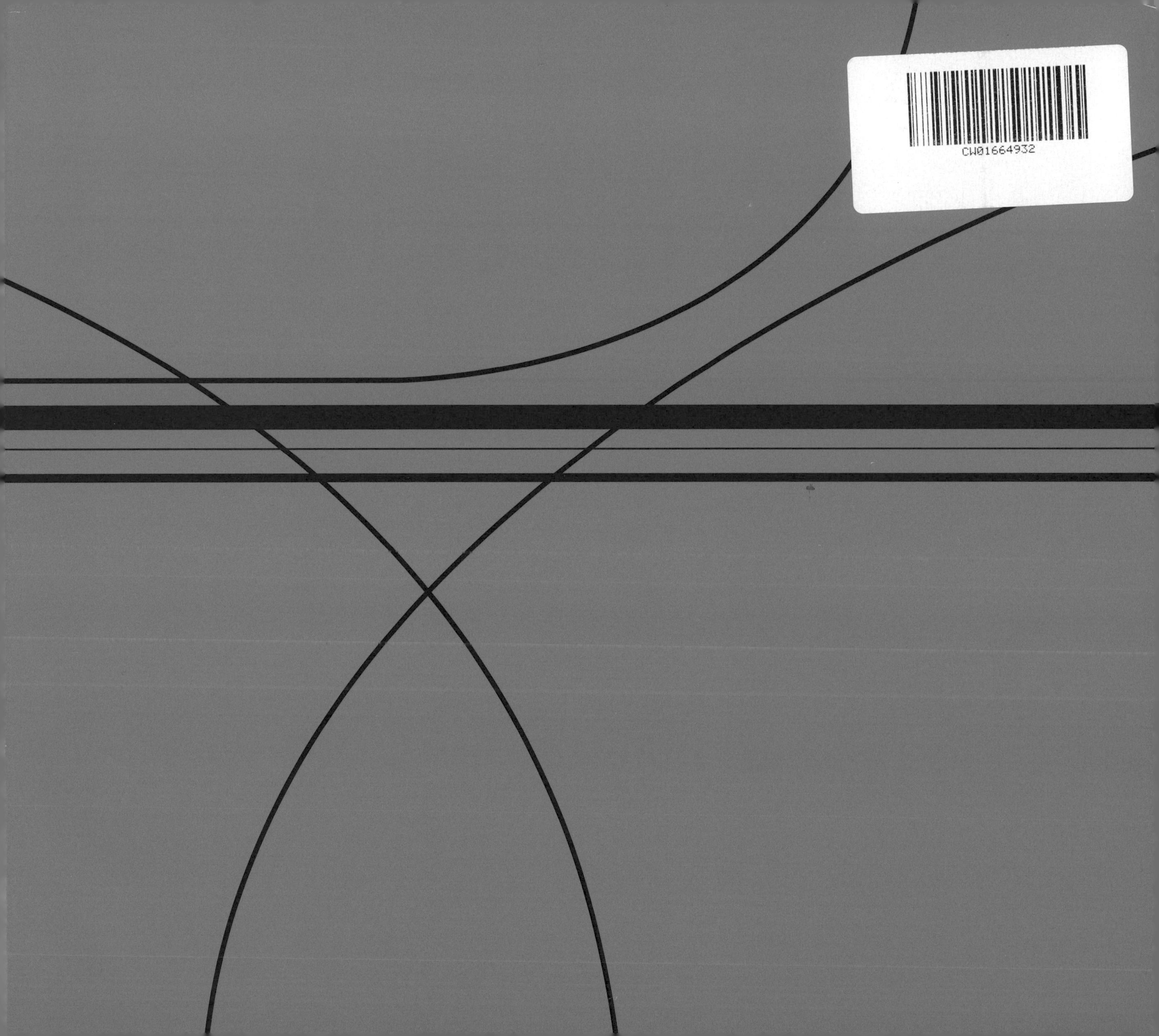

THE RIGHT LINE

SEGRAVE FOULKES

THE RIGHT LINE

THE POLITICS, THE PLANNING AND THE AGAINST-THE-ODDS GAMBLE BEHIND BRITAIN'S FIRST HIGH-SPEED RAILWAY

NICHOLAS FAITH

WITH A FOREWORD BY PROFESSOR SIR PETER HALL

The Right Line
The politics, the planning and the against-the-odds gamble behind Britain's first high-speed railway

Published in 2007 by Segrave Foulkes Publishers
8 King's Road, Kingston KT2 5HR, UK
segrave.foulkes@btopenworld.com

Designed by Lizzie Ballantyne

Set in Berkeley Old Style and Officina Sans
Printed in England by Beacon Press
using pureprint® environmental print technology which minimises the impact on the environment. All electricity comes from renewable sources; inks throughout are vegetable oil-based; 90% of dry waste and 95% of cleaning solvent associated with this product has been recycled. The paper is made at an ISO14001 and EMAS accredited paper mill.
Beacon Press is a carbon-neutral business; it runs an ISO14001 and EMAS accredited environmental management system. It has won the Queens Award for Enterprise: Sustainable Development.

ISBN 978-1-898618-03-4

ACKNOWLEDGEMENTS

I am indebted to Arup for suggesting that I should investigate and write this extraordinary story. My special thanks to Mark Bostock and Terry Hill, the chairman, for facilitating this.

This book could never have taken shape without Chris Foulkes and Carrie Segrave, who not only edited and produced it in fine form but also did a great deal of the research, not only in the depths of electronic Hansard but in other less likely sources, and added immeasurably to the book's content as well as its form. Lizzie Ballantyne came up with the imaginative solution to the problems posed by the book's design, while Jonothan Carver lavished his talents on providing the many maps which form a key element in the book's contents.

I'm also grateful to the following witnesses (and to those who preferred to remain anonymous), many of whom not only agreed to be interviewed but in many cases also submitted with considerable patience to a deluge of further e-mails and telephone calls: Lord Bruce-Lockhart, Lord Heseltine, Lord Howe of Aberavon, Lord Marsh, Lord Turnbull, Right Hon John Prescott, Right Hon Sir Malcolm Rifkind, Right Hon Stephen Timms, Professor Sir Peter Hall, Mike Ash, John Couch, Alastair Dick, Alan Dyke, Bernard Gambrill, Sam Higginson, Steven Hoier, Gill Howarth, Andrew Lee, Malcolm Noyce, the late Mike Odling, John Palmer, Julia Prescott, Caroline Simpson, Malcolm Southgate, Colin Stannard, Theo Steel, Maureen Tomison, Nick Wakefield, John Welsby, Pam Williams.

And from Arup, Sir Philip Dowson, Sir Duncan Michael, Sir Jack Zunz, Nick Banks, Julian Dawson, Richard Foster, Ian Gardner, Daniel Imade, Paul Johnson, Jørgen Nissen, Pauline Shirley, Michael Somers.

Nicholas Faith
London, September 2007

CONTENTS

FOREWORD

This, by any standards, is an extraordinary tale: a story of a grand engineering project in a country that distrusts grand projects, conceived by a tiny group of mavericks inside an extraordinary company that had become successful by breaking all known rules, fighting virtually the whole of the nation's political and bureaucratic and professional establishment with apparently negligible chance of success – and, against impossible odds, winning. On 6 November 2007, as the Queen opens the Channel Tunnel Rail Link, this small band will celebrate a moment of euphoria known to very few in a lifetime. And, if there is justice in the world, a moment of recognition of their extraordinary achievement.

The Right Line is a story of much more than that: a story of endless vacillation on the part of politicians, of desperation and chronic short-sightedness on the part of established professional cadres, of conflicting political and bureaucratic agendas, miraculously and quite suddenly ended in 1990 by Michael Heseltine's return to his old job as Secretary of State for the Environment. Critical, as background, is Britain in the 1980s: a country dominated by the Thatcherite agenda of dismantling the great nationalised behemoths created by a radical Labour government under Clement Attlee forty years earlier. Already, as the tale begins to unfold, the telephone system and the gas and electricity industries had been privatised. Now it was the turn of rail. But by that point Thatcher's ministers had already decided that it had been a mistake to replace public monopolies by private ones. They wanted to break up British Rail – they knew not how. At the same time, Thatcher and François Mitterrand signed the historic Treaty of Canterbury to build a fixed link across the Channel – but, at Thatcher's insistence, no public money must be used to build it or any associated works.

This left British Rail with an almost impossible dilemma. This part of their rail system, between the Channel Tunnel and London, was perhaps the worst in their whole network. Built on the cheap by Victorian entrepreneurs, it was barely capable of doing its main job of ferrying commuters to work and back. As it approached central London, it was effectively already full up. As an interim solution, they found a lesser-used line across Kent, formerly used by boat trains until flying had killed them off. The straightest piece of railway in Britain, eighteen miles from Ashford to Tonbridge, it could be electrified to take the load for a few years. But beyond that, a solution had to be found.

The Right Line demonstrates how the British Rail establishment, faced with this problem, proceeded systematically to find the worst possible answer. Their engineers, wedded to the idea of following motorways and then existing rail lines into London, devised a route that threatened 5,000 homes with severe impacts from construction and long-term noise blight. They thus achieved the unlikely outcome of maximising possible opposition, both across rural Kent and in the South-East London suburbs. This took the form of countless local protest movements. But in Kent, by happy accident, was a county council with a strong political mission to create a highly effective professional service. And, almost inevitably, this led officials and politicians to focus on practicable alternatives.

None of this might have turned the tide in itself, if it had not been for Arup. Much of this book is about the extraordinary ethos of this company, bequeathed to it by its Danish founder, Ove Arup, who ironically died in 1988 just as the saga is reaching its climax. It was an unusual combination of Victorian miserliness – Arup became notorious for presenting their clients with monthly bills and paying Scrooge-like salaries – and a strong sense of partnership, which demanded that profits be ploughed back into the business. But more than this: because the founder was obsessed with ideas and chronically uninterested in management, employees had extraordinary freedom to do what they liked, developing lateral-thinking solutions to problems that would never occur in a conventionally-run company. Indeed, the firm's rise to international fame rested in large measure on their success in finding an engineering solution to building the architect Jørn Utzon's brilliant but poorly-conceived Sydney Opera House, which almost anyone else would have abandoned as Mission Impossible.

It was precisely this freedom that was exploited by a tiny group inside the company, which developed an alternative route for the new rail line, diverting from the BR route in mid-Kent and swinging sharply north-west through the North Downs and across the huge chalk pits of Kent Thamesside, before plunging under the Thames to run through East London. Broadly equivalent in cost to the British Rail line, it had two unique advantages: it demolished no houses, impacted a mere 200, and could potentially bring huge regeneration benefits to the blighted areas through which it would run.

Despite the support both of the embattled groups in Kent and South-East London, and more from the Borough of Newham, foreseeing huge benefits from regeneration around a station at Stratford, the Arup line might still not have won the day. For it faced massive opposition from entrenched interests in BR and the Department of Transport. What finally swung the decision was a classic example of Harold Macmillan's famous political dictum, events, dear boy, events. Thatcher was forced out and Michael Heseltine, who made his pre-emptive bid to take over from her, was beaten by John Major. Major, seeking to defuse what he saw as a smoking bomb left by Thatcher, the Poll Tax, appointed his rival to his old job at the DoE, where a decade earlier he had achieved such notable success with the regeneration of London Docklands. Arriving back with the famous greeting to his civil servants, 'it would be idle to pretend that this was the limit of my ambition', he nonetheless flung himself into a project even larger than Docklands: the regeneration of the East Thames Corridor – later Thames Gateway – which he announced to the public in March 1991.

The final chapters, which describe a drama of almost gladiatorial quality fought out over the summer of 1991, highlight Heseltine's personal achievement. Immortally described by Thatcher as 'not one of us', philosophically he was an interventionist on a positively French scale – save that, always, his *grands projets* would require big injections of public money in order to attract even larger sums from the private sector. And this was the master plan he conceived that summer: by backing the Arup line, by paying what it would take to make it happen, he could bring in private capital to carry most of the burden of building the new railway and then, even more importantly, finance the regeneration megaprojects that would follow around its stations. His passion for the grand design, his extraordinary power of advocacy backed by total conviction of the rightness of his cause, his knowledge that he carried unique clout within the ranks of the Tory conferences, brought him victory. At critical junctures, most notably in a June meeting when Arup came to make their case, he was able by sheer moral power and authority to bulldoze the conventional ranks of the opposition. By October, when his victory was announced first to the party conference and then to Parliament, this part of the story was over.

That was not the end of the tale, nor of the accompanying drama. Much more was to come: the realisation of the Arup vision in the London and Continental Railway company, the complex interactions of the engineering and financial interests within it that culminated in the winning bid to build and operate the new line, the massive financial failure and rescue in the early days of John Prescott's stewardship of Heseltine's old department. That part of the tale, where Prescott played a role equivalent to that of his predecessor, is big enough and exciting enough to deserve a volume to itself – which, before long, it will get. Meanwhile, *The Right Line* has sufficient drama for one book – and enough lessons, too, for students of politics and government, not to mention all the ex-students, still learning their trades on the job, who have much to learn from the many mistakes and rare successes of their predecessors.

Professor Sir Peter Hall
London, August 2007

1 2 3 4 5 6 7 8 9 10 11 12

THE VISION THING

Where there is no vision, the people perish

Proverbs, 29:18

Not a scene from a thriller, but a team from the International Olympic Committee en route through the new high-speed rail tunnel that now links St Pancras to Stratford and the site of the 2012 Olympics

In February 2005 a team from the International Olympic Committee came to London to inspect the capital's transport system. The visit was important, for the system's well publicised problems were one of the major question-marks hanging over London's bid to host the 2012 Games. In a masterly stroke of public relations the delegates were whisked in minutes – albeit in Land Rovers, not a train – along the just-completed rail tunnel that now connects St Pancras to Stratford's station, a few hundred yards from the proposed main Olympic site.

This gesture provided a triumphant underscoring of the seriousness of London's bid. In the event, its unexpected victory was largely due to the way that the bid was based on the vision of a regenerated East London, symbolised and demonstrated by the ultra-fast railway link – Britain's first – from London to the Channel Tunnel via Stratford.

The story of the new line, originally dubbed Channel Tunnel Rail Link (CTRL) and now, optimistically, High Speed 1 (HS1) is a most enlightening and entertaining one. This book attempts to explain how this, as opposed to the many projects still lurking in Whitehall's filing cabinets, actually, finally, came to be built in the right place – as well as the reasons why it took over two decades. It recounts how the new line had several false starts, with much money wasted, a great deal of hot air expended and many lives unfairly blighted. It describes how the solution that virtually everyone now hails as obvious only emerged from a group of outsiders. And how it was derided and dismissed by official opinion. It tells how no-one's house was knocked down (though one was moved), in contrast to the hundreds earmarked for demolition in the original, and the two dozen in the final, British Rail schemes. It shows how rather than disturbing the peace of inoffensive suburbanites it instead unlocked the potential of thousands of acres of derelict land.

The idea of an Olympic bid, its location and the many advantages for London's East End – above all as a catalyst for a dramatic step-change in so long-neglected a part of the capital – had first been publicly put forward in detail by Mark Bostock of engineering firm Arup in May 2000. This was over a decade after Arup had first performed the same task, of analysis and promotion, for the concept of a fast rail link to the Channel Tunnel through Stratford. At that time, of course, the line's promoters had no reason to include the Olympics in their calculations.

The saga of the fast link reaches its climax on 14 November 2007 – thirteen years to the day after a train first left Waterloo for Paris – when a Eurostar leaves St Pancras Station for the same destination. This time, though, the journey lasts a mere two and a quarter hours, not three hours as it did in 1994. Trains from that day on travel along the first stretch of main-line railway built in Britain since 1899, when the Great Central reached London's Marylebone Station from Manchester and Queen Victoria was on the throne. A century later, a mere 68 miles (just under 110 km) of track has taken over twenty years since the Channel Tunnel Treaty was signed by Mrs Thatcher and President Mitterrand: a period which has witnessed the reign of no fewer than fourteen Ministers of Transport. By contrast, the 22 years after the opening of the Liverpool to Manchester Railway in 1830 saw the construction of all the main routes connecting England's major cities – without benefit of any ministerial involvement.

The length of time now required to devise, finance and at last press 'go' on the new link is not, though, unusual for big schemes – in Britain at least. Terminal 5 at Heathrow, the second-largest such project in recent years (and, like the fast link, proof that major infrastructure can sometimes be delivered in Britain on time and on budget) took 23 years all told, even though it involved far fewer planning and construction problems. But many such plans remain more or less in limbo, without any definite date for the actual construction. Typically, while for a generation Parisians have been travelling on the RER[1] fast lines across their capital, neither one of the London equivalents, Crossrail and Thameslink, have as yet received an unequivocal, cash-on-the-table go-ahead. (At time of writing, Thameslink is further along the process – but it is worth noting that is was originally called 'Thameslink 2000'....)

The fast link was a once-in-a-century opportunity, and it was only fully grasped by a lucky combination of two far-sighted politicians, from different parties and at different times, and a group of imaginative engineers. In this improbable trio were two deputy prime ministers, Michael Heseltine and John Prescott; the third member, Arup, is the engineering consultancy founded in 1946 by the engineer-extraordinaire Ove Arup. Without the involvement of these three at crucial moments, a completed rail line, and in the best place, would never have emerged from a primaeval swamp of official muddle and ideological posturing.

1 RER: Réseau Express Régional.

Both of the politicians were totally untypical of the political and administrative Establishment. And they could not have been more different. Michael Heseltine, more a visionary tycoon than a politician, rescued the project from political and planning paralysis in pursuit of his vision for the regeneration of the 'Thames Gateway': London's long-neglected backyard out along the Thames to the east of the City. For his part John Prescott, probably the last example of the old-fashioned, trades-union, working-class politician, was later to rescue it a second time, from financial disaster, with a well-thought-out refinancing scheme. Prescott understood the transport needs of London and the South-East, and was the only British politician who had thought through the strictly transport advantages of the project. As a result he provided the conceptual underpinning for a sensible partnership between the public and private sectors. Prescott had also supported Arup's proposition when shadow transport secretary of state, as he envisaged the CTRL as the start of his dream for a TGV-style fast rail network in the UK.

As for Arup, its founder had died in 1988 – but he bequeathed his vision of imaginative project engineering, along with an ability to think both big and beyond the obvious, to his successors. Arup isn't really an organisation; more a natural organism that had grown almost by accident since it was created after the Second World War by the eponymous engineer-philosopher. It now employs over 9,000 people across the world, linking hundreds of technical specialists – by no means all connected with engineering – but all of whom share the founder's self-confidence, his vision and his assumption that there was no limit to the ideas, however far-fetched, that he and his colleagues could translate into reality. It was his firm that worked out the way to bring the fast line into London: from the east, benefiting run-down Stratford and North Kent and reprieving the crowded suburbs of South-East London.

Without such diverse but essential talents, the fast rail link would either not have been built at all or would have been constructed later, would have offered an inferior service to the Continent, fewer of the advantages for commuters and above all would have been built on the wrong route, failing to provide any spur to the regeneration of the deprived areas.

But perhaps the single most important strand of the story is the sheer inability of the British governmental machine to arrive at a decision. In other instances, this failure to make up the administrative mind has resulted in bets being expensively hedged: in the 1950s this country financed three types of V-bombers to deliver atomic bombs, and three different types of nuclear reactor – the third added by the ministry involved almost as an insurance policy. This ingrained indecision seems to be based on a very British dislike of the '*führerprinzip*'. Worse, the deep-rooted reluctance to reach a conclusion leads to an over-reliance on hordes of consultants (in the case of the CTRL, I gave up counting after I reached fifty) in order to forestall any criticism. The 'decision-makers' reached for consultants in much the same way as an alcoholic reaches for the whisky bottle.

LONDON, STRATFORD, THE THAMES GATEWAY AND HS1

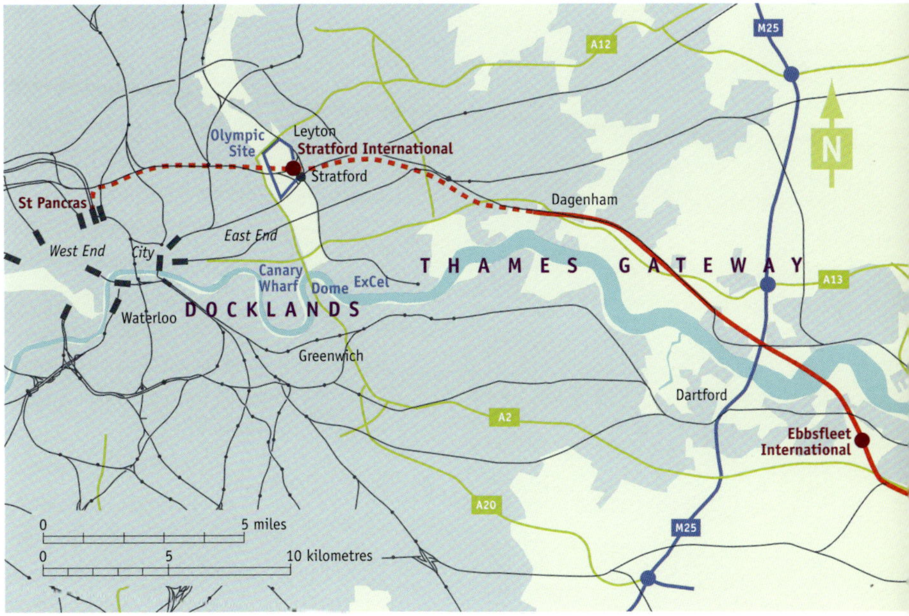

The HS1 high speed line (red) showing its relationship to Central London, Docklands, Stratford, the Thames Gateway zone and the 2012 Olympic site

Facing page: London's Olympic site, in the lower Lea Valley around Stratford's new international station, lies within sight of the towers of the City of London – and even, just visible, the London Eye

Overarching any such project there is the English mindset, which has led to a planning system in which everyone is consulted – giving the impression of a nation of Groucho Marxes singing, as he did, 'whatever it is I'm against it'. It can take eight years to plan a road which will be built in a mere two. The objectors, naturally dubbed NIMBYs ('Not In My Back Yard'), have a noble ancestry: the first was none other than William Wordsworth, aghast at the intrusion of railways into his precious Lake District.[2]

The easiest target for blame is that Rolls-Royce of a bureaucracy, Britain's Civil Service. Its critics claim that it prefers the car to possess only two gears, neutral and reverse. But its defenders can point to the behaviour of the Department of the Environment when Michael Heseltine was at its helm as proof that the Rollers are only too happy to follow any minister – and there are precious few of them – who know their own mind and who possess definite, and realistic, ideas that they want implemented. The major rebuke that one can make to the civil servants is that their vision is necessarily confined to their own baronies, whose interests they, and their political masters, naturally defend against any interference from (or collaboration with) rival

2 It may not have been his finest, but his sonnet on the matter was certainly heartfelt: see Chapter 5.

departments. Such defensiveness is naturally fiercest in a department, like that of Transport, low down the Whitehall pecking order, and results in an inability to 'think outside the box' of its own remit. Arup, partly through an inherent confidence, seems to have been the only institutional player in the story – other than, surprisingly, Kent County Council – capable of 'joined-up thinking'. It thus filled a gap in the machinery of government, which did not possess (and still doesn't) a strategic framework for roads and railways that combines broader social and environmental elements with narrow transport views.

The Channel Tunnel Rail Link's protagonists were also faced by Margaret Thatcher's refusal to spend public money on it, having already left the construction of the Tunnel itself purely to the private sector. The problem was exacerbated by an ever-increasing, and increasingly unrealistic, list of requirements tacked on to the original scheme – most bizarrely, night trains to the Continent.

The most obvious contrast is with the French, naturally proud of *grands projets* like their LGVs (Lignes de Grande Vitesse). Of course this has a lot to do with the passionate interest – and pride – in their advanced railway system shown by that nation, and indeed most other European countries, all of which have regularly invested far larger sums in their rail networks over the past fifty years than has the UK. This forms an unhappy contrast to the grudging British attitude to railways in general, and the late lamented British Railways (BR) in particular. The difference was summed up by the *Financial Times*: it pointed out that in the UK provision for public transport has traditionally been regarded as a drain on public funds, whereas in Continental Europe it is regarded as part of the infrastructure of civilised life.

But in the end, perhaps the best explanation behind the seeming inability to act of the British people (and not just the media or the Establishment, who merely reflect their character) is a national lack of decisiveness, so well expressed in a comment on his British contemporaries by the South African-born poet Roy Campbell:

> *You praise the firm restraint with which they write,*
> *I'm with you there, of course:*
> *They use the snaffle and the curb all right,*
> *But where's the bloody horse?*

Campbell wrote these lines in 1939; nothing much seems to have changed since then.

CONTINENT STILL CUT OFF

newspaper placard from between the wars: it began: 'Fog in Channel...'

Almighty God in his wisdom, a few millennia earlier, had laid down a chalk strip from Folkestone to Calais, which was the ideal substance in which to bore a tunnel under the Channel.

Lord Marsh, *Off The Rails*

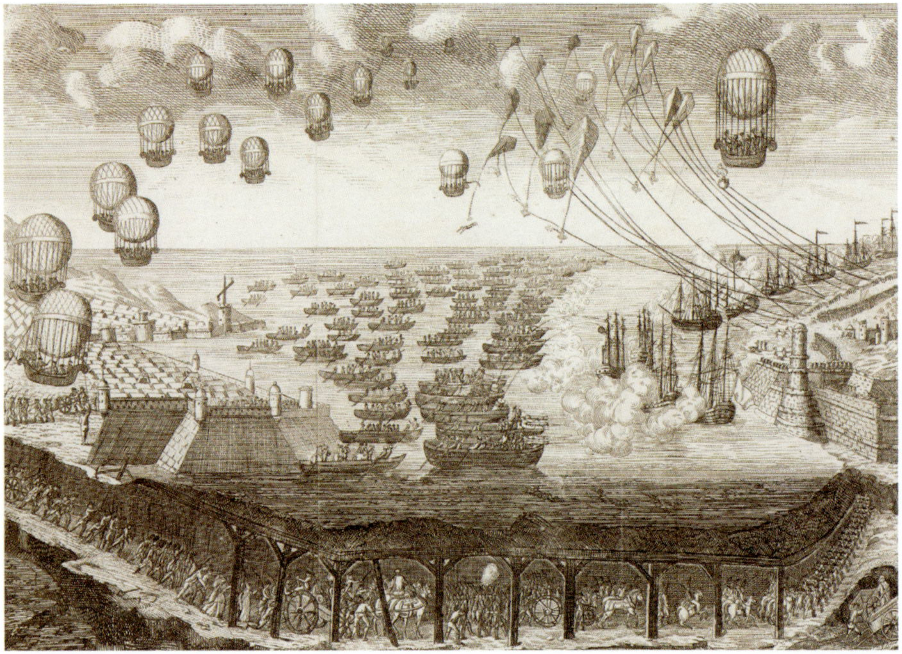

A fanciful depiction of Napoleon's plans for the invasion of England which included a Channel tunnel

■ At some point between 8000 and 7000 BC the Atlantic Ocean and the North Sea broke through the 'land bridge' which had until then linked Britain to the Continent of Europe, thus creating the English Channel. No-one made any serious attempt to join the two sides together again for the following eight millennia, until in 1803 a French engineer proposed a tunnel – to be an immersed cast-iron tube – that would help Napoleon with his planned invasion of Britain. One hundred and seventy years (and a steady stream of more, or less, serious schemes) later, the French and British parliaments finally passed the legislation allowing consortia to start tunnelling.

In the meantime, comprehensive railway networks were constructed in both countries, together with ever-faster steamships; and these had dramatically reduced the travel time between the two capitals. Already by 1852 it took a mere twelve hours – down from four days (or a matter of weeks, if the winds were contrary) in Napoleon's time, to make the journey. And 350,000 people each year – most of them English – were doing so.

Passengers for the new steam packets, which had begun in 1818, could travel by train (from 1843) from London to Dover or Folkestone. From the 1860s they had a choice of rail routes, built and run by competing companies from different London termini – and, in the case of the London, Chatham & Dover, several different routes into the capital as well. This legacy of tangled rail lines was to blight later efforts to introduce speedy, efficient services. But once at the coast travellers had to consign themselves to an 'uncertain, dilatory, expensive and health-disturbing sea voyage', to quote *Railway Times* in 1873. To the newly-punctual Victorians, by now accustomed to trains which ran to timetables, ships and sailors were annoyingly imprecise. Steamers often had to wait for the tide before entering harbour, and some captains would not sail at all – timetable or no timetable – if they did not have a shipful of passengers.

Channel tunnels were endlessly promoted, in more or less practicable guises, throughout the 19th century. The first person to envisage a special railway link (in his case, from Manchester via London, through a Channel tunnel, then on to Paris) was a visionary Victorian entrepreneur, Sir Edward Watkin. Watkin was the man responsible for the Great Central, the last major railway line built in Britain, which reached London in 1899. A man described as 'imperious, incredibly energetic and dogged with restless ambition', Watkin had his finger in innumerable railway pies.

Such was the fragmented state of Britain's railways that his route from Manchester to the coast involved eleven separate companies – including the Metropolitan Railway, which enabled trains to pass directly through London on their way to the Channel. Sadly, his dream of a tunnel soon faded: Watkin fell foul of the Crown Estate, which owns the foreshore along Britain's coasts, when he started digging a trial shaft at Folkestone without first obtaining permission – though not before he had uncovered an unexpected seam of coal, thick enough to remain profitable for over half a century.

Sir Edward Watkin, the imperious Victorian railway entrepreneur who planned not just a tunnel but a rail link as well

By the early 20th century new tunnelling machines and, above all, the development of electric traction for trains – the only practicable form of power for so long an underground railway – had made the idea of a tunnel a truly rational proposition. In 1906 the American businessman and statesman, William G McAdoo, declared that 'the time has come … when groundless prejudice must disappear and this important project, demanded by civilisation, become a reality. The Channel tunnels are of interest not to England and France alone, but to the entire civilized world, because they would become an important link in the direct line of the world's most important traffic'.

Yet a number of obstacles, practical, economic, financial and political, prevented the tunnel's construction during the first 85 years of the 20th century. The biggest blockage, however, was fear – mainly from the British side: an unappetising blend of ignorance, arrogance, hysteria and xenophobia only too typical of attitudes throughout the period. As late as 1949 the Foreign Office could declare that a tunnel would undermine 'that unquestioning sense of superiority over the peoples of the Continent which forms an essential element in British self-confidence'.

But the most regular and ferocious objections to the tunnel were 'strategic' (a word I deliberately put into quotation marks), raised by many of Britain's most distinguished military men and collected in an official Blue Book, 386 pages in length and published in 1882. It was such pressure from the military that halted the one serious attempt at a

CROSSING THE CHANNEL: SAIL TO STEAM

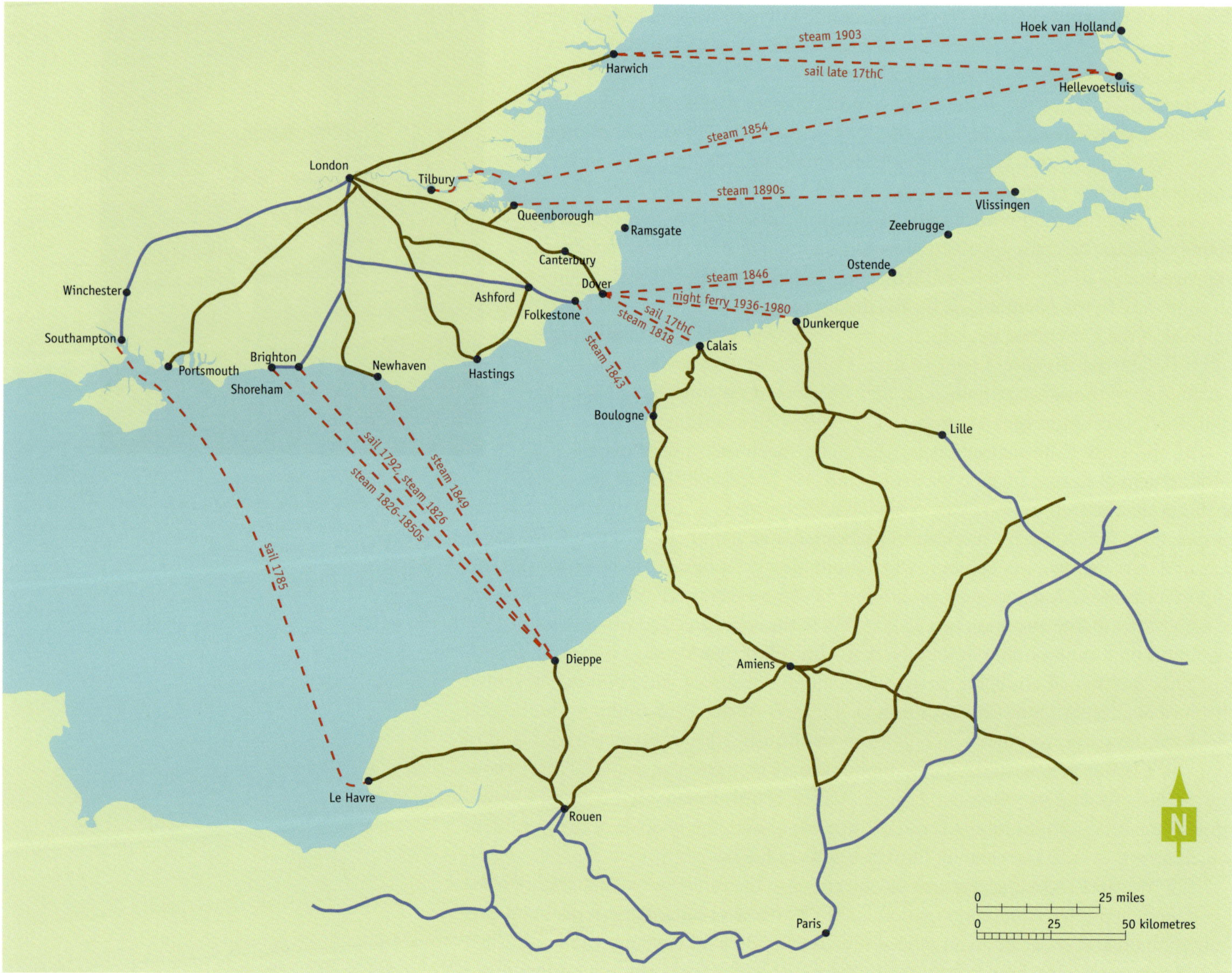

— Railways open 1843 — Railways open 1861

tunnel, which got well over a mile (2km) across – from both ends – in the early 1880s. This was despite an assurance by its promoters that a plug could be fixed halfway along, with a soldier kept permanently on guard to pull it if the perfidious French tried anything....

The panic was reignited in the late 1890s by Field Marshal Sir Garnet Wolseley, then Commander-in-Chief of the British army, who believed that foreign forces would use a tunnel to invade the 'sceptr'd isle'. This fear was shown to be nonsensical when the German General Von Moltke turned the argument on its head: if a tunnel were built, he said, it would enable the British to transport troops and materials to France and would 'prove fatal to Germany in the case of a conflict'. This opinion was shared by Marshal Foch, who believed that 'if the tunnel had been built, the carnage [of World War I] would have been over in half the time'.

Even in Britain there were a few saner voices. Before 1914 the pioneer Socialist MP Keir Hardie dismissed the military opposition as 'neurotic foolishness'; in 1919 David Lloyd George, the then Prime Minister, tried to reignite interest in a tunnel at the Paris Peace Conference; between the wars Winston Churchill ridiculed the diehards, pointing out that the Admiralty had variously rejected the use of steam power, derided the propeller and discounted the submarine! Indeed the fears, all absurd, melted away immediately the tunnel actually opened.

All the time the journey between London and Paris was speeding up. By 1891 it was down to seven and a half hours; by 1914 it took seven hours, and by the 1930s the glamorous Golden Arrow/Flèche d'Or service had refined that down to just over six and half – a timing which by then had to compete with the early air services flying from Croydon to Le Bourget.[1]

From 1936 you could even travel in undisturbed comfort on a night-train ferry from London to Paris and Brussels: the coaches were loaded on board ship, allowing

The British section of the Golden Arrow Boat Train route was hauled by steam until 1961

Facing page: until 1818, when the first steamship appeared on the Dover–Calais route, travellers from Britain to the Continent had to rely on sailing ships. In England the railways speeded journeys from 1843 onwards, but the French lines did not reach the coast until 1848.

1 The Golden Arrow's London-Dover time in the 1930s was 90 minutes.

Victoria Station, the terminus of the Night Ferry to Paris and Brussels. The airline advertisement visible in the background hints at its fate.

passengers to leave Victoria at 10 p.m. and arrive after a night's sleep before 9 a.m. at Paris's Gare du Nord. When it was abandoned, as late as 1980, night-time travellers were left almost stranded.[2] But, in an ominous development for the railways, 1936 also saw the launch of the *Autocarrier*, the first car-carrying ferry.

By the 1950s, Harold Macmillan had admitted that there were no legitimate military objections to a tunnel; then finally, in 1966, Prime Ministers Harold Wilson and Georges Pompidou announced a definite decision that a tunnel would be built – a decision which, in a sense, formed part of the European dream that brought Britain into the Common Market in 1973 (as well as a serious gesture to the French, who had banned our entry ten years earlier). Moreover the commercial outlook was promising, for the number of travellers between London and Paris had shown a steady increase, from a million a year in 1960 to two and a half million by 1978.

Once negotiations started, a marked contrast emerged between the attitudes of British Rail and France's national railway system, SNCF.[3] In Britain Dr Michael Bonavia, the BR official responsible, described himself as merely 'a channel of communication and coordinator of departmental views'; in France, the Tunnel project was directly coordinated

2 As one MP, Nigel Spearing, put it in a debate in 1990: 'Had I travelled overnight to or from Brussels fifty-five years ago, I should have had a much better deal, as I did a few years ago when I could go to Victoria station on foot, climb aboard a sleeper and wake somewhere past Lille. Alas, the Night Ferry has disappeared and its substitute is poor. The overnight train advertised as travelling to places such as Cologne and Brussels stops at every station between Bromley and Faversham. Returning this morning, we had a two-hour wait at Dover and joined the first commuter train at 4.45 from Dover Priory, which was naturally liable to be overcrowded as it neared Victoria. That is the standard to which British Rail treats us'.

3 *Société Nationale des Chemins de Fer.*

by the deputy director-general of the SNCF. Writing in 1987 Bonavia lamented 'the delays and indecision on the part of both ministers and civil servants.... Years were wasted and, naturally, every year the estimated cost increased. Had the tunnel been built between, say, 1964 and 1970, the first cost, and hence the interest charges, would have been much lower'.[4]

Also apparent early on was the Treasury's obsession with cutting costs – in the mid-1960s they even proposed that Direct Current electric traction should be used, to remove the need for the taller (and thus more expensive) tunnel required for the overhead wires of the far more efficient Alternating Current. During the early 1970s the Treasury insisted above all that the new line should pass commercial tests – that there should be no question of subsidising it. The project was also viewed in a vacuum, entirely separately from environmental costs and development benefits – a theme that was to reverberate throughout the whole story.

The Treasury's opposition was only one of the factors that were to bedevil the project for the rest of the century. These first became apparent in the early 1970s, in a series of events which amounted to a dress-rehearsal for later difficulties – a rehearsal which stopped only when the project was abandoned by the Labour government in January 1975. To make matters worse, some of BR's chairmen had wavered in their support for the project; but fortunately in 1971 a new one was appointed. Richard (now Lord) Marsh was the son and grandson of railwaymen and had been Labour's Minister of Transport in the 1960s. He was a firm champion of the Channel Tunnel – but he underestimated the internal opposition, notably of BR's profitable shipping division (which ran the Channel ferries), and the suspicion of the managers of the Southern Region, on whose already-overcrowded lines the trains from the Tunnel would run.

They had a point. The railways through Kent and into London from the south-east showed the British rail system at its worst. Its tangled history, the inheritance of the dreams of a group of dubious Victorian entrepreneurs, had left the legacy of a complex, twisty, constricted-gauged network, memorably described by Alastair Morton[5] as a 'congealing mess'.[6]

Moreover any attempt to build a new rail route, or even to improve or enlarge the existing ones, was bedevilled by the fact that Kent, pathway for invaders since before Roman times, was naturally full of historical remains from the previous 2,000 years. Even more important was the reaction of its inhabitants. The usual description of Kent as the Garden of England implies, correctly, that it is full of people and their houses,

President Pompidou of France and Prime Minister Edward Heath shake hands over the signing of the first, ill-fated Channel Tunnel Treaty at Chequers in 1973

4 *The Channel Tunnel Story* (David & Charles, 1987).

5 Co-chairman of Eurotunnel, 1987-1996; knighted 1992.

6 The irrationality of the network is exemplified by the lines from the eastern corner of Kent, which terminate at the westernmost platforms at Victoria – itself the westernmost of the London stations serving the South-East.

■ LONDON, KENT & THE THAMES ESTUARY

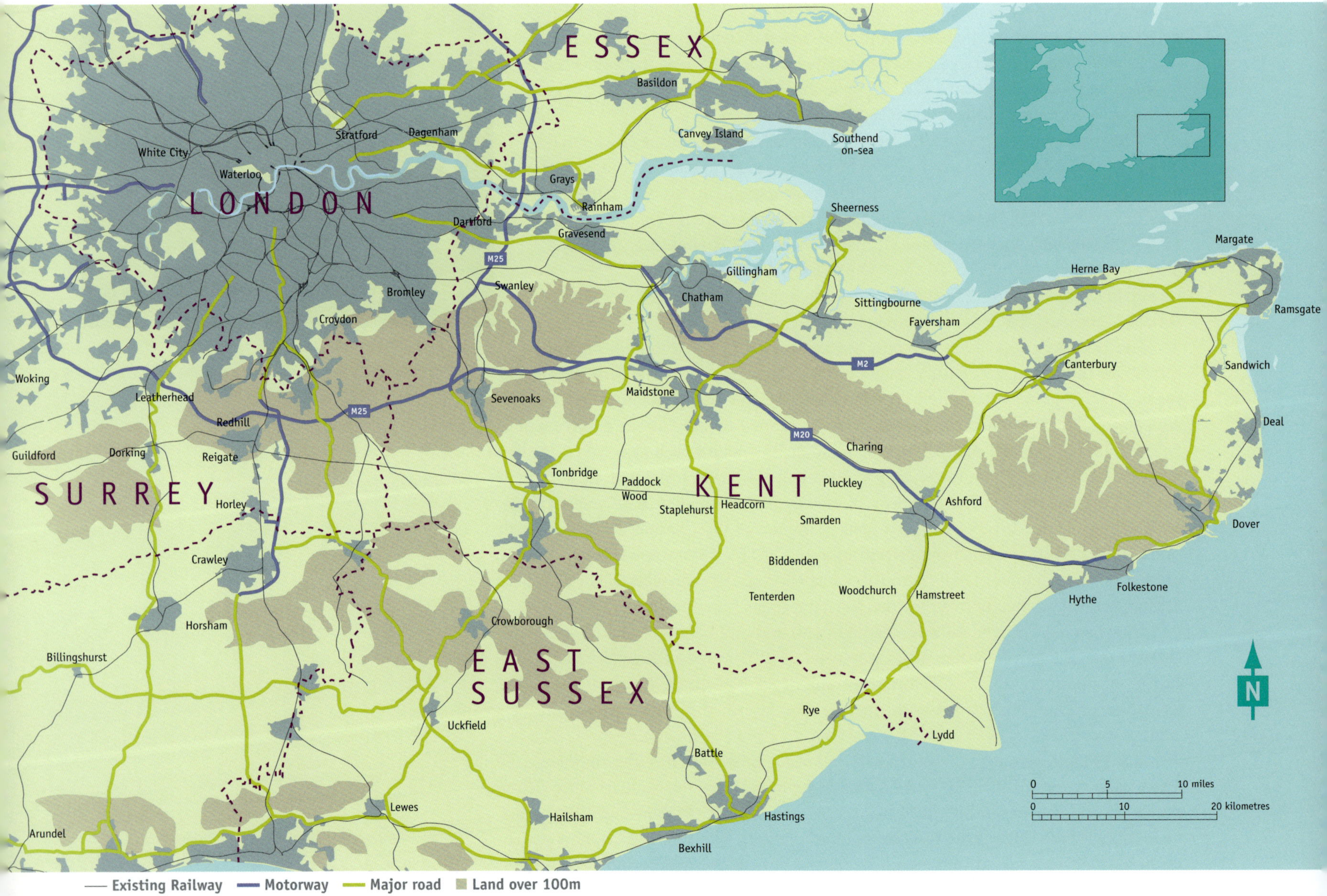

towns and villages – and influential people at that: one BR manager groaned that 'there were more judges in southern Kent than in the whole of the rest of the country'.

Opposition to any rail link was reinforced by the exaggerated traffic estimates being promulgated before the Tunnel opened – one 1970s forecast envisaged up to 170 trains (enormous, noisy trains, the protesters urged) each day. Worse, BR proved unable to cope with an investment of any size and scope; the only new railway they had been allowed to build since 1945 was a twenty-mile stretch to by-pass a newly-dug coal mine at Selby in Yorkshire. Their inadequacy was made much worse by the impossible timetables set by political considerations, by the cack-handed relationship with the public inevitable from such an inward-looking organisation, and by the inability they shared with the whole political establishment to consider wider factors like the environment or urban planning. Not surprisingly BR's management was, and remained, obsessed with their desire to site any new line alongside existing rail tracks: this is what they were used to doing, as with the complex and expensive upgrade of the West Coast Main Line. (If there was any thought that this would lessen conflicts with those affected by the new line, this seems unlikely: more tracks, and thus a much wider rail corridor, would still entail demolition and disruption, especially in urban areas.)

Marsh, and even more his senior managers, were fully aware that BR's investment budget was permanently stretched and everlastingly under threat. At that time, too, the situation in Whitehall was far from ideal. In 1970 a newly-formed Department of the Environment had embraced the Ministry of Transport, and had become rather dysfunctional after the departure of Peter Walker as Secretary of State in 1972. Although John Peyton, the Minister of Transport, was a Tunnel enthusiast, the project was bedevilled by the DoE's inability to consider proposals either promptly or constructively.

David McKenna, director of Southern Region and BR's most enthusiastic proponent of the Tunnel project, pleaded for 'some indication of a more strategic view of tunnel thinking', while Marsh said with characteristic bluntness that the choice lay between a 'bodged job done reluctantly on the cheap and a first-class railway.' To make matters worse, the different methodologies employed by BR and Whitehall ensured that forecasts of passenger traffic varied widely. The need for speed in decision-making – and in the trains themselves – was emphasised by the SNCF's revelation of their plans for what soon became the TGV (Train à Grande Vitesse), designed to travel across France on dedicated lines (LGVs) at speeds of up to 300kph. Britain's best at the time, the West Coast Main Line, reached a mere 125mph (200kph).

THE 'CONGEALING MESS'

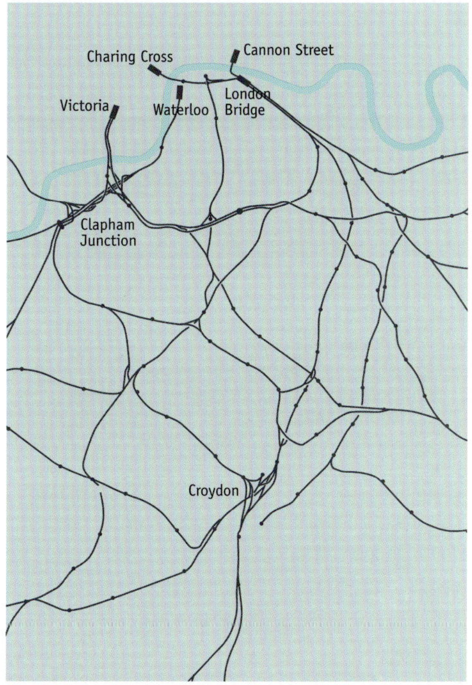

Alastair Morton's description of the South London and Kent rail system was rude but accurate: Victorian entrepeneurs had left a legacy of lines which crossed, merged and duplicated – and which were used at full capacity in rush hours.

Facing page: Between London and the Channel Tunnel lies Kent: close-knit countryside with an intricate web of hills, valleys and villages.

■ LONDON TO PARIS: A TIMELINE

The coasts of France and England are visible from each other, and this has tantalised generations of dreamers and engineers. A brief chronicle of the labyrinthine politicking and start–stop–start story of the Tunnel and the Fast Link begins here, and runs through the chapters to 2007.

1800s

1802

- During brief peace in the Anglo/French wars, mining engineer Albert Mathieu-Favier designs a tunnel from Cap Gris Nez to Folkestone, with an artificial island for ventilation and horse-drawn passenger and freight wagons

1803

- War recommences: Tessier de Mottrays proposes tunnel, in the form of immersed cast-iron tube on the Channel bed, to Napoleon

1818

- Steam packet boats begin service Dover–Calais

1826

- Steam packets Brighton–Dieppe

1834-1866

- French engineer Aimé de Gamond revives submerged-tube idea; then a bridge. His descents to sea-bed to study geology attract wide praise, but political opposition in England prevents progress.

Nevertheless BR responded gallantly to the challenge to construct 68 miles of high-speed line. By late 1970 a report by Livesey & Henderson, one of the first of the innumerable consultants involved over the following three decades, advised a line either leading directly to Victoria – historic destination of trains from the Channel – or, by skirting London to the south and west, exploiting the then-underused West London Line, ending at Olympia. In 1973, with Anglo-French agreement on Stage Two of the preliminary studies for the Tunnel, the project was given impetus from the top: the Conservative government had come to feel that a fast rail link would be essential.

BR then proposed no less than four alternative routes across Kent from the Tunnel to London (see map on page 27). Public reaction, says a study of the process by the Harvard Design School, 'was immediate and totally averse'. The project was further bedevilled by the way the railways in Kent and Surrey had been constructed to a very restrictive loading gauge – too small, naturally, to admit trains of European height and width. And then the timing depended on whether the new line was to be an orthodox railway, or one of the new ultra-fast TGV-type lines that could reduce the London–Paris time to a mere two and a half hours.

From the four routes originally explored, in 1974 BR settled on one which would by-pass Ashford and then use existing, under-used, lines across Kent and Surrey from Tonbridge to Redhill, with two alternative routes to South Croydon and then on to Victoria, using the slope of the site to build a raft above the existing tracks. Sadly this constricted site proved unsuitable for the length of trains proposed for the international service. So Bonavia and his colleagues followed the consultants' radical ideas, with a by-pass ending up not, as they had proposed, at Olympia, but a couple of miles further north at White City, where there was ample room for a terminus. It also had excellent rail connections to the lines to the West and North of England and, although several miles west of central London, it was served by two Underground lines. But, characteristically, the site was chosen purely because it was convenient for BR, not its customers; and without any discussion over the environment or development possibilities.

Nevertheless arguments still raged over routes. A low-investment adaptation of the 'boat train' route to Victoria was anathema to the French, who claimed (probably rightly) that, quite apart from the additional journey times involved, the capacity constraints would be contrary to a schedule in the Channel Tunnel Treaty which committed both sides to adequate investment to provide the 'necessary road and rail access'.

The silliest organisation with which BR had to deal was undoubtedly the then Greater London Council. It objected to the White City plan (without giving its reasons) and mentioned ten other sites – some with neither rail or tube links – apparently plucked at random from a map of London. Their final choice, at Surrey Docks east of Tower Bridge, was ruled out on environmental grounds. But then, any terminus was going to face opposition from the locals: due to the over-optimistic forecasts of Tunnel passenger numbers, traffic gridlock around the chosen site was widely predicted. The inhabitants of Hammersmith didn't want the White City terminus, and Bob Mellish, MP for Bermondsey, said of the Surrey Docks idea that 'they are not having that either'.

By mid-1973, BR had called the DoE's bluff by refusing to compromise and had been given the go-ahead to plan the White City route. This, though, left the planners less than a year (before the ratification of the Anglo-French treaty) to provide a detailed blueprint for a route which would also – and notably unlike the TGVs – carry freight trains: it thus could not have the steep gradients of the new French lines. To BR, the line that they had picked was the natural route, for much of it was along a stretch of railway – the Pluckley to Edenbridge line – far straighter and less crowded than any other through Kent.

The proposals naturally added fuel to the opponents of a Channel Tunnel, for any new railway line would directly affect the people along the route. As Bonavia points out, 'the simple xenophobia, the dislike of strengthening links with Europe that was to distinguish much of the debate over Britain's entry into the Common Market … spilled over on to the tunnel'. Even BR was divided, with its Southern Region still naturally objecting to the use of scarce managerial resources and the complications involved in any new route. Inevitably BR's ideas were attacked on all sorts of grounds – including that its plans were supposedly based on out-of-date maps. BR tried hard, offering a full pre-threat price when buying houses and payments to cover the costs of disturbance during construction, and attempting to explain that there was little or no noise problem – inhabitants of Kensington, they said, had never objected previously when noisy freight trains had used the West London Line….

But BR's underlying arrogance was shown clearly when the Royal Institute of British Architects came up with a perfectly rational report commenting, for instance, that 'no data or evidence' supported BR's choice of White City, and that 'no proper multi-disciplinary team was appointed' to assess the effect on the environment: 'landscape appears to be something one adjusts after the event'. In Bonavia's words,

1800s

1843

- South-Eastern Railway reaches Folkestone from London, via Redhill and Ashford, and begins steam packet service to Boulogne (1 hour 45 minutes), making Paris to London 14 hours. After the railway reaches Boulogne in 1848, this is reduced to 12 hours 30 minutes.

1861

- London, Chatham & Dover Railway reaches Dover

1882

- British and French companies sink shafts near Folkestone, Kent and Sangatte, France, and the British Channel Tunnel Company employs Colonel Beaumont, the inventor of the first rotary boring machine, to build a mile-long pilot tunnel on English side of Channel

1884

- London to Paris (via Folkestone–Boulogne) 8 hours

1891

- London to Paris 7 hours 30 minutes.

The young Geoffrey Howe QC, MP – and author of a trenchant report on the noise likely to be caused by trains from the Chunnel, which would have passed through his Surrey consituency

the British Rail team merely pointed to 'the hideous slabs with which [architects] had covered Central London since 1945', and in effect told RIBA to shut up.

A foretaste of the objections that were to be made in the late 1980s came from MPs in the Tory bastions of Kent and Surrey, the heart of the new route. These included a bright young barrister: the future Chancellor of the Exchequer, Geoffrey Howe. Elected in 1974 as MP for Reigate, one of the constituencies most affected by BR's plans, Howe remembers a meeting objecting to the disturbance. He pointed out that fewer freight trains – a particular bugbear of the objectors – would run along the lines than they had in the 1920s. Nevertheless he was commissioned by the objectors in Kent and Surrey (combined in Surrey and Kent Action on Rail) to draft a report (titled 'An Arrow through the Heart of Kent'). This concentrated on noise pollution, a factor which was mentioned at the time as a major reason for the abandonment of the rail link project.[7] The report was so cogently argued that it formed the basis for a European Directive which enshrined the concept that environmental damage had to be designed out at source, rather than ameliorated once a project had been decided upon – a directive incorporated into British law in July 1988.[8]

The cost of the route depended on several major factors: notably whether the line should be built to the UIC B+1 gauge,[9] whether the trains would run on existing tracks, and how much of it should be in tunnel, or on routes widened from two to four tracks. Fully aware that too high a cost would alarm its masters in Whitehall, BR initially proposed what they called a 'charm price' of £99 million: i.e., the most they thought the government would accept. This was soon revised to £114 million, but in the following eighteen months soared to £337 million – well above BR's total annual investment figure. Inflation accounted for some of the rise, but 'add-ons' like provision for freight traffic, quadruple tracks, new by-passes and above all a 'long tunnel' between South Croydon and the Thames at Chelsea Reach were responsible for most of the additional sums. By now BR was thoroughly fed up with the continuing criticisms and the insistence on putting an increasing proportion of the line in a tunnel. As one BR man cried out: 'why don't they just join the London Underground with the Paris Metro?'

Outsiders were also becoming alarmed. In March 1973 *The Economist* condemned the whole Tunnel proposal because it did not mention what the magazine perceived as the critical issue: the extent of the necessary investment in high-speed railways between the respective capitals. Meanwhile the DoE was worried that the evidence provided by BR was 'sadly defective', while the Treasury continued to bleat that the project had to

Facing page: BR proposed four routes, and finally setttled on Route One – with the addition of a tunnel from Croydon to the Thames. The London terminus was to be at White City.

7 The noise issue prompted a Kent GP to write to the *British Medical Journal* with his concerns about the '300 trains every 24 hours at speeds of up to 180mph, creating possible sound levels of 85Db' which 'BR would have us believe would have no ill effects on the inhabitants between Cheriton and White City'.

8 See Chapter 5.

9 The Union International des Chemins de Fer lays down different types of loading gauge. Even if the rails are all laid 4' 8½" apart, the width and height of the trains vary (and bridges and tunnels are built to these gauges); and the figures for the Southern Region were far lower than those in France or many other countries on the Continent – and many lines in Britain for that matter. See diagram page 51.

BR'S 1973 ROUTES

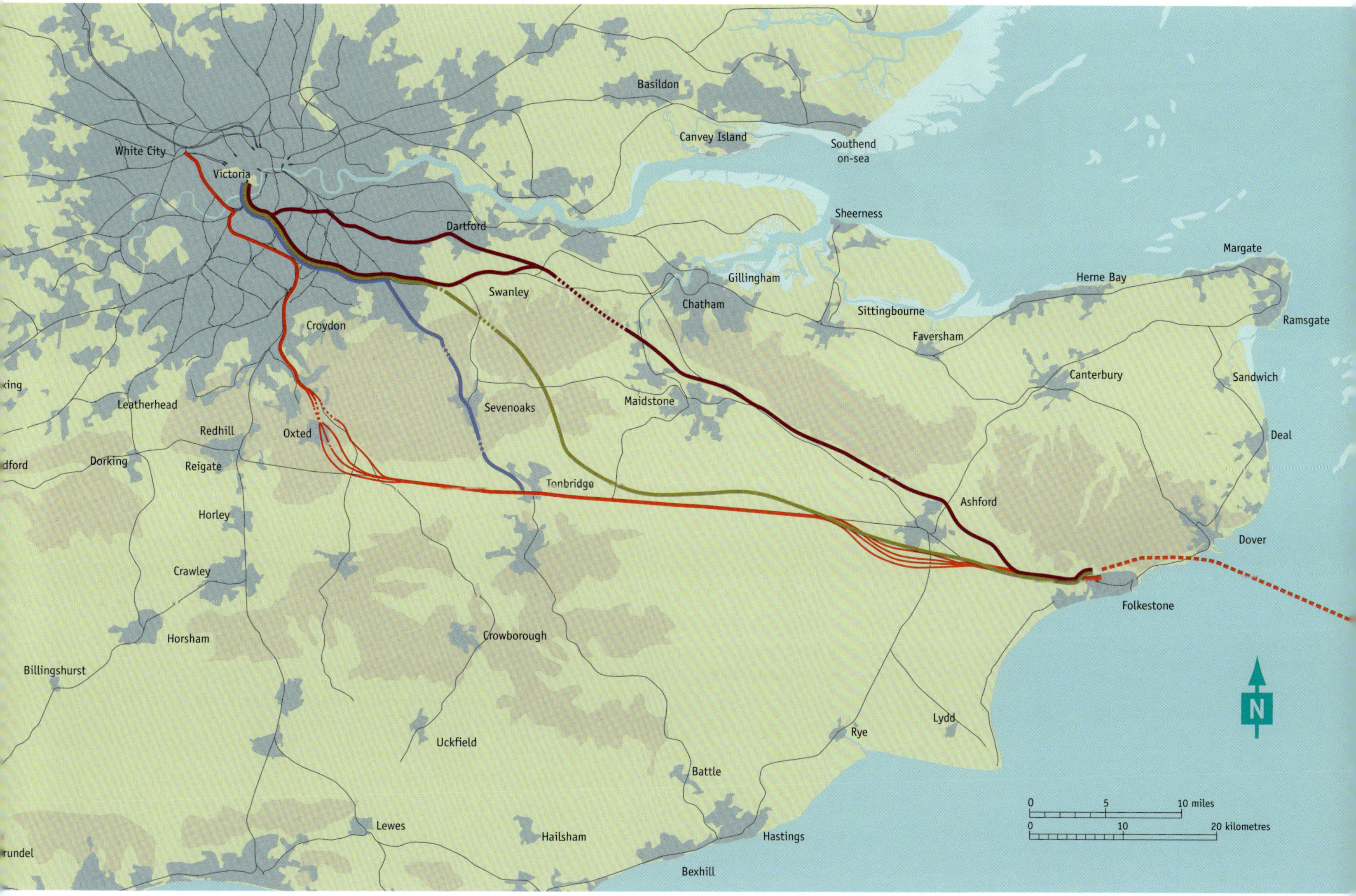

Route 1 Route 2 Route 3 Route 4 Land over 100m

Anthony Crosland, whose decision it was to abandon the Channel Tunnel project in January 1975

pass commercial tests and must never be subsidised. Doubts were increased by legal opinion that an (inevitably time-consuming) planning enquiry might be necessary. With the additions and the onset of the inflation surge caused by the first oil crisis, costs of the rail link mounted further to £373 million – almost as much as the £450 million that was Britain's share of the construction costs of the Tunnel itself. (But even this apparently impossible figure of £373 million was approximately the cost of the consultants hired in expensive droves in the late 1980s and early 1990s.)

In his memoirs Richard Marsh does admit that 'the very able railway staff who dealt with the early estimates [for the rail link] did so in a rather cursory fashion, because they could not believe that the government would ever renege on the project'. But it was Secretary of State Peyton who summed up the basic dilemma: 'we need attractive main-line services for the passengers using the Tunnel route', but 'if the rail investment is too expensive it could wreck the project [the Tunnel]. We must get this right and time is short' – in fact far too short, given the complexity of the factors BR faced and the shilly-shallying by a suspicious DoE.

The vastly increased estimate put out by BR marked the whole idea of a fast link with a lasting stain. As Mrs Thatcher, then newly-elected as Tory leader, put it after the project had been abandoned: 'the Channel Tunnel would not have been heavy on public expenditure. It was the rail link that would have involved the expenditure'.[10]

At the time the cost increase provided a convenient let-out for the newly-elected Labour government that took over in a crisis atmosphere in February 1974. The minister responsible was Anthony Crosland, whose Department of the Environment embraced Transport. In the words of an old friend, Crosland was a 'compulsively devious fellow' with no real love for railways: he believed that most of the subsidies they were given went to undeserving – i.e. Tory-voting – commuters to London.[11] On 14 January 1975 the Cabinet approved Crosland's decision to abandon the whole Tunnel project – without previously telling the French.[12]

When BR produced an estimate for the rail link reduced by £100 million, it was told it was too late even though Marsh, for one, did not think 'that any minister had ever seen the changed figures'. In fact, of course, knowledge of the sudden reduction in the costs would merely have underscored the government's suspicions about the solidity of BR's estimates. Nevertheless Marsh, more than the ministers, understood the political implications of the decision to abandon the whole project. To him it was 'a typical

10 House of Commons 22 May 1975.

11 Though he told Nicholas Comfort (*The Channel Tunnel and its High-speed Links*, Oakwood Press 2006) that 'he was sorry that he couldn't do something for the railways'!

12 Though a 1km trial bore was allowed to continue – and was maintained thereafter by the Department of Transport.

example of the frivolous way in which major decisions are taken … particularly since many people, including myself, had been assuring French officials only weeks before, with the full support of ministers, that there was no question of the UK ratting on the project; but we did just that'.

Crosland provided three explanations of the decision to abandon the project unilaterally, none of them related to the underlying reality of the situation. The 'devious fellow' certainly sprayed the blame around pretty freely: when he announced the decision to abandon the Tunnel in the House of Commons he attributed it to the 'quite unacceptable' terms posed by the contractors – though they had merely been protecting their legal position and were quite prepared to negotiate. He told at least one journalist – and repeated the statement to a Parliamentary colleague – that the choice was between two major projects, the Tunnel and Concorde: an absurd comparison, but one which had the advantage of pinning the blame on his rival Tony Benn, Concorde's stoutest supporter. More importantly in the previous November he had told MPs that 'the cost of the high-speed rail link had so increased that the government felt unable to proceed with it'.

This strengthened the myth that 'if the rail investment is too expensive it could wreck the Chunnel project', a non-sequitur which became only too fashionable in Whitehall.[13] The final part of the treaty with France was due to be signed by 1 July 1975 'or later by agreement', so Crosland simply proposed putting back the timetable 'to enable alternative lower-cost options to be thoroughly examined' – ignoring the fact that the government had already accepted BR's plans, and French objections ensured that the government could never have gone for a low-cost solution.

But the basic reason for abandonment of the Tunnel, dumped at the same time as was another high-profile, far less realistic, project – an airport proposed for Maplin Sands off the Essex coast – was simply that Britain was by then in full economic melt-down and could not afford any expensive projects at all. The country's ever-worsening financial situation, combined with the inflationary effects of the first oil crisis, put a kibosh to all of them. In early January 1975 the FT All-Share Index had fallen to 146, its lowest for twenty years;[14] although it had rallied strongly in the following weeks no-one was sure that this was not merely what the City calls 'a dead-cat bounce' and not the sign of a real recovery. Even more ominously, the lead story in the issue of *The Times* that reported Crosland's announcement was that average wages were rising at an annual rate of 32 per cent.

1924

- British Imperial Defence Committee rejects Tunnel plan

1955-60

- Private companies undertake Anglo-French studies into a 'Fixed Link'

1963

- British Ministry of Transport study supports a Tunnel

1964–1970

- British and French transport ministers authorize joint consortium to undertake geological and engineering surveys of sea-bed in preparation for a Tunnel – which British minister Ernest Marples describes as 'a certainty'

February 1967

- British and French governments invite private-sector bids for a Fixed Link

13 Richard Gibb, in *The Channel Tunnel: a Geograhical Perspective* (Wiley, 1994) believes that the government deliberately accepted BR's most expensive option to provide an excuse for abandoning the project. I believe that the government simply went along with BR's view without thinking much about it.

14 The index was lower in real terms than the all-time nadir of 40.4, reached in 1940 in the week of Dunkirk.

1971–1975

March 1971

- French and British Governments sign agreement with two consortia to allow further studies into a Tunnel

20 October 1972

- Governments commit to Phase One (of three) involving detailed studies

1973

- British Government decides train link to London necessary: BR publishes first attempt at route

June 1973

- Phase One studies complete

17 November 1973

- President Pompidou and Prime Minister Edward Heath preside over the signing of the Anglo-French Channel Tunnel treaty at Chequers

November 1973

- Phase Two begins: construction of access works, service tunnels and rail yards

20 January 1975

- Channel Tunnel cancelled unilaterally by British Government on grounds of cost. However government allows trial bore of 1km tunnel to continue – which indicates feasibility of scheme (this section maintained in good order until the 1980s by Department of Transport).

The abandonment of the Tunnel was also intimately linked to the ferocious battle over the forthcoming referendum on Britain's continuing membership of what was then the European Common Market: it was taken as a sop to the antis within the Labour party. Barbara Castle, earlier an enthusiast, confided to her diary that she nursed a 'kind of earthy feeling that an island is an island and should not be violated'. In his diary Tony Benn, a staunch anti-European who had earlier noted how the Channel Tunnel 'has now become inextricably linked with the Common Market', called the announcement of the abandonment 'very good news'.

Henry Woodhouse, the transport solicitor for the DoE, pinpointed the real cause of the disaster. 'A fatal mistake was made by the planners in the 1960s', he noted, 'when they decided to put to one side the question of the Rail Link. The result was … that by the early 1970s the Tunnel project itself had been developed very fully and adequately, but when it was decided to undertake the Rail Link as well, the scheme for this came along in an exceedingly half-baked condition.' Woodhouse blames British Rail – a typical piece of buck-passing since the DoE was far more responsible, if only because it always took so long to reply to BR's plans.

A report a few months later in May 1975 by the distinguished economist Sir Alec Cairncross expressed the general Whitehall view that 'the additional investment in any of the rail links so far proposed is unlikely to provide an adequate return'. This opinion separated the Tunnel from its rail links, and henceforth BR had to justify its plans in financial terms quite independently of the Tunnel. Other near-fatal long-term effects left successive governments sceptical of any budgets put forward by BR, while in its turn BR was scared stiff of proposing other than a minimal project. No wonder one cynic could say that 'Britain is no longer separated from Europe by the Channel. It is separated by Kent'.

1 2 3 4 5 6 7 8 9 10 11 12

TOGETHER, AT LONG, LONG LAST

The further off from England the nearer is to France –
Then turn not pale, beloved snail, but come and join the dance

Lewis Carroll, Alice in Wonderland

Another red book: French President François Mitterrand and British PM Margaret Thatcher at the signing of the Channel Tunnel Treaty in Canterbury Cathedral in February 1986

'A remarkable feature of the Channel Tunnel's long gestation', wrote Richard Gibb[1], 'has been its ability to recover momentum'. Within four years of the dramatic British abandonment of the project, Sir Peter Parker, the chairman of BR, together with his colleagues from the SNCF, had resurrected it by proposing a single-track rail tunnel – inevitably called the 'Mousehole' – running alternate 'flights' of trains from either side of the Channel. In 1980 the Minister of Transport, Norman Fowler, set out the new Conservative government's position: a tunnel could go ahead if, and only if, it was funded by private capital. Nevertheless for nearly a decade the pace was being set by 'Flexilink', the ferry operators' ferocious PR campaign which took advantage of primeval British fears of rabies, garlic and foreigners in general. In 1982 this attitude was given respectable intellectual backing when Cairncross produced another analysis, this one demonstrating that there was no need for a fixed link and forecasting that any such project would not be financially successful.

But in June 1984 the outlook suddenly cleared after Mrs Thatcher had succeeded in extracting a major budget rebate from our European 'partners' and was anxious to promote a free-trade area within the EEC. According to Sir Nicholas Henderson, the first chairman of Eurotunnel, she 'wished to make some positive move towards our European partners, with whom we had been wrangling for so long'; and what would be more suitable than 'a project which can show visibly how the technology of this age has moved to link the Continent and Britain closer together'[2] – though, needless to add so far as Mrs Thatcher was concerned, it would have to be built as a private project without involving any public money.

Within eighteen months[3] a treaty had been agreed between Mrs Thatcher and the French President François Mitterrand, and bids had been invited to build the tunnel. Nine more or less practicable schemes were proposed, the most implausible being a suspension bridge kept in place by heavy-lift airships. The contenders were soon winnowed down to four: Channel Expressway, involving twin-bore tunnels taking road and rail; Eurobridge, a suspension bridge with spans of three miles (4.8km) supporting a motorway in a tube; Euroroute, backed by Nigel Broackes of Trafalgar House (one of Mrs Thatcher's favourite businessmen), involving a tunnel and two bridges to allow road travel; and the Channel Tunnel Group offering twin-bore rail tunnels.

1 Richard Gibb (ed), *The Channel Tunnel, A Geographical Perspective* (Wiley, 1994).

2 *Channels and Tunnels* (Weidenfeld & Nicolson, 1987).

3 The announcement was in Lille on 20 January 1986; the signature was at Canterbury on February 13.

Mrs Thatcher disliked railways: BR was that undesirable animal, a public monopoly; moreover, the rail unions had forced her into a climb-down early in her reign. So her natural preference was for a road-based scheme; but bridges would have been an impractical proposition, if only because they would have to be built over one of the world's busiest seaways. By the end of 1985 the Channel Tunnel Group had won the day. The speed of the decision – a mere 81 days spent deciding whether a link ought to be built at all and if so in what form – was largely due to the insistence of Nicholas Ridley, the arch-Thatcherite Minister of Transport, who was keen not to lose the momentum so crucial to so long-delayed a project.

Artist's impression of the Euroroute bridge/tunnel which would take a roadway across the Channel: the promoters' slogan, pitched squarely at the 1980s motor-car mania, was 'you drive all the way'

The parliamentary Bill implementing the decision was in hybrid form, a device which had often been used by railway companies in the 19th century. They 'affect the private interests of a particular person or organisation', so that a Select Committee examining such a Bill can consider only specific, private interests, although it becomes a normal public Bill once through the committee stage. In the event the Select Committee received no fewer than 4,852 petitions – a warning that any attempt to introduce ambitious plans for a rail link would have attracted thousands more. As Holliday[4] put it, 'by avoiding discussion of a rail link during the Bill's passage [the government] hoped to reduce the potential for organised resistance by local authorities, interested bodies, communities, action groups and individuals'. Any major rail project 'was simply too contentious to be explored'. Fortunately, the Hybrid Bill procedure enabled the government to throw out all the petitions apart from the 70 which involved specific impacts. This accelerated process ensured that the Bill had hurtled through Parliament by February 1987.

In its final form the Act was a triumph of Thatcherite thinking. It avoided any discussion of wider issues like regional policy, planning or the environment and concentrated almost exclusively on the transport aspects of the project – the only remotely environmental clause protected historic buildings and woods. Financially it distinguished between the private-sector nature of the Tunnel itself and the public-sector funding required for improving the existing rail infrastructure to serve it. It crucially omitted the powers required to build a wholly new rail link to the Tunnel, assuming that the construction of such a line could be left to Mrs Thatcher's beloved private sector. The Tunnel itself was a national commitment, but the rail link was by no means central to her thinking – nor to that of ministers like Nicholas Ridley. Like her, he focused on the 'consumer choice' offered by the Shuttle service carrying cars and lorries through the

4 In Holliday, I., Marcou, G., & Vickerman, R. (eds) *The Channel Tunnel: Public Policy, Regional Development and European Integration* (Belhaven 1991).

1978

- BR and SNCF – British and French railways – start planning for a single-track Tunnel (nicknamed 'The Mousehole') between Folkestone and Calais

Early 1981

- Joint BR/SNCF proposal for a twin-bore Tunnel submitted to both governments

1981

11 September

- President François Mitterrand and Prime Minister Margaret Thatcher agree at summit talks to commission Anglo-French study group on the Channel Tunnel

1982

May

- Revised BR/SNCF proposal for twin-bore rail tunnel being considered by British Cabinet when news of sinking of HMS Sheffield during Falklands War is received. UK government defers decision until report of UK/French Study Group: in June 1982 this also reports in favour of twin-bore tunnel scheme.

Tunnel – a service which filled a gap in the European motorway network. So the rail link was merely an afterthought – and one, as she insisted, that would not attract a subsidy: after all its competitors, the ferries and airlines, had to operate without one.

Mrs Thatcher's objections were not in fact to state aid to the link itself, but only to state aid to BR as a publicly-owned body – objections reinforced by the belief she shared with most politicians, that the 1970s Tunnel scheme had been scuppered by BR's inordinate financial demands. As a result the 1987 Act included a ban on government subsidies if the link were built by a public-sector body, but it did not preclude subsidising a private-sector operation. Since BR was at the time the only game in town, this effectively stopped state aid to the link, unless such aid were to be deemed to help commuters, or for regional development – or if the link were to be built by the private sector. In a debate on May 1990 the Labour MP Joan Ruddock poured scorn on the need to provide 'a new commuter service from Kent to King's Cross in an attempt to attract public subsidy. What a ludicrous way to devise a national infrastructure plan for the 21st century!'

If BR wanted money for new investment, it had to approach the Treasury with its plans to ensure that they fulfilled the magic – and unrealistic – figure of an eight per cent return: i.e., were investments rather than state subsidy. Not surprisingly Mrs Thatcher's attitude was backed by David Shaw, the Tory MP for Dover, who proposed Section 42 of the Bill: this ensured that the Government would not put money into the Tunnel to subsidise unfair competition by international rail with the ferries sailing from his constituency. But BR was allowed funds for modifying the track and signalling between London and the Kent coast, and Kent County Council gained cash for roads around Ashford and near Folkestone. The Secretary of State was also allowed to approve investment in the rolling-stock and locomotives, as well as BR's proposal for a terminal at Waterloo Station and a possible station at Ashford, with the passenger-handling facilities they required.

The Department of Transport (DoT) was in no condition to help BR. As Peter Hennessy[5] put it, it was 'a Cinderella within Whitehall', sometimes merely one sub-department of an over-arching Department of the Environment. Its ministers rarely lasted more than a couple of years – there were no fewer than seven in the last 11 years of the Tory government. They were either – like John Moore and Paul Channon – on their way down the political ladder or, like Malcolm Rifkind, on their way up (in his case to Defence and then Foreign Secretary). As for Cecil Parkinson, who was minister during

5 *Whitehall* (Fontana, 1990).

sixteen crucial months during 1989 and 1990, he was working his way back after a spell out of office thanks to his personal problems, and, as one insider put it, 'never seemed able to fully recover the characteristic dynamism he had before' (indeed, was reported as asking friends whether he was on the way up or down....)

Whatever their position on the political greasy pole, they all naturally tended to be 'transient and embarrassed phantoms', in the words of Benjamin Disraeli. They were fully aware that their stay would be too short for any major decision or achievement, and that any initiative they undertook would be credited – or debited for that matter – to their successors. This ministerial transience has dogged any and all ambitious plans for the railways over the years. As *The Economist* summed it up: 'one day the transport minister makes welcoming noises; the next day, his successor says, sorry, they can't be afforded – you'll have to make do with a tube extension to Docklands'. *The Economist* was referring to Crossrail, the obviously essential, still-unbuilt, underground rail link across Central London, akin to the Paris RER; it could, however, have been writing about many another such scheme.

Meanwhile, at the Channel Tunnel.... assembling the boring machine under Dover as the English and the French inch towards each other

To make matters worse, throughout the late 1980s and the first half of the 1990 the DoT was traumatised – there really is no other term for it – by an unprecedented series of accidents. On 6 March 1987, during John Moore's brief stay at the department and barely a month after the passage of the Channel Tunnel Act, came the sinking of the cross-Channel ferry *Herald of Free Enterprise*, drowning 193 passengers and crew. This was the worst peacetime calamity to affect a ship registered in Britain since the *Titanic* seventy years earlier. The only positive effect was to silence the previously strident voices of the ferry operators. Eight months later, a fire at King's Cross Underground station killed 32 people – the worst ever accident in London's deep tube system.[6]

The next month witnessed another fatal crash, killing 35, at Clapham Junction on

6 The disaster at Moorgate Station in 1975 which killed 33 people was on the Metropolitan Line, just below the surface and thus more akin to an accident on a surface line than to one on the deep Underground.

Eurotunnel's Alastair Morton

one of the busiest railway lines into London – an event which traumatised Moore's unlucky successor, Paul Channon, and induced him to set up a lengthy, unprecedented and largely useless judicial enquiry into the accident. Within a few months yet another crash on London's commuter system, this time at Purley, killed five and injured 88 unlucky people. And then, before the end of 1988, even worse was to come. Just before Christmas all the 270 passengers and crew in a Pan Am airliner were killed at Lockerbie in Southern Scotland.

Under the circumstances, coping with the CTRL was largely left to junior ministers: David Mitchell (of the family that owned El Vino's Wine Bars) for two years until July 1989, followed by Roger Freeman. In May 1990, at the only major debate devoted to the CTRL, Freeman – then newly appointed – had to admit that he had 'approached the debate with some caution as I am new to the job and do not want to put my foot in it'. At the end, he agreed with the description given by one MP of the debate as being 'in effect, a five-hour tutorial for a new minister'.

So British Rail was left on its own. It had performed brilliantly as a railway operator, a facilities manager, throughout its 40-year life, even though it had been permanently starved of funds by a short-sighted and all-powerful Treasury. Its budgets were set one year at a time, so long-term planning was virtually impossible. Nevertheless by the time the Channel Tunnel Treaty was passed, BR was enjoying something of a golden age. Sir Robert (Bob) Reid, an experienced railwayman who had been chairman since 1983, had transformed the organisation into a market-oriented concern. Indeed he was probably the only railwayman in Europe to treat railways as a business, by dividing it into operating, rather than geographical, sectors.

John Palmer, BR's 'banker' at the DoT, brokered a deal with the ultra-Thatcherite Transport Secretary, Nicholas Ridley – a personal friend of Reid's, with whom he used to go shooting, and the only Secretary of State for Transport in recent times to last four years and to make a positive contribution to its problems. Reid used the funds from the sale of peripheral subsidiaries like BR's hotels to invest in the railways, and in the five years to 1989 had reduced the subsidy from the Treasury by nearly a half.

At the time the Treasury was too preoccupied with privatising most of the other nationalised industries to pay much attention to British Rail. Nevertheless the 'golden age' was bound to be temporary, since BR only had a few businesses it could sell – and profit from the redevelopment of stations like Liverpool Street went straight to the Treasury anyway. Even in this halcyon period BR's biggest project, electrification of the main line from London to Newcastle and Edinburgh, suffered from the usual financial constraints.

It did not help that British Rail was rather taken aback by the sheer speed of the Channel Tunnel Treaty. Thanks to the previous false starts, it had not given much attention to the problems involved in linking the Tunnel with London before the Bill was presented to Parliament – although in late 1985 it had provided the government with a preliminary estimate. In any case, the first few months following the passage of the Act were spent in an argument between BR and SNCF and Alastair Morton, the newly-appointed co-chairman of Eurotunnel, over the terms of the agreement by which their trains would be able to use the Tunnel – terms which were settled only in May 1987. From then on Bob Reid, a great believer in delegation, let his team get on with it.

Unfortunately BR had become one of the country's favourite Aunt Sallies, its achievements unnoticed, every mistake broadcast to the nation – an attitude that in 1994 led to the disastrous way in which it was privatised, when Kenneth Clarke as Chancellor of the Exchequer approved the plans of officials obsessed with smashing the organisation into 192 fragments in the name of 'competition'. Clarke echoed the feelings of many of his fellow-countrymen when he said that 'anything was better than BR'. Inevitably the same attitude bedevilled it when it was rushing to fulfil the government's plans for the rail links to the 'Chunnel' (as the press had dubbed it).

BR produced its 'first report' on 'Britain and the Channel Link' (it meant the Tunnel) in 1986. It promised 'no new main lines will be built in Great Britain' – a promise that lasted a bare two years. There being no plans for a new line, the first priority was a scramble to provide an adequate service to and through the Chunnel by the planned opening date in 1993. BR accomplished this task extremely efficiently, thus avoiding the penalty-clause in the Treaty (if road and rail links had not been 'properly constructed' by the time the tunnel opened, the offending country would have had to pay compensation). The job was made easier because, under the contract with Eurotunnel, trains could take up to three hours on their journey from London to Paris: not a demanding target, even with the slow journey through Kent, since the French had already committed to their LGV which allowed Paris–Tunnel journeys of an hour and a half.

So BR had to cobble up a route by improving existing, and already crowded, ones. What is usually overlooked is that it costs far more in time and trouble to modify or widen existing lines than to build new ones – getting 'possessions' of the line for engineering works inevitably dislocates existing traffic. Indeed, BR was faced with stitching into its existing routes what was in effect a mini-TGV – a train which, in the

1983

October

- Nicholas Ridley becomes Secretary of State for Transport

1982–1984

- Private companies carry out studies and indicate interest in building privately-financed 'Fixed Channel Link'
- Joint British/French banking study investigates feasibility of financing scheme

1984

15 November

- Secretary of State for Transport and his French counterparts announce both governments willing to give the necessary political guarantees to facilitate fixed link – providing this is financed without public support or government financial guarantees. Ministers set up working parties to prepare guidelines for potential promoters.

29 November

- Agreement endorsed by British Prime Minister and French President

Facing page: the 1986 solution envisaged use of Boat Train Route One – through Tonbridge and Sevenoaks – while the main freight line was via Redhill. 'No new main lines' was BR's promise at the time.

words of Nicholas Comfort,[7] would be 'capable of operating over the Southern Region's third-rail electrified tracks with their sharp curves, steep gradients, tight clearances, speed restrictions and (even) manually-operated level crossings'.

Trying to thread these monster trains through an ever-increasing horde of commuter services posed another problem. The French were already complaining about the number of slots for the international trains – especially the impossibility of finding any access to and from central London between 8–9 a.m. during the morning rush hour, and the limitation to three trains an hour in the early evening instead of the four they needed. At first they quite simply could not understand the constraints under which BR claimed it was working, but a single visit by a French team forced them to recognise the real situation – as well as BR's professionalism.

British Rail entrusted the job of planning the new service to Malcolm Southgate, the former manager of its biggest region, the Midland; he was rather loosely supervised by David Kirby, BR's joint managing director. The first problem faced by him and his – originally tiny – team was to work with the SNCF to commission the very special new trains required. Designing them was a nightmare. They had to have short, narrow carriages to cope with the British loading gauge and the twists and turns of the route, and, worse, they had to be able to accept three very different power supplies,[8] no fewer than four signalling systems[9] – and two different platform heights!

Fortunately, this time some funds were in place. As one leading railwayman put it, 'we were so afraid of a repetition of the 1970s that we underplayed our request to a mere £500 million. As a result, and for the first time ever, the Department of Transport actually increased the figures'.

There followed an intricate series of negotiations over the extremely lucrative £180 million contract to build the new trains – especially as in reality there was only one candidate, a joint venture between the British GEC and the French Alsthom companies, whose rail-related businesses had merged during the time the trains were being built. As with the Chunnel itself, the terms of the contract were too loose, with minimal damages for delays. (In the event the trains were a year late – but then, so was the construction of the Tunnel.)

John Welsby, who replaced Kirby in 1987 as joint managing director, succeeded in persuading the SNCF to form a joint venture to manage the purchase of the Eurostar trains which, managerially anyway, went well. Because of their complexity, the eighteen-car trains (31 of them) cost £23 million each – a total of over £700 million, and by far the

7 Nicholas Comfort, a former Lobby correspondent of the *Daily Telegraph*, is also an expert on the Tunnel.

8 Main lines in France and Britain 25kv overhead; London and South East England 750 volts DC. Some of France 1.5kv overhead – and if the trains ventured to Germany or Switzerland yet another power supply would be involved.

9 The Thalys trains plying between France, Belgium, Holland and Germany have to cope with eight.

BRITISH RAIL: THE 1986 ROUTE

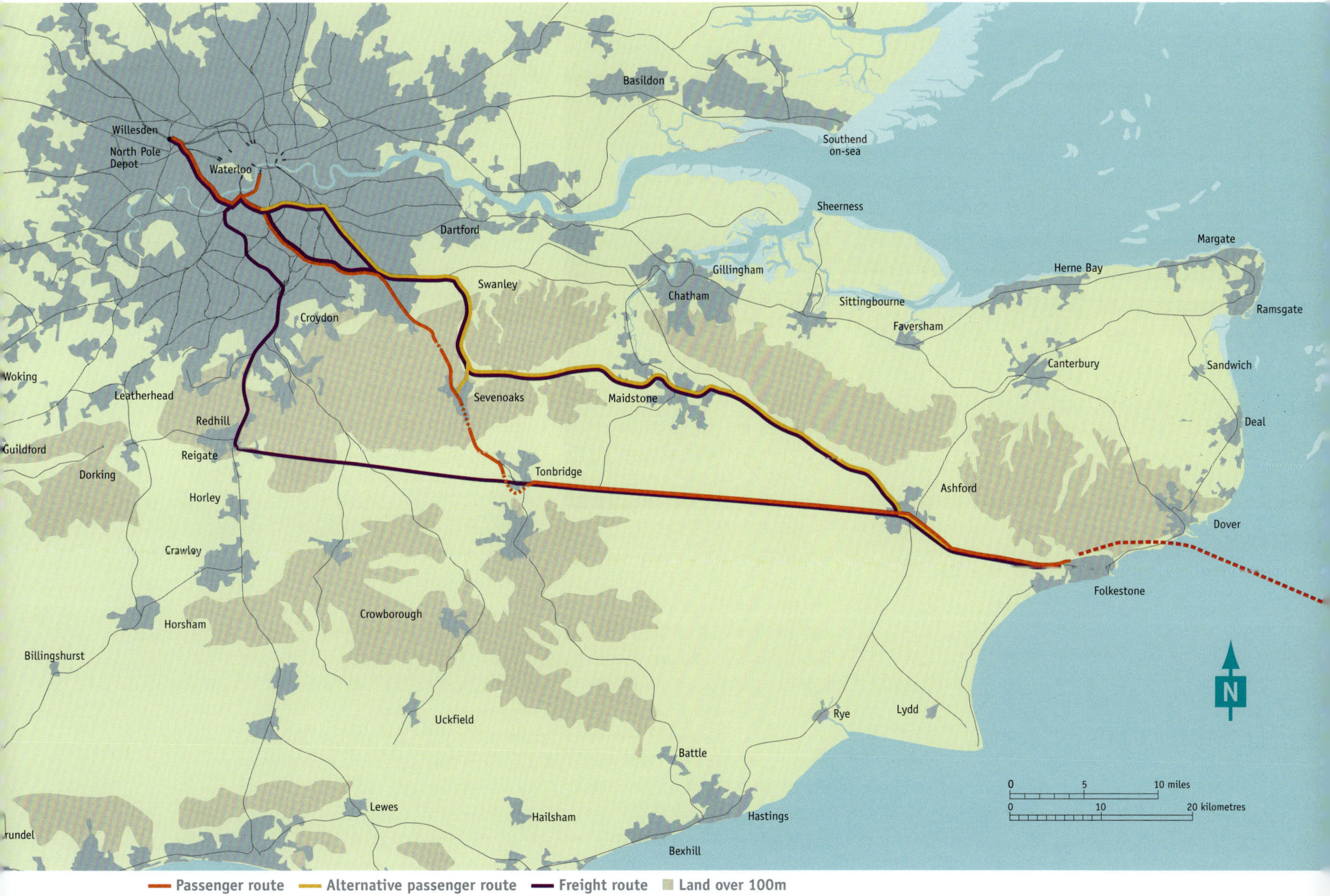

Victorian infrastructure, mediaeval landscape – and 1980s trains: the Garden of England lay between the Channel Tunnel and the capital

largest item in the entire, £1.7 billion, budget for the Tunnel's rail infrastructure. Unfortunately, at the beginning the brand new train-sets proved unreliable. In a classic case of what the British press inevitably termed 'le coq-up', the Eurostar provided to take the press on its first trip through the Tunnel proved faulty and another had to be fetched down from the depot. (Journalists who complained that there was no back-up train at Waterloo were not to know that there was indeed one, but that it too was dysfunctional....) Despite all these first-day gremlins, one trial train showed what could be done when it took just under two hours and twenty minutes between the two capitals over BR's Victorian tracks.

So far as the route was concerned Malcolm Southgate – like everyone else in BR at the time – naturally assumed that the solution lay in what was proudly named the Number One Boat Train Route – which by British Rail's modest standards was 'quite fast' but still took 70 minutes, or 85 at peak times, for the 68-mile journey to the coast. Since BR had found in the 1970s that Victoria Station was too constricted for Eurostar's eighteen-carriage trains, a new terminus was needed. The obvious solution was Waterloo, which had four platforms at the northern end of the station previously used for parcels and the lines to Windsor. These could be connected with the Boat Train route by a simple viaduct in Battersea, just south of the Thames, joining the lines to Waterloo through Vauxhall – a route also providing flexibility to use other Southern Region termini.

At Waterloo itself, the relative isolation of the four platforms provided room for a magnificent, dedicated new station, designed by Nicholas Grimshaw and commissioned in 1990 at a cost of £130 million. Trains would emerge from its sinuous curve and run, via a new flyover at Stewart's Lane, through Herne Hill, Orpington, Sevenoaks, Tonbridge and Ashford – essentially BTR 1 (see map page 39). Improvements east of Tonbridge would permit 100mph running, allowing London–Paris journeys of 3 hours 15 minutes.

In fact, the most elaborate rail improvements needed were those made to the West London Line through Battersea and Chelsea for the Eurostar trains to reach their new depot, on the Western Main Line at North Pole near Wormwood Scrubs. This depot alone cost £80 million.

So much, for the time being, for London to Paris. Unfortunately however, BR was also saddled with demands based on the notion that services from Britain's provinces to Paris or Brussels could be a practical proposition. This derived from Section 40 of the Channel Tunnel Act, based on an amendment proposed by Peter Snape, a former railwayman and MP for a Birmingham constituency. It provided for 'an increase in the proportion of the passengers and goods carried between places in the United Kingdom and places outside the United Kingdom that is carried by international through-service … the provision or improvement of international through-services serving various parts of the United Kingdom'.

Section 40 responded to – and further prompted – continuing pressure from outside London. In early 1989 *The Independent* carried an apocalyptic, and totally unjustified, report that 'the north-south divide will widen, industry in the regions will be left to wither and die, and investment in the overcrowded South-East will be sucked into northern France unless the government moves to ensure fast, smooth, regional access to the Channel Tunnel'. A few months later the House of Commons Welsh Affairs committee issued a report, 'The Channel Tunnel, Implications for Wales'. Later on an MP from Stockton, in the North-East, showed the basis of the provincial case when he declared that 'the real villains of the piece [are] the London community who want to shut out what will be a very important development in the north'.

The regional MPs who backed Snape's proposals seem, sensibly enough, to have been thinking more in terms of direct access to the Tunnel by freight rather than passengers, but the government clearly panicked and planned for expensive passenger services as well. In fact as John Armitt, who as head of Union Railways[10] had been responsible for the new link, told the Royal Academy of Engineering in 1995, the fast link would 'provide additional capacity … for freight trains' only indirectly, 'primarily by freeing capacity on existing lines' as fast passenger trains switched to the new link.

So far as passenger traffic was concerned, the lobbyists were living in what the late President Reagan so memorably described as 'La-La land'. One forecaster even stated that the West Midlands would be 'only five and a half hours from Paris', when it was clearly recognised at the time that three hours was the limit for which trains could compete with air services, city centre to city centre.[11] Even in the 1980s there were an increasing

10 Union Railways: the agency company of the British Railways Board created in 1992 to plan the CTRL.

11 A figure which I gave in *Return Train*, a major survey in *The Economist* in 1986 and which went unchallenged.

1985

2 April

- 'Invitation to Promoters' extended by Transport Secretary Nicholas Ridley, requiring proposals to be submitted by 31 October. All proposals to be assessed before year end and both governments to agree final choice by end of January 1986.

November 1985–January 1986

- Nine schemes to build a Fixed Link submitted; five rejected in the first round. Shortlisted are: Channel Tunnel Group; Euroroute; Channel Expressway; Eurobridge. Assessment criteria range from financial solidity to effect on navigation and veterinary controls.

number of air services from Birmingham, Manchester and Glasgow to Paris, albeit with high fares. Nevertheless as one weary railway executive puts it 'if Glasgow had a service, Bristol wanted one as well'.

The pressure may have been totally unrealistic, but it came from many sources. In the words of Graham Allen, an MP for Nottingham, 'those who look after our interests include the Channel Tunnel Group, which comprises the most powerful and influential bodies in the North-West. They include the North-West local authorities; Rail Forum; Greater Manchester Economic Development Ltd; Central Manchester, Merseyside and Trafford Park development corporations; English Estates; chambers of commerce in the North-West of England, and the Confederation of British Industry in the North-West. Those voices wanting to be heard in the debate are not insignificant – and it is not an insignificant issue'. In response to pressures like these British Rail had to invest £145 million to provide the trains for an ambitious schedule. One train a day would run from Glasgow via Edinburgh and the East Coast Main Line, two along the West Coast Main Line, and there would also be a daily service from Manchester to Paris.

The estimates appear to have been based on the – totally untested – assumption that the new provincial services must inevitably attract a decent proportion of the available traffic. BR's 1986 report forecast that 'nearly half' the British passengers for services through the Tunnel would come from outside South-East England. To make matters worse, through trains could be run only on main lines that had already been electrified (rather than using diesel locomotives), thus eliminating for instance all traffic west of London – though there were proposals at the time that the Great Western lines could be electrified in view of the promise offered by the Tunnel.

The delusion that the estimates were reasonable persisted until the Tunnel actually opened for business. In the May 1990 debate in the House of Commons – the only one exclusively devoted to a rail link – MPs solemnly discussed the requirements of a businessman travelling by train from Milan to the north of England or from the north to Milan. He would, they decided, have to stop in London to change trains – this at a time when the pioneering Trans-European Expresses (TEEs), pride of the international rail system on the Continent in the 1960s and 1970s, were being abandoned in the face of competition from road and air. Looking ahead to the Tunnel's opening, BR produced a regional timetable in 1988, complete with traditional timetable footnotes: passengers on the eight-hour trek from Carlisle to Paris had to remember to change at Crewe....

In a startlingly unreal statement at the October 1994 Tory party conference Dr Brian

Mawhinney, then Minister of Transport, asserted that regional Eurostar services would begin 'at the start of 1996'. In reality, as a report commissioned in 2004 put it, such services would not only be unremunerative, but 'any social, environmental, or other non-financial benefits from the introduction of a regional service would be too small to compensate for failure to make a profit'. Yet as late as 1995 John Armitt could state that 'a direct Eurostar from Newcastle could reach Paris in under six hours'. To which the only answer, in a decade when cheap flights from regional airports like Newcastle[12] had become the norm is, 'so what?'

But the least realistic investment was in the 139 carriages of special Nightstar stock, ordered in 1992 at a cool £1 million apiece. According to the alluring publicity material, The Channel Tunnel Night Train, 'a hotel on wheels', represented 'A Renaissance in Overnight Travel' – of which there was no sign anywhere else in Europe. Nevertheless BR felt it had to appease the politicians – although, to be fair, it dragged its feet against the political tide, fully aware of the absurdity of the proposal. The Nightstar offered night sleepers from Glasgow, Manchester, Plymouth and Swansea to Paris (with numerous stops in England along the way) as well as from London to Amsterdam and to various German cities. Its defenders point out that, at the time, the air fare from London to Frankfurt, one of its destinations, was as much as £484.

The trains, decked out in two shades of green, with room for up to 400 passengers, provided lavish sleeping accommodation (some with own toilets and showers), open carriages, buffet bars, accommodation for disabled passengers, the train captain and customs officials. The prospect was thought to be so serious that the proponents were even afraid of a competition enquiry by the European Commission. Unbelievably, the normally penny-pinching Treasury never queried any of the expenditure involved. In 1998 John Prescott, then the head of a super-ministry including Transport, complained

The dream of Swansea to Paris by night was destined to remain unfulfilled.... From the brochure for the service that never was.

12 A typical Newcastle–Paris Charles de Gaulle flight time in 2007 is 100 minutes, and the airport is six miles from Newcastle city centre.

1986

20 January

- Prime Minister Thatcher and President Mitterrand meet at Lille to announce that the consortium of Channel Tunnel Group and France Manche will receive a 55-year concession to build and operate the Tunnel

13 February

- Thatcher and Mitterrand meet at Canterbury Cathedral for the signing of the Channel Fixed Link Treaty

14 March

- Concession Agreement between Transport Secretary Nicholas Ridley, his French opposite number J Auroux, Nicholas Henderson for the Channel Tunnel Group, J-P Parayre for France Manche

that 'this week I've been asked to pay for specially designed sleeper trains which didn't work, have never been used and are now lying idle in a field'.[13]

The provision of space for customs and immigration was a sore point, as British Rail realised early on in their planning.[14] The trains' planners had hoped to avoid problems with British immigration officials, but both they and the customs authorities were decidedly unsympathetic. At first customs claimed they would need one and half coaches on each train, although today they provide only two – little-used – customs compartments and a couple of cells. Until 2000 they refused to allow freight to be cleared other than at Willesden. For its part, the immigration service vetoed attempts to fill up half-empty Eurostars at Ashford – international trains, they decided, must not 'stop at any platform open to domestic traffic' south of the terminal. By contrast the only check on the Belfast–Dublin service, constantly threatened by terrorists at the time, was from ticket collectors, while the French have cheerfully allowed domestic passengers to travel on Eurostars from Paris to Calais. BR presciently raised the issue of customs checks as early as 1986, but nothing was achieved.

By contrast some of the expenditure, especially on improvements to the tracks, proved extremely useful. The power supply along the route in Kent had to be strengthened to provide for the requirements of the enormous eighteen-coach trains, so these were the only routes that did not have to have a similar upgrade carried out when faster, heavier trains were introduced on commuter routes in the late 1990s. Twenty miles (32km) of track between Tonbridge and Redhill were electrified to handle international freight.

More importantly, within London, as *Modern Railways* noted, the plans involved 'the construction [at a cost of £148 million] of virtually a new railway over the central section of the North London Line' – a crucial bypass round North London – as well as the electrification of the West London Line north from Clapham Junction to Willesden Junction to enable Eurostars to reach their depot. On the North London Line the track had to be lowered to accommodate Eurostar trains, and many bridges and other structures had to be strengthened, as did the track itself. Chelsea Railway Bridge on the West London Line – where previously, as one railwayman put it 'we had to tiptoe across at 15mph' – was strengthened to bring speeds up to 45mph (72kph).

All these improvements have proved essential as both freight and passenger traffic round and through London have increased so dramatically in the past twenty years. They also provide the option for an 'Orbirail' service: a kind of Outer Circle Line on largely existing lines now being considered by Transport for London.

13 They found a home in, of all places, Canada, which paid a reported £12 million for the lot. But it took until 2007 to find a use for the seven regional Eurostars, which had cost £180 million: they have been leased to SNCF. 'I am sure we can get them back if we want them', said a Eurostar manager.

14 See their 1986 Channel Tunnel report.

SLOW TRACKS TO A FAST TRAIN

We'll probably build the BR line now and then, a couple of years after we're re-elected, we'll think about the national interest and build the other one as well

Anonymous cabinet minister, February 1990

The first impetus for a new and fast link to the Channel Tunnel came from a surprising source, Kent County Council (KCC). In many ways Kent was an old-fashioned, pre-Thatcher, Tory county – but its county council was dominated not (as in so many others) by country gentlemen, but by distinguished figures who had retired to the hamlets and villages nestling in the rolling countryside so typical of 'the Garden of England'. In the early 1980s one example of the new inhabitants was Mike Odling, a former senior executive from ICI. Tony Hart, chairman of the Council and himself a former accountant, appointed Odling as chairman of its combined development, planning and transport committee.

He and his colleagues saw the need for a new culture within the Council: 'a go-go attitude' that would 'combine public service and making things happen'. To achieve their aim they set about recruiting the best local-government 'civil service' they could, offering pay rates comparable with similar ranks in ICI. They immediately hired a distinguished group of department heads (who later went on to major roles within the engineering profession and local government), who were also 'kept on a light lead'. The new team could thus, in Odling's words, 'come to a complete overview of what was going to happen'. The changes in the way the council was run – 'more professional, more innovative, less reactive' – combined with its impeccable Thatcherite credentials, made it far more influential in Whitehall than other councils.

Not surprisingly, then, KCC's councillors belied the usual Tory-council image and provided the most comprehensively integrated of plans for their county's future. By contrast Cecil Parkinson, marking his return to government in 1989, voiced the Thatcherite suspicion of strategic long-term plans. 'Eastern Europe', he declared, 'is littered with examples of countries which have just decided that this is not a good idea'. As a senior civil servant in the DoT wrote in May 1990: 'the government's view on long-term, comprehensive transport planning for all modes is ... that the complexity and inflexibility of such a policy renders it unsuitable as a means of dealing with the transport requirements of the rapidly-changing economic and social scene we are now witnessing in London'. But such was KCC's professionalism – and its political clout – that during the 1980s it attracted around £500 million of public funds from the DoT, especially for roads: not just the main roads from London to the coast, but also connecting roads from north to south. But, Odling insisted, 'roads had to fit into the landscape' – and so, of course, did any projected railway line. In fact KCC's attitude was similar to that of Eurotunnel chairman Alastair Morton, who claimed to have been the first person to propose (in March 1988) a new high-speed line along one of the existing transport corridors, a suggestion very similar to the eventual outcome.

The KCC's attitude towards the tunnel itself was also constructive – as was inevitable from a group of men who often felt that they had more in common with their counterparts in Northern France, whom they frequently visited, than those in the rest of England. Others, and not only in Kent, 'looked on a new rail link as a restraint, not a resource', says Odling. The Council, together with David Mitchell, the junior minister of transport, had formed the Kent Joint Consultative Committee to study the effects of the Tunnel and produce the Kent Impact Study, published in August 1987. It was supposedly designed merely to map out the expanded road network required to cope with traffic to and from the tunnel, but the KCC took a broader view, analysing the need for new rail infrastructure in what was the sole study (from government, or indeed anyone else) to examine the environmental and other non-transport results of the rail links.

Of course Kent did not forget its own, narrower interests: the study also emphasised the need for a station at Ashford (allowed for, but not insisted on, in the Channel Tunnel Act) which, it claimed, would result in 14,000 additional jobs. These were badly needed – coincidentally, partly because of the closure of the Kent coalfield discovered by Watkin's tunnellers a hundred years earlier. Ashford, says Odling, was a 'prerequisite to permission'.

The study provided the necessary shock to Whitehall, and the Minister immediately announced that BR had appointed a team 'to study the implications of such a need, if and when it was proved necessary' – a sure sign of the stately pace of the whole process. BR's, and Whitehall's, reluctance to face facts was not just an automatic Thatcherite reaction but was seemingly deeply embedded in the British consciousness, for by the late 1980s Britain was virtually the only major European country not to be building, or at least planning, a network of TGV-type lines.

Meanwhile, however, the forecasts of traffic through the Tunnel were rising, and this was the crucial factor that at last drove demands for a high-speed train link. As they rose a widespread fear grew, both in those affected by the rail services and those who were to run them, that the existing infrastructure would be overwhelmed. Capacity, not speed, was the issue.

The idea of a fast link began to ride up the Whitehall agenda, with everyone trying to square the circle, refusing to accept that although one was necessary, it could not be built without involving substantial sums of public money. Alastair Morton was charging around demanding action – to which a Treasury official replied that: 'although BR thinks

1986

- British Rail begins planning for rail routes to Tunnel using existing Boat Train Routes with upgrades, and freight routes similar to those proposed in 1973–4. It promises 'no new main lines'.

March

- Kent Joint Consultative Committee (Kent JCC) set up to assess effect of Tunnel on the county

April

- Kent JCC sets up Kent Impact Study

May

- John Moore is Secretary of State for Transport

June-November

- Parliamentary Select Committee considers Channel Tunnel Bill, receives 4,852 petitions: these lead to just 70 amendments

CROSS-CHANNEL TRAFFIC: PREDICTIONS. . .

1882: Sir Edward Watkin

Passenger journeys between Great Britain and France

Rail/ship	0.46
With Channel Tunnel, predicted, first year	4.5

The 1970s: unexpected decline

Total market, air and surface, between Great Britain and mainland Europe

	1973	1974
Passenger journeys	30	28

1986: BR's predictions

Total market, air and surface, between Great Britain and mainland Europe

	1983 *(actual)*	1993	2003
Passenger journeys	46	67	98
Rail share (Tunnel from 1993)	3.1	15.6	20.4

1993: Eurotunnel's predictions

Total market, air and surface, between Great Britain and mainland Europe

	1995*	1996*	2003†	2013†
Total cross-Channel journeys	74	78	101	136
Tunnel (Eurostar) share	9	11	17	22

*Sources: *Eurotunnel; †Traffic & Revenue Consultants*
All figures in tables above are passenger journeys in millions

he is wrong, we do not intend to obstruct anybody else who wants to put *their* money where *his* mouth is' (his emphasis!) As the Treasury warned, the documents so far circulated were 'unblemished by figures' and this, the dominant department, was not sure 'that the private sector will build and finance it on acceptable terms'.

But then, the whole process had become a farce – partly because of the rules laid down by the DoT on behalf of the Treasury that: 'rail services have to be run on a commercial basis ... The Ryrie[1] rules say that private-sector participation in a public-sector project must bring with it benefits which would not arise if the project were funded by the public sector'. In fact there was an unspoken assumption that some public money would inevitably be involved, though BR was not informed of the fact.

Ironically, in fact, all those traffic forecasts were flawed – if only because they assumed a static situation, with the Channel Tunnel's competitors unable to adapt their prices and their range of services to the threats posed by the new international railway services. The opposite proved to be true. Once the Tunnel opened ferries proved to be very flexible in their pricing policies, while air fares were sharply reduced from their elevated 1980s level and airlines provided an increasing range of services – from regional airports, as well as London – to, and of course beyond, Brussels and Paris. The forecasters also apparently assumed that there was no limit to the number of travellers wanting to go to Brussels and, more especially, Paris. Today of course, thanks to ever-cheaper air fares, couples looking for a suitable destination for a romantic weekend can choose between dozens of destinations, from Prague to Morocco.

Forecasters' inability to cope with forseeable changes in modes of transport had already been demonstrated with startling relevance in the late 1950s, when the Boeing 707 first started flying across the Atlantic. At the same time the Ministry of Transport was persuaded by Cunard, which was seeking – and indeed received – government financial aid for the QE2, that their twice-weekly service from Southampton to New York was a permanent fixture. In the event, of course, it took only a few years for the whole idea of regular steamship services anywhere in the world to pass into maritime history, and the Cunarders to transmute into cruise liners. The 1980s Chunnel forecasts uncannily echoed those of Sir Edward Watkin a century earlier: he predicted that 250 trains a day, in each direction, would use his proposed Tunnel.[2] The 1880s rail traffic to the Channel ports totalled 16 trains a day each way.

It was too late, in the mid-1990s, when Andrew Barker, head of the transport research team at SG Warburg, pointed out some more fundamental flaws in the Tunnel

1 See Chapter 12.

2 The *Railway Times*, reporting Watkin's evidence to a Parliamentary select committee.

traffic forecasts.[3] 'Each year's revenue forecast … is based on 450 assumptions (15 assumptions in each of 30 different market segments). Two of the assumptions in each market segment (underlying growth rate, 'generative factor') have some scientific basis; the others (market share, distribution of traffic into twelve different fare bands) are purely subjective and based on the forecasters' personal experience of the market'.

Even he was being too kind, for the 'generative factor' – that the mere existence of a new rail link would inevitably generate substantial new traffic – proved over-optimistic. All the forecasts were based on wishful thinking: most obviously so in the case of Eurotunnel, desperate for puffed-up figures that would help the company to raise money. Not surprisingly, the estimates were increased by two million passengers a year when Eurotunnel applied for its third chunk of equity capital. There was also an assumption that holiday traffic would switch from charter flights to charter trains – a market segment that has totally failed to materialise. Had the relatively pessimistic BR estimates been taken seriously, there would, for instance, have been no immediate need for a second London terminus.

These fanciful traffic forecasts piled further pressure on BR, which had believed that from 13.4 million to 15.6 million passengers a year would use the service when the tunnel opened.[4] Eurotunnel's figure of 15.4 million was not the highest: SNCF's figure was a million more. But the most absurd of all came from the Policy Unit at Ten Downing Street (which even the cautious Dr Gourvish[5] describes as 'gung-ho'): this referred to 48 million passenger trips and 60 million tons of freight by 2003. In reality Eurostar carried fewer than eight million people in 2006 – and this was after the first stage of the fast link had opened. The forecasts disagreed so wildly that the date when the existing tracks would become overcrowded varied between the turn of the century and 'well into the 21st century'.

At the time none of these predictions were ever seriously challenged, even though the forecasters should have hedged their bets and pointed out that they were necessarily only approximations since they were made a full seven years before the Tunnel was due to open. In reality, even if every passenger who went by air had switched to the Channel Tunnel, the figures would not have stood up.

One major flaw was that they were all produced by economists, so they tended to be based on the value of the time factor – enormously important in dealing with the planning of roads – but largely ignored the relative costs of different means of travel. In at least one case, it was assumed that the full potential of the Tunnel would be realised

CROSS-CHANNEL TRAFFIC: . . . AND OUTCOMES

Channel Tunnel actual (Eurostar)*	
1998	6.7
1999	7.0
2000	7.0
2001	7.0
2002	6.6
2003	6.3
2004	7.3
2005	7.5
2006	7.9

*Excludes passenger journeys by car/coach on the Shuttle
Figures are passenger journeys in millions

3 Quoted in *Freud in the City* by David Freud (Bene Factum Publishing, 2006).

4 Figures from BR's 1986 report.

5 Dr Terry Gourvish is the director of the Business History Unit at the LSE and is author of the standard two-volume history of British Rail. In 2006 Routledge published his book *The Official History of Britain and the Channel Tunnel* in the Government Official History Series. He interviewed most of the politicians and civil servants involved and therefore invariably confines the story to Whitehall, reflecting exclusively the attitudes of his interviewees.

from the moment it opened, in complete contradiction of any normal expectations, which allow for a build-up, rather than an immediate rush to a new facility.

Moreover there was a distinct element of wishful thinking. The figures all took as their base the total traffic between everywhere in Britain and all parts of France, assuming that passengers would continue on from Paris or London by rail. Eurotunnel, anxious to boost passenger traffic once the Tunnel was open, re-did its estimates once more. It became clear – to Eurotunnel – that a fast rail link would attract more passengers: ten per cent more, in fact, if the London–Paris journey were to be cut by half an hour. Unfortunately BR's attempts to cool the over-enthusiasm were stymied by the roaring success of the first TGV, that from Paris to Lyon, which from its opening in 1981 enjoyed traffic levels well above the most optimistic forecasts – though the air fares were expensive and the two cities offered an incomparable and guaranteed traffic flow.[6]

The saddest story is that of freight, where rail is generally more economic on journeys of over 500 miles. Again BR's estimates were modest, increasing from a figure of 6.2 million tons per annum when the Tunnel opened to a mere 8.5 million thirty years later – as against SNCF's estimates of 7.2 and 16.4 million. Unlike other estimates these were based on real figures, calculating that the tunnel would capture a fifth of the 'unitised' international traffic – the same proportion that BR captured on runs of over 200 miles – a total helped by the assumed increased speeds possible. And indeed the traffic is there – as witness the success of the lorry shuttles which took far more than their estimated share of cross-Channel traffic. It's just that rail has been unable to capture more than a sliver of it.

There are many reasons for this failure, including the general incompetence of SNCF's freight division and the obstacles placed in the way of opening France's rails to international traffic by management and unions. To make matters worse the extremely expensive, dual-voltage Class 92 electric locomotives specially constructed for the freight trains proved virtually useless, since French railwaymen refused to let them loose on their precious tracks. As for the Germans, they were unwilling to deprive their North Sea ports of traffic by routing it through the Tunnel. In the event, traffic slumped by a half from over three million tons in 1998 (itself only half the original forecasts) to 1.5 million in 2002, as a result of the security problems created by illegal immigrants trying to smuggle themselves aboard the trains. But a senior railwayman gave me a much more fundamental answer. 'When a freight manager is sending his cargo anywhere', he said, 'he needs to know exactly who's responsible for its progress' – an impossible task, given

6 Air passenger numbers on the route halved; by 1990 ten times as many went by train as by plane.

the way Europe's highly independent, not to say idiosyncratic, rail systems are managed.

There were also two technical problems: any new line would have far steeper gradients than SNCF recommended,[7] and the tracks in Britain would need to be upgraded to a 'Berne Gauge' to enable them to transport wagons built to the bigger Continental loading gauge. Only a few British routes could carry the crucial 9ft 6in-high containers increasingly employed by shipping companies – and only provided that they were carried on special, and expensive, wagons which were lower and had smaller wheels.

The demand for a new line was increased by subtle – and sometimes not so subtle – pressure from the French. Typically, when he opened the French high-speed link to the Tunnel on 18 May 1993, a year before the Tunnel itself was completed, President Mitterrand predicted, quite correctly, that: 'passengers will race at a great pace across the plains of northern France, rush through the Tunnel on a fast track – and then be able to daydream at very low speed, admiring the English countryside'.[8] On every Eurostar, as Nicholas Comfort remarks, soon after reaching France 'the train captain will announce that the train has reached its maximum speed of 186mph (300kph) – whether it has or not' (a habit abandoned in 2003, following the opening of the first section of the fast link).

Inevitably, as every commentator on the contrast between the French and British approaches to the link has remarked, the French got there first and more efficiently. Although the treaty establishing the Tunnel did not contain any reference to new railway links, nevertheless within a couple of years the French had taken action. André Bénard, the French co-chairman of Eurotunnel, made a promise to Alastair Morton to organise the project. Bénard was in a position to make good his pledge. A *polytechnicien* and former director of Shell, he simply arranged a dinner party for some of his influential friends and they decided that the link was required. And that, in France, was that.

It helped that the French love major schemes, and are quite prepared to tolerate the problems they cause. This attitude is reflected in their planning system which – in stark contrast to its British equivalent – actually encourages *grands projets*, with objections steam-rollered once a project has received its *declaration d'utilité publique*. And so far as the French are concerned, that is the end of the matter. As a French lawyer told a British civil servant, 'if you take action against a *declaration d'utilité publique* you're regarded as a traitor; not a proper republican'.

The result is that for the past thirty years the French have gone nap on their ever-expanding network of LGVs,[9] and the LGV Nord would have been built in the 1970s before the LGV Sud-Est from Paris to Lyon if the Tunnel had gone ahead then. France is

LOADING GAUGES

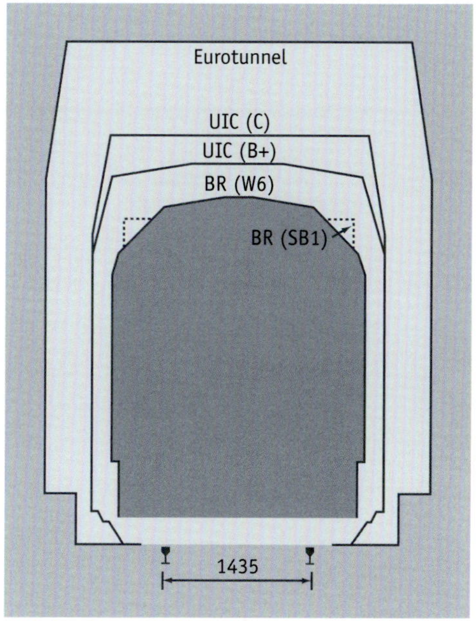

The BR loading gauge was smaller than the UIC (B+) gauge used in continental Europe. This meant that many lines in England were too constricted for through-running of freight trains from the Tunnel.

7 The French maximum gradient for mixed-use tracks was 1:83 as against 1:40 for the CTRL and TGV.

8 A remark described by a Labour MP as 'not a graceful gesture about the beauties of the English landscape: it was a humiliating put-down of the government's incompetence'. (Michael Meacher, January 1995). A British commentator in the late 1980s described the discrepancy as 'a looming humiliation'.

9 Lignes de Grande Vitesse, on which run TGVs, Trains de Grande Vitesse.

a big country, with more space to build and fewer people to object – though the line through the southern part of the Rhône Valley aroused some ire in the early 1990s. But there is a limiting factor. French authorities believe that '*tout passe par Paris*' – that the only important lines are those which fan out from the capital. The result is that France's network of traditional railway routes – itself much reduced since 1945 – has been largely neglected over the past three decades, with fewer and fewer trains travelling at ever-slower speeds even between major centres[10] as the quality of the track deteriorates.

Moreover the LGV to the Chunnel was merely a branch line on the main route from Paris through Lille to Brussels, for the French reduced the cost – to a mere £1.85 billion for the whole 333-km (207-mile) route – by avoiding the old Boat Train route via Amiens. In doing so they added 32km (20 miles) to the journey, making maximum use of the line from Paris to Brussels, by going via Lille. Indeed at a time when Kent's NIMBYs were howling at the possible proximity of a new railway line, the Amiennais were – and remain – furious that they had been by-passed.[11] France had its high-speed rail link ready in 1993 – a year before the Channel Tunnel opened – while the Belgians' was completed around 1997, the same year as the full LGV Nord. The French then went on to build a line by-passing Paris to join the LGV Sud-Est via Charles de Gaulle Airport.

The French planning process went further: the French, though not the English, version of the Channel Tunnel bid document contained clauses ensuring that a successful bidder would have to cooperate in helping to regenerate the Nord-Pas de Calais region, seriously depressed with the decline of its coal and textile industries. Success was further guaranteed because the mayor of Lille was Pierre Mauroy, President Mitterrand's first Prime Minister from 1981–1984, who remained a power in the land – and in the Socialist Party – after his dismissal. Despite initial objections from the Ministry of Finance, vast sums of money were poured into his fiefdom dressed up as a part of a major plan, transforming Lille into a splendid city (though neither the LGV nor the other investments helped his wider region, which remains to this day one of the most depressed in France). But aside from this, the French had one fundamental advantage: when it came to the line itself they had only to build through deserted countryside between Lille and Calais – and indeed between the outskirts of Paris and Lille. '112 kilometres of Eff-all' in the words of one embittered BR official, 'as against the same length of well-tended garden in Kent'.

Indeed, only too often, comparisons with the French situation are misleading. At first the SNCF took issue with the cost per kilometre of the proposed fast English link.

10 There are virtually no trains between Lyon and Bordeaux, and it takes seven hours to travel from Bordeaux to Marseilles, a distance of 645km, covered by autoroute in around five and threequarter hours.

11 A direct route is promised sometime before 2020.

THE FRENCH TGV NETWORK

CTRL ACCESS TO CENTRAL LONDON & TGV ACCESS TO PARIS

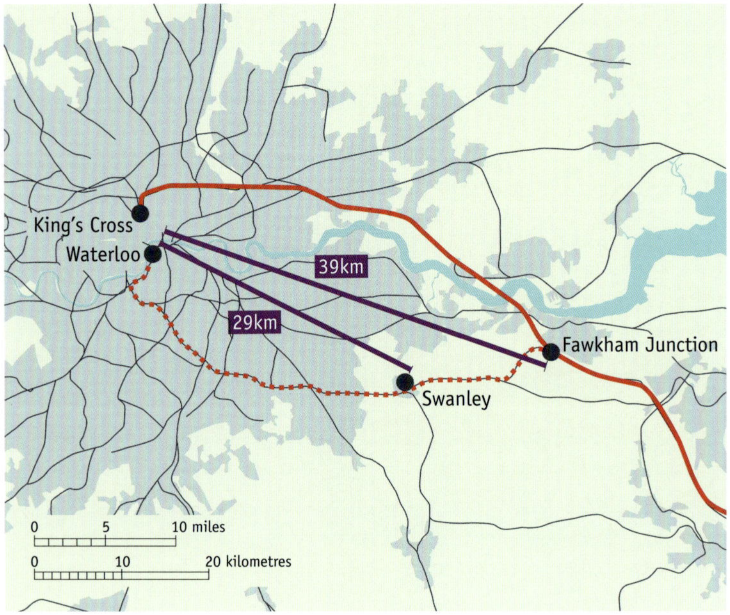

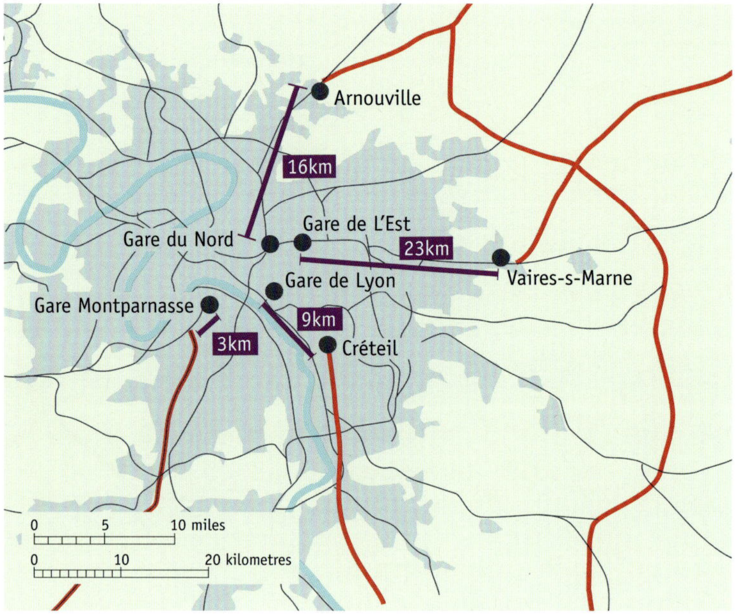

Above left: London's sprawling suburbs and busy commuter lines forced CTRL planners to either put up with slow running over the 29km (18 miles) from Swanley to Waterloo or dig a long tunnel. Even after CTRL 1 opened in 2003, Eurostars had to use 39km (24 miles) of slow track through South-East London (dotted line)

Above right: Paris, a smaller city with fewer rail commuters, allowed engineers to push the LGVs far closer in – and emptier tracks eased access to the termini

They came to Britain to look at the simplest section of the line, that from the Medway to Ashford, to study the design and the cost. They could get down to within 15 per cent of the British cost – but no closer.[12]

Costs in France are also drastically reduced by the way that their LGVs can join normal tracks some miles from their Parisian terminals, thus eliminating the need for – inevitably highly expensive and contentious – lines through the approaches to their final destination.[13] Happily for them, the French had ample capacity on the lines leading to their Paris termini, available thanks to the lack of any serious commuter traffic into Paris on the historic rail network – a mere nothing compared with the hordes who descend on London's termini every day (see maps above). Similarly, the Japanese could reach the centre of their cities on lines through land still vacant before post-war reconstruction when routing their Shinkansen (Bullet Trains).

A taste of the advantages offered by a fast link has come since 2003, when the fast railway from the tunnel to the outskirts of London was opened. Eurostar's punctuality rose from 78 to 91.5 per cent, and the improvement in speed and reliability immediately and increasingly attracted more passengers away from the airlines. But, alas, the Paris solution was impossible given the congestion on London's commuter railways.

The British were forced, albeit belatedly, to accept that growing pressure on existing routes meant that any new line would have to be built all the way into a terminal in central London. The congestion factor also applied to the terminus. In Paris they merely tacked on four new platforms to the Gare du Nord, a startling contrast to the magnificent and complex new station squeezed in at Waterloo. One man in an ideal position to compare the two attitudes was Sir Bob Reid I,[14] who had spent his seven years as chairman of BR loyally producing plans covering a mere five years: far too short a time for any major project. In early 1990, just before his retirement, he returned from a visit to France saying that it would take BR twenty years to catch up with the French. As a result he made a passionate plea for plans that would bring us in line with those being introduced by the French and Belgian governments.

The fundamental neglect of the need for a properly-financed rail system meant that the fast link to the Channel was on the radar at either Ten Downing Street or the Treasury only two or three times during the entire twenty-year process. It was simply assumed that BR would put the London section in a tunnel to Waterloo. This attitude was summed up in May 1990 by Harriet Harman, the Labour MP for Peckham, one of the parts of London most affected. On the 19th she noted how Michael Portillo[15] when Minister of State for Transport had sat through a previous debate[16] on the subject 'with a studied, neutral expression on his face. He listened to one side; he listened to the other; then he got up and said, "of course, it's nothing to do with me". That is not good enough. The Secretary of State for Transport said that the plan for the route was a private matter for British Rail and its partners. That is no way to treat the issue.'

Ms Harman grew more eloquent: 'Banks, property developers, British Rail and Members of Parliament with constituency interests have been fighting like rats in a sack – while the national interest wanders lonely and afraid, with no-one to look after it.'

Nevertheless the attempts by the government to distance itself from the scheme continued for some time. As late as November 1990 the then minister responsible, Roger Freeman, visited Stratford; while he asked BR's director of the South-East Region to consider the proposals for redeveloping the station, at the same time he stated firmly that 'it was for BR to evaluate' the idea of Stratford as an international station. Likewise on several occasions Mrs Thatcher made it clear that the whole affair was the sole responsibility of British Rail.

12 I am grateful to rail consultant Alan Dyke (a founder-member of the CTRL team and later MD for LCR's Union Railways) for this clarification: *"SNCF does not account for all its costs or charges when it uses its existing assets when building a new line, while BR had to pay market price for all assets used. The taxation system used in the UK is also quite different from France, so our contractors had to include more tax costs than SNCF."* The main difference in construction costs between northern France and southern England was the terrain and population centres. Labour rates between the two were also somewhat different, being much higher in southern England.

13 When building the LGV to the west and south-west, the French discovered an unused pair of tracks leading for several miles into the Gare Montparnasse – an unthinkable discovery in London.The fairest comparison is between the British and the Germans, who took nearly a quarter of a century to build a new line from Frankfurt to Cologne thanks to the efforts of Germany's ever-vigilant environmentalists.

14 His successor had the same name and was naturally referred to as Bob Reid II.

15 Once Portillo did get involved 'he was first class', says one Kent councillor. 'You could have a meaningful dialogue with him: things happened as a consequence.'

16 On 2 December 1988.

In December 1988 the lie was given by a normally loyal Tory, Sir John Stanley, MP for Tonbridge and Malling. Sir John emphasised that the fast link was 'the responsibility not only of British Rail, but of the Government.

'The proposals published by British Rail can only have been published with the approval of the Secretary of State for Transport. He must have approved publication, because he initiated these studies. The Government must have known that, by sanctioning the act of publication, they would confer instantaneous and severe planning blight from one end of Kent to the other. Therefore, a real responsibility lies with the Government, as well as with British Rail, to clear up the severe difficulties created.'

But the pressure for a new line was not only political. During the 1970s and early 1980s commuter traffic into London from Kent had declined steadily, thus making available an increasing number of 'paths' for rail traffic from South-East Kent. Traffic on the route, says Theo Steel (then of BR), 'was totally dominated by employment in Central London' – but then this began to soar again as the country went into the boom of the 1980s. After 1984 the number of passengers, far from falling (as BR had become accustomed to expect) rose at a steady pace of four per cent annually, and BR was aware that its new Networker trains could attract even more passengers, as indeed they did. The 500,000 commuters carried to the capital by train in 1988 were, records the '89 edition of the *London Property Guide*, 'a figure not seen since 1971' and were part of a general upsurge: 'across the country, and especially on express lines into London, rail travel is at its highest since 1961'.[17]

By this time a new executive, John Welsby, was responsible for the line at BR. In 1979 he had been brought in from a job as transport economist at the DoT as a trouble-shooter, originally to sort out the problems of BR's engineering division to prepare it for privatisation. He had gone on to undertake equally thorny jobs, including reorganising BR's provincial services and its procurement business. In November 1987 he was appointed to the BR board, of which he subsequently became chairman, and was put in full-time charge of the Channel link project after Kirby, for whom it had been only one of many responsibilities, had been promoted to vice-chairman.

Welsby was a highly effective operations and facilities manager, a classic British Rail man who 'fought the good fight' to keep BR intact. But his experience as a civil servant and a railway executive had not equipped him with the diplomatic and planning skills involved in not only devising a new railway, but also in the even more complex task of persuading a myriad of interest groups to accept the inevitable intrusion into their cosy worlds.

17 The dependence on employment in the City was then dramatically demonstrated during the slump of the early 1990s, for by 1992 passenger numbers from East Kent had shrunk back to their earlier level.

But by now Whitehall was in panic mode and, as one of the planners put it, 'we were always having to defend half-worked-out projects'. By July 1988, forecasts issued by BR in its first detailed report on the subject,[18] 'led it to conclude that there was a need for a CTRL' – and also (thanks entirely to those ludicrous traffic forecasts) for two London termini. But, as with the route, four locations made it to the shortlist (from 42 possibles): King's Cross Low Level, St Pancras, White City and Stratford.[19]

To Hammersmith Borough Council, the idea of a terminus at White City was as unappetising in the late 1980s as it had been 15 years earlier. But to the council of the deprived borough of Newham, centred round Stratford, the alternatives held out a wonderful, unprecedented opportunity for Stratford to be either the line's terminal or a station along the route. It might be said that they were PIMBYs – Please In My Back Yard.

They were led by an unlikely figure, Stephen Timms. He was a mathematician from Cambridge who had moved to one of the less-salubrious corners of Newham while working in IT. In 1984 he was elected as a Labour member of the local council (the start of a political career which was to lead him to the Cabinet as Chief Secretary to the

Above left: Kent's legacy of built-on-the-cheap 19th-century railways, with their tight, twisting curves and numerous little bridges and short tunnels contrasts with the TGV Nord (**above right**), striding across the empty landscape of the Pas de Calais

18 Channel Tunnel Rail Services: BR study report on long-term route and terminal capacity.

19 Another six out of 42 initial prospects made it to the detailed assessment: these were Euston High and Low Level, Smithfield, Bishopsgate, London Bridge Low Level, Stratford High Level and Temple Mills.

1987

February

- The Channel Tunnel Act receives Royal Assent
- Waterloo chosen as first London terminal

July

- British Rail (BR) begins a study of long-term capacity needed for Channel Tunnel services

29 July

- President Mitterrand and Prime Minister Thatcher meet at Elysée Palace, Paris, to sign agreement for construction of the Channel Tunnel

August

- Kent Impact Study report accepted by government

1988

January

- Kent JCC sets up monitoring group to report on strategy

Treasury within 20 years). In 1986 he became chairman of Newham's environment committee, and Leader of the Council four years on. At the time, he says, 'East London was at rock bottom; the docks and their associated industries had disappeared and the unemployment rate was 20 per cent'.

Before BR had announced the four chosen sites for the second terminus, Timms had fought a successful battle in Parliament with the London Docklands Development Corporation (LDDC) to get Canning Town a station on the Docklands Light Railway's new extension to Beckton – even though this involved a kink in the route. 'This gave us the confidence that we could get something done', he says – and he immediately saw BR's CTRL proposals 'as a fantastic opportunity'.

His reasoning was simple: historically Stratford had, in effect, been a 'railway town' in the middle of East London, and already had a good set of local rail connections, so a new international station on 120 acres of little-used railway land was the obvious way of regenerating the borough. Sadly, throughout the saga BR fought a stubborn rearguard battle to avoid surrendering the whole site. Although prepared to abandon some of its sprawling buildings it wanted to relocate carriage sidings there, and to build new carriage-cleaning sheds.

BR's report, which also contained the various forecasts plus high-, medium- and low-growth scenarios for Kent's domestic services, drew the conclusion that without a new link, and because of the 'severe peaks each morning and evening … some [international] passengers will be unable to travel at the hour of their choice on about 55 days in the year'. These unfortunates, said BR, 'will generally be accommodated on trains with empty seats at other times of day'.[20] It had often used differential pricing to force passengers off domestic trains at peak hours, and was perfectly prepared to continue this practice on the service to the Channel over the existing tracks.

British Rail's caution was based on its own traffic forecasts, less unrealistic than anyone else's; besides, it saw no urgent need for a faster journey time, in any case preferring to wait until the Tunnel opened. For BR was by no means eager to promote the new line. 'We never wanted a CTRL', said one senior railwayman; 'we were quite happy with a slower route'. In the peak hours freight trains would be banned from the Channel line, and only three international passenger trains could be fitted in – 'all with extended journey times'.

Above all, BR had not understood that Kent was not so much the Garden of England but thousands of gardens, so that any new railway had to be confined to an existing road

20 Or even 'other days of the week'.

corridor. John Welsby and his team made a bad start. BR had decided on four different possible alignments in both halves of the route, blithely assuring the rest of Whitehall that the publication of the four alternative route corridors would not create any blight....[21]

Inevitably an early draft of BR's proposals leaked: to the *Sunday Times* in April 1988.[22] They were published, with maps (of a sort) in BR's report three months later and were a total disaster – even though Route Four, based on the old Boat Train Route No 1 so beloved of BR, had already been discarded. But even then the reasoning was merely that it 'looks unattractive on grounds of both cost and journey-time' – not because it ran slap through Sevenoaks and a number of villages on the way. The map on page 63 – and British Rail's own contemporary map, reproduced on page 60 – show that between them the three remaining routes threatened the whole heart of Kent and a great swathe of South-East London.

Obviously the extent of the blight was far greater than if the plan had been confined to a single route. It also proposed four sites for the second station, deemed to be required because the forecasts anticipated more than the 13 million passengers possible at Waterloo – echoes of the 1970s. The plan also offered the possibility of using the new railway for domestic services, thus relieving the strain on the existing network and allowing for the possiblity of government subsidy.

Before announcing his decision John Welsby met Kent Council's Mike Odling, with Mike Cottell, the County Surveyor (and later President of the Institution of Civil Engineers). It seemed to Odling that Welsby 'had simply drawn four lines on a map'. One went through the Bourne Valley 'an absolutely glorious part of Kent' where Odling himself lived. 'Cottell asked Welsby how much work had been done. It was clearly minimal work – and minimal thought, too.' Odling told him that 'we already had a transport corridor, the M20, and that BR should work on that'. For the KCC was aware, as BR so obviously wasn't, of the vital importance of the environmental dimension in the choice of route; although it has to be said that none of the major organisations devoted to the protection of the environment seemed to be concerned at the time.

In effect it had taken a county council to plan an international railway – if only, as Odling points out, because 'there was no liaison between the Department of Transport and the Department of the Environment.' Not surprisingly the meeting at which Welsby presented BR's plans to KCC was not a success. 'We sent Welsby away with a flea in his ear', Odling said, after pointing out that 'you've not built a railway for 100 years and you can't do it like this, environmentally or politically'. Indeed Kent had proved not only that

21 ...and repeating precisely the mistake it had made in 1973.

22 The *Sunday Times* must have had an early version of the report, for it described three routes: Option 1 was essentially the 1973 route, Option 2 followed the M20 and Option 3 was close to the eventual route, crossing the Medway then under the Thames into Essex, to Stratford and then to King's Cross. Both Options 1 and 3 ended at King's Cross.

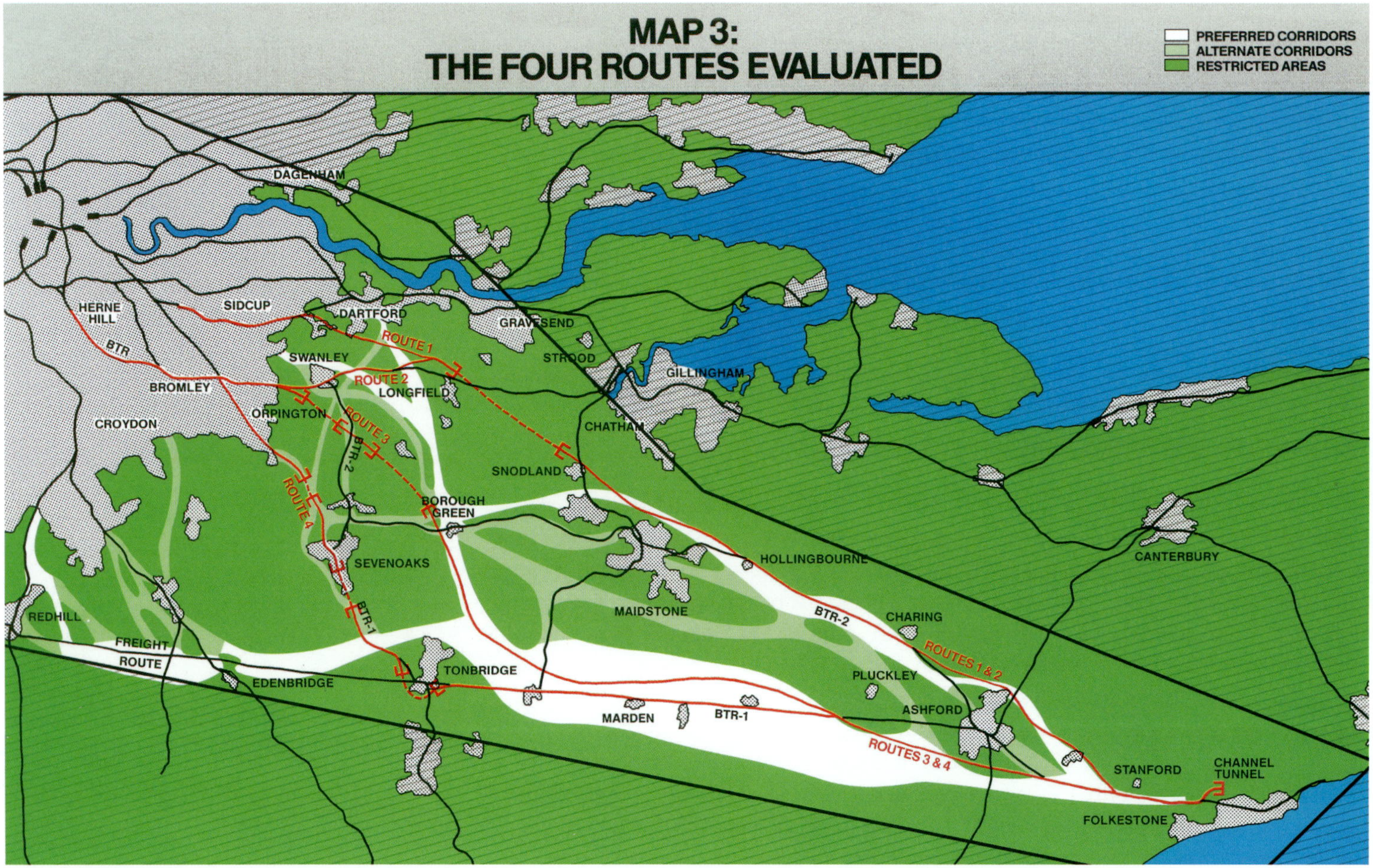

Map reproduced from BR's July 1988 report: the white belts showed 'preferred corridors' up to six miles wide – and the routes could follow any line within them

it was – uniquely in the Thacherite years – capable of 'joined-up government': it was also better able to plan a railway than BR. British Rail took no notice, and then went public; but even after the announcement (in July 1988), the government continued to distance itself from the whole venture. According to the official history, 'Channon took the view that it was BR's report and that it was for BR to defend it'. This did not stop him from announcing the idea of a public–private partnership to build the new line at the Tory Party conference in early October. But by then (to no-one's surprise except BR's), massive protests were threatening the whole project. As Odling put it: 'Kent went up in smoke' – and so, too, did the whole of South-East London.

1 2 3 4 **5** 6 7 8 9 10 11 12

LIVE IN KENT AND BE CONTENT

pre-war advertisement for Southern Electrics

A high-speed line does not weave its way around hills, mills and manors; it proceeds with the tact of a Roman road, using brute power to drive its trains up steel hillsides.

The Economist, 16 July 1988

Facing page: July 1988 saw the publication of BR's report, with four possible routes from the Channel Tunnel to London. It already faced competition from the RACHEL and TALIS schemes, neither of which threatened the Weald of Kent with its wealthy and influential inhabitants.

■ Over a century before the term 'NIMBY' – Not in My Back Yard – had been coined, no less a person than William Wordsworth had launched the concept. Attempting to defend his precious corner of the Lake District from intrusion by that smoky monster, the railway train, he penned a famous sonnet which begins with the stirring words: 'Is then no nook of English ground secure from rash assault?'[1] By the end of the 1980s the NIMBYs were rampant, and the multiplicity of choices for the fast line put forward by BR gave them an unrivalled reason to object – far more so than with a new motorway, when only a single route is presented to the public.

BR's proposals thus caused uproar, for they not only greatly enlarged the areas affected by potential blight, but ensured that the threat was imprecise. The four routes – see map opposite – covered a wedge-shaped swathe of land across Kent's most prosperous central belt, the county's 'fillet', housing, usually in some comfort, the rich and influential inhabitants of the Weald – a stark contrast to the relatively poor east and north of the county. What is more, the routes ran through 'Preferred Corridors' that were as much as six miles wide, shown on maps bereft of contours, motorways or local government boundaries. Indeed, BR stressed that the maps were merely a 'general indication' of the routes – and that precise alignments would come later. And one must remember that this was not simply a case of some middle-class objections to losing a little of the serenity of their homes to an intermittent rattling of trains: London and the South-East were at the climax of a dramatic property price boom, and for most people their home now represented by far their biggest (for many, their only) tangible asset. At a stroke, all homes the length and breadth of all four 'routes' were at best devalued, at least unsaleable, at worst under threat of demolition. People were trapped.

To make matters worse, looming in the background was the ominous figure of Alastair Morton, Eurotunnel's co-chairman, naturally fuming at any delay ('the French will not know whether to laugh or cry'). In particular he simply could not understand why BR had even suggested Route Three, which ran straight across the Weald. Here the heavy clay soil meant that much of the line would have to be raised on bunds,[2] thus greatly increasing the visual intrusion on the landscape. And, to boot, greatly exacerbating the noise problem of what *The Economist* referred to as 'low-flying trains': a central feature of the protesters' complaints.

Inevitably there was an immediate and violent reaction throughout Kent and South-East London. British Rail had been naïve, as it was throughout the whole saga – a reaction typical of many a large, introverted organisation both public and private –

1 The remaining lines of the sonnet are:

. . . Schemes of retirement sown
In youth, and 'mid the busy world kept pure
As when their earliest flowers of hope were blown,
Must perish;—how can they this blight endure?
And must he too the ruthless change bemoan
Who scorns a false utilitarian lure
'Mid his paternal fields at random thrown?
Baffle the threat, bright Scene, from Orresthead
Given to the pausing traveller's rapturous glance:
Plead for thy peace, thou beautiful romance
Of nature; and, if human hearts be dead,
Speak, passing winds; ye torrents, with your strong
And constant voice, protest against the wrong.

2 Originally an Urdu word, which became railwaymen's term for embankments.

1988: BR, TALIS & RACHEL

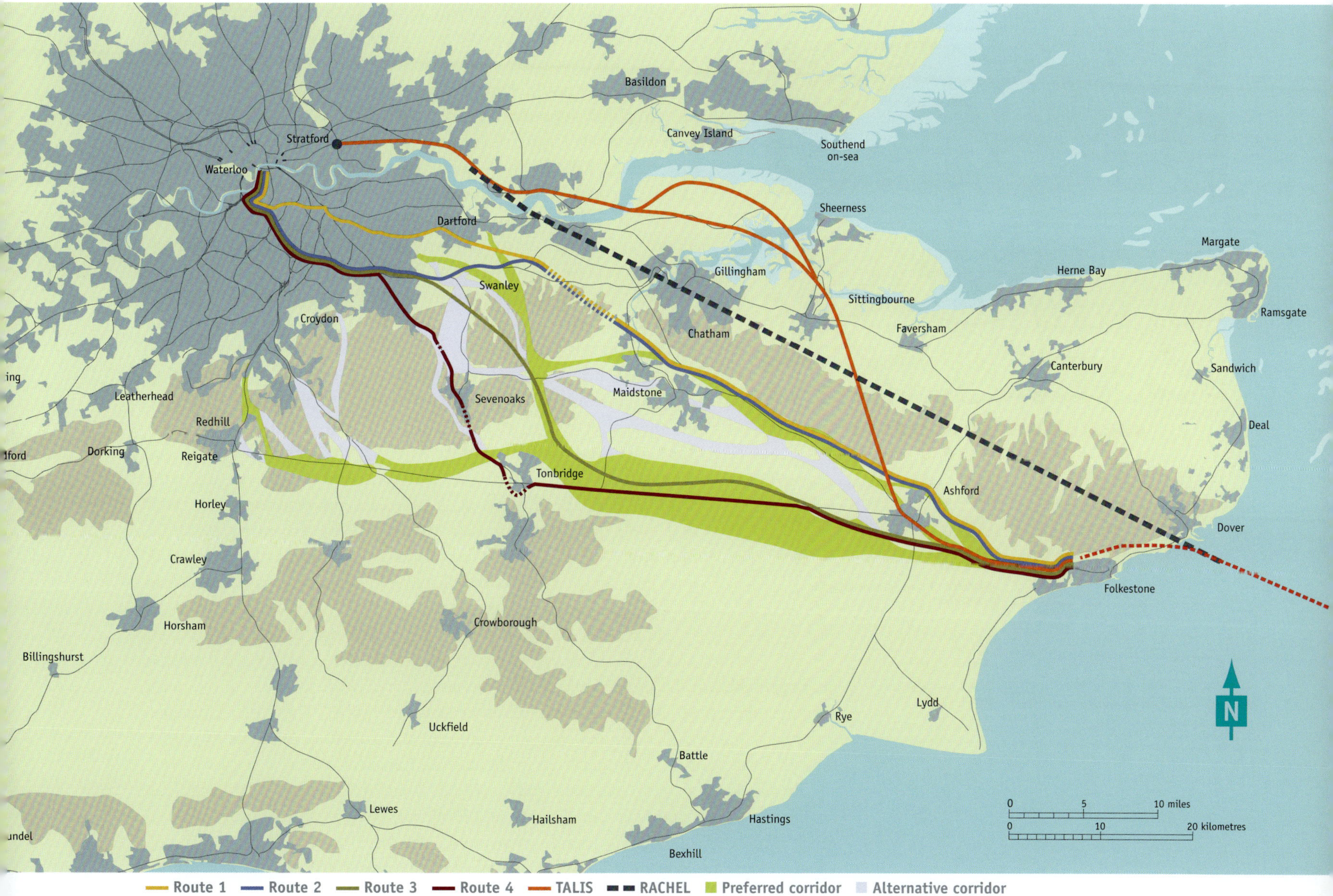

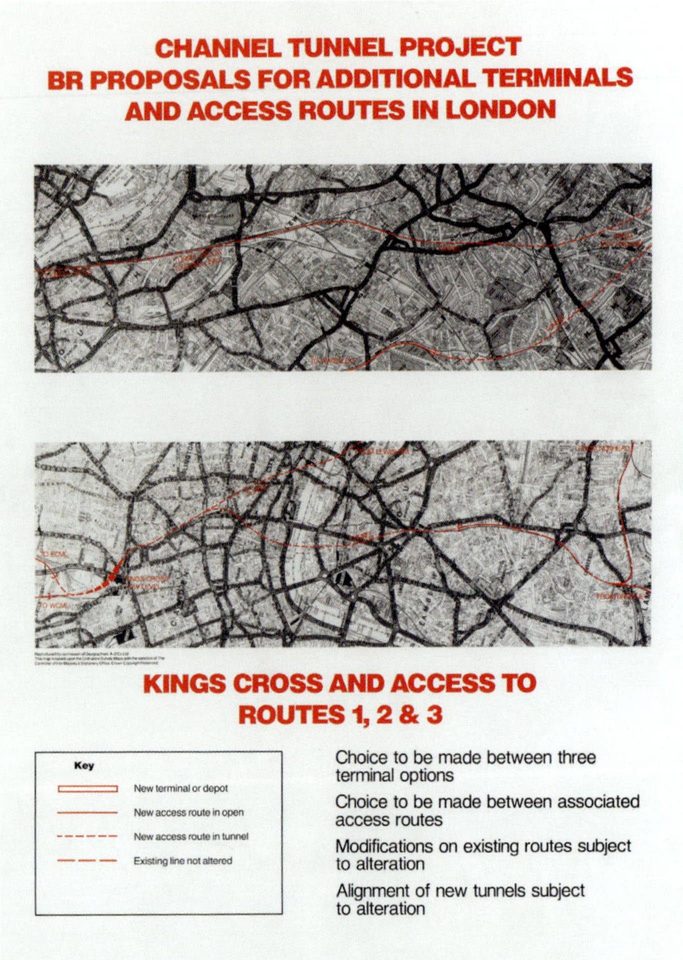

BR's 'attempt to be open' with Londoners backfired, as locals contemplated poorly-produced maps with several choices of route – all 'subject to alteration'

indeed, so naïve that it simply could not understand what was happening. One clue was the reaction from one planner towards a proposal that they called an 'outline possibility'. 'Maybe', he said, 'with hindsight we should have planned more deeply at the start and delayed public announcement and consultation….' As a colleague put it: 'it was purely an attempt on our part to be open about consultation possibilities. I don't think we envisaged the reaction that this would cause'. Of course it had not helped that BR had only a tiny team trying to sketch out the route – the same problem had afflicted its pioneering, tilting Advanced Passenger Train, crippled because only five engineers were assigned to it.

But then British Rail simply could not cope, either with the ridiculous timetable imposed on it by the DoT, or in dealing with the public. Crucially, in the total absence of any alternative guidance from Whitehall, BR looked at the link from a purely transport point of view. As one British Rail veteran put it: 'as it is a BR project they have no alternative but to exclude all the property benefits'. Malcolm Southgate, BR's project manager, saw that 'the prime need from our point of view is the transport network, to connect the UK with Europe's high-speed network. If there are any planning gains, well and good; but our proposals should not be driven by planning opportunities. We're trying to produce a new transport infrastructure for a new century. I think the proponents of the alternative solutions have got the cart before the horse'.

In fact, if it did pause to consider such things, British Rail got them wrong. In a throwaway paragraph, it said that it had rejected a route via Dagenham, on the north bank of the Thames estuary, 'because of its conflict with current and proposed developments south of the Dartford Tunnel'. These 'developments' – the recycling of the enormous, disused chalk pits – provided an opportunity, rather than an obstacle, to the eventual route in the form of Ebbsfleet station.

British Rail's naïvety was especially evident when it came to considering the environment. 'We simply assumed' said one BR official, 'that because railways were so much more environmentally friendly than roads, the fast link would be welcomed'. Characteristically Bernard Gambrill, a member of the rail link team and a chartered engineer, was brought in to cover the environmental portfolio after the chief engineer saw him studying a book on wild flowers, his passion outside his work.

One of BR's few defenders was the redoubtable Ann Widdecombe, the MP for Maidstone. In December 1988 – the first time the House of Commons had discussed the projected fast link – she sensibly refused to 'join in the general bashing of British Rail that has been prevalent recently.

'British Rail had a hopeless task. It had to produce four hideous propositions, take them into the heart of Kent and sell them to people who were to be affected by them. Inevitably, it has been castigated for mistakes which it undoubtedly made. The people trying to sell the proposals were not public relations men but British Rail officials. They did a good job, and are continuing to do so, under difficult circumstances.'

Nevertheless such was British Rail's status as a national punch-ball that every error was pointed up and magnified. Today people still recall how BR used an out-of-date map, and thus had not realised that one of its chosen routes went through Oakhive, a newly-built housing estate between Maidstone and the Medway towns. Similarly a report for BR from Environmental Resources (ERL) on properties affected was, to the protesters, 'completely invalid', since it included a school which had not existed since 1977 and failed to show sheltered and other housing. To make matters worse Nick Alexander, BR's study-group leader, revealed that the initial route plans were indeed produced on a map overlaid 'with greaseproof paper on the kitchen table'.[3]

Within a few months BR reported that they had received 'comments' – a huge understatement – from 'nineteen action groups, 52 District or Parish councils and over 10,000 individuals or groups'. These covered South-East London and much of Kent. In the eloquent words of Nigel Thomas,[4] 'the revolt that followed [BR's proposals] shook the Tory Party to the core. A revolutionary mob in waxed green jackets is enough to bring any Home Counties MP out in a rash. An attempt to smear the campaigners as NIMBYs never really got off the ground for, as the then environment secretary Nicholas Ridley pointed out when he objected to a scheme affecting his own home, "who isn't guilty of that?"'

The worst problem was the sheer uncertainty provoked by BR's proposals. As Harriet Harman put it, 'the difficulties of my constituents have been made much worse by the continuing uncertainty surrounding the route of the link.... One of the commonest complaints that I receive is that people do not know where they stand because the route has not yet been decided'.

3 A Kent MP also reported that villagers in his constituency were told by a BR official that he had used his children's crayons and his wife's greaseproof paper to draw up the route. (Jacques Arnold MP, Hansard January 1995).

4 *Sunday Times Magazine*, 6 May 1990.

Four Secretaries of State for Transport in a mere seven years: *top left* Nicholas Ridley (October 83–May 86); *top right* John Moore (May 86–June 87); *lower left* Paul Channon (June 87–July 89); *lower right* Cecil Parkinson (July 89–November 90)

But it was not a party political matter: every MP and councillor of every persuasion was active. Kent had thirteen MPs (all Tories, five of them ministers), each of them objecting in his or her own way. Attitudes ranged from that of one councillor who exploded 'who wants an effing railway anyway?' to Michael Howard, MP for Folkestone, who took every complaint on its merits, accepting only the clearly genuine ones. In most cases MPs 'were perfectly reasonable in private and then played to the gallery of their constituents in public', remembers one BR planner wryly. The London MPs included the vociferous Kate Hoey, Labour, whose Vauxhall seat would be affected by developments at Waterloo and the increased road traffic that they would create, as well as Simon Hughes, the Liberal MP for Bermondsey.

In fact the line divided into two. The route of the first two-thirds (later CTRL1), from the Tunnel to the London side of the North Downs, was relatively straightforward; on this the panic, largely avoidable, was almost entirely created by the publication of the four routes. Naturally the proposals sparked off the establishment of numerous protest groups such as CHARGE (Channel Action Residents' Groups Executive). The most effective perhaps was the A2 action group North Downs Rail Concern, presided over by Andrew Rowe, the local MP – though the Darent Valley NIMBYs were also a force to be reckoned with, blooded by their success in opposing the M25.[5] The Bourne Valley group proved their professionalism by churning out newsletters with a print-run of 10,000, then getting them out to the hamlets in 24 hours via a pyramid distribution network.

Many more joined the fundamentalist opposition under the banner 'Sink the Link'. This involved every type of demonstration, most noisily a van going round the county armed with a loudspeaker blaring forth the imagined sound of a TGV. There were 14,000 signatures in a petition to Kent County Hall. No less than 6,000 souls marched through Maidstone one January Saturday. There was even a witches' rally to demonstrate about BR's apparent plans to desecrate one particularly holy Circle, the Countess Stones of Kit's Coty.

British Rail simply could not cope with the sheer professionalism of the 'Men of Kent'. 'In Kent' said Mike Odling of the County Council, 'there is a mobile and able population.... You don't go into a public meeting without doing your homework. You had to assume that there was an expert in the room.' Moreover they were well connected. The council, he said, found it necessary 'to tap influential people in the Commons, the

5 The motorway's alignment through their valley proved so contentious that it was the very last section to be finished.

Lords, industry.... Kent County Council's range of contacts was enormous. We could find anybody to do anything'.[6] In the council, too, this was not a party political matter. 'There was a general sense that it was bigger than any group of people.'

Fortunately for British Rail, the more rational opposition represented by the KCC dominated the discussion. It was well expressed by Sandy Bruce-Lockhart, a fruit farmer from a distinguished family, who had been closely involved in the Weald of Kent Preservation Society. Odling helped persuade him to take up politics: he stood for the council; within a few years he had taken over Odling's committee chairmanship and he soon rose through the political ranks to head first the Kent County Council and then, as Lord Bruce-Lockhart, the Local Government Association. As he says: 'we had a more rational and pragmatic view of the national interest'. Indeed KCC had a surprisingly constructive attitude and, 'while accepting the need for new rail capacity', rejected all BR's options 'in their present form'. Right through the planning process the council kept a beady eye on the project. In 1988 they checked up on BR's plans through consultants who confirmed that a new line was indeed necessary, and later compared the proposed noise limits with those prevailing in France and Germany. Unfortunately British Rail could seemingly respond only with pamphlets couched in technical language: 'the level of railway noise at which 20 per cent of people will be highly annoyed is about 72 to 75dbA....'

But British Rail had seen nothing yet: the last third of the route lay through London, as defined by the boundaries of the Greater London Council. Threading a new line through the capital's densely populated south-eastern approaches was always going to be a nightmare. The result, wrote Thomas in the *Sunday Times*, was 'a mass mobilisation of the inner suburbs led by the young professional and business classes armed with skills of management, organisation, planning, research, communication

OPTIONS FOR A SECOND LONDON TERMINUS

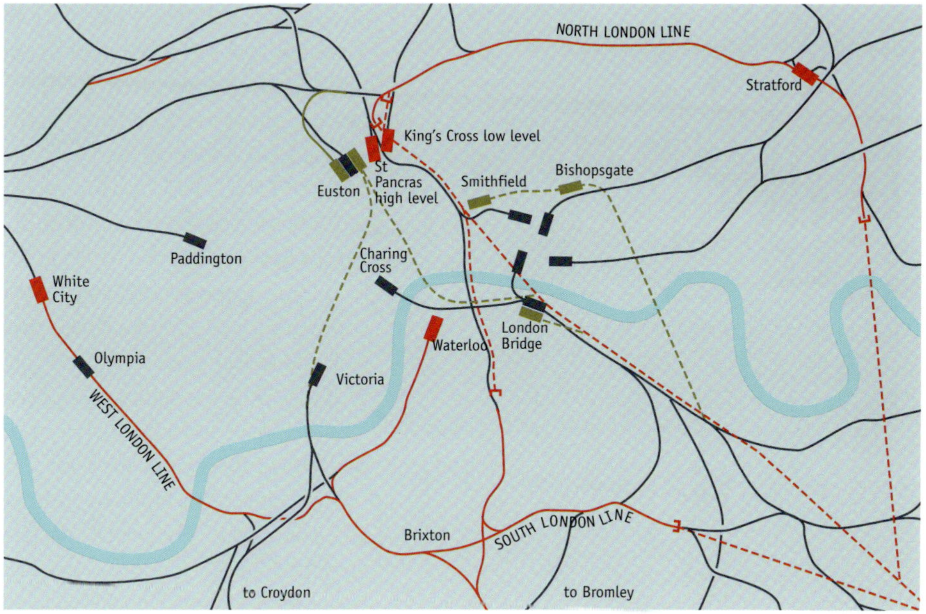

BR's July 1988 report ruled out several possibles (shown in green above) for a second terminus. Shortlisted were (in red): St Pancras, King's Cross Low Level, White City and Stratford

6 Typically, the father of Roger Freeman, the junior Minister of State responsible between 1990 and 1992, had managed ICI's pension funds; naturally, Odling knew him.

and media relations – the very qualities hitherto lacking at BR'. Unfortunately Mrs Thatcher had just abolished the GLC, so coping with BR's plans was left to individual boroughs. Not surprisingly they and the pressure-groups they spawned were not united, since each one was trying to move the route to someone else's back-yard. To the Kent groups were swiftly added PEARL (Peckham and Camberwell Action on the Rail Link), BATTL (Brockley), THROTTL (Telegraph Hill Residents), DARLINK (Dulwich)... and a dozen others.

In dealing with the thousands of homeowners who found themselves threatened by its plans, BR was also hamstrung by the archaic nature of the way it could pay compensation to those affected. In theory this was covered by what is called the National Compensation Code even though, as Bernard Gambrill points out, 'it is not national, provides little monetary compensation and it is not codified'. But the whole situtation seems to have been both chaotic and illogical. By contrast, in France SNCF was able to offer those disturbed a generous rate, paid up front (though unlike the British the French victims had to pay their own transaction costs).

There was a chance to compare the distinction between road and rail when the Bill covering the BR route for the fast link was being examined by Parliamentary Select Committees, since the Bill also included the widening of the A2/M2 – the old Dover Road. When the widening had been mooted it looked as if the Highways Agency had been buying almost any property offered to it in the corridor before it had received the powers required to undertake the work.

Again it was Widdecombe who pointed up the absurdity of the situation: 'It is difficult to produce a full package of measures to deal with a completely new set of circumstances, but surely it was realised that the day would inevitably come when a new railway track would have be be built. It must have been realised that we could not go on for ever without any expansion of the rail network. It must have been clear that any major railway construction project would have presented complex and manifold problems. However, insufficient thought was given before the proposals were announced to ensuring that the necessary laws were on the statute book or that British Rail, as a nationalised industry, was given firm guidance.... The issues are complex. We have built no new railways since the turn of the century and our compensation laws are therefore inadequate and in a mess. The laws that apply to motorways do not apply in the same way to railways ... BR is not obliged to provide compensation to persons affected by the route until the bill to authorise the scheme receives Royal Assent.' But, as she pointed out,

BR had recognised the problem and started to offer the ex-gratia payments which were the only way it could help those affected. Nevertheless BR had been very slow off the mark. It wasn't until May 1989, for instance, that it appointed a company called Terraquest to produce a record of all the properties that would, or could, be affected. By this time, maps of the proposed routes had been in the public domain for over a year.

In January 1989 British Rail suddenly announced that a low-level station at King's Cross was their preferred choice for the second London terminal. Originally BR had said that it would need to spend two years studying the alternatives, but greed greatly speeded up the study. British Rail was hoping to take advantage of the plans put forward by two major property developers, Rosehaugh and Stanhope, linked as the London Regeneration Consortium (LRC) to develop the unoccupied railway lands[7] across the canal to the north of both King's Cross and St Pancras (and not anywhere near anyone's Back Yards). There was even talk that the developers would combine with the irrepressible Alastair Morton to build a new fast line as well. 'The new Channel Tunnel and the new King's Cross station will both be ready by 1993; so we are only debating how to connect them', said Morton.[8]

John Welsby presents BR's favourite route, March 1989

As a result BR hoped to get a station for free, and put forward a Bill covering the development within a mere six weeks – without warning the DoT. Stratford was dismissed because of the 'constricted' site, a longer journey and thus more expense, while St Pancras, the most likely alternative, was excluded because it would involve moving the Midland Main Line's domestic services. It would also require new tracks on the North London Line from Stratford, whereas the tunnel to King's Cross could join with 'Thameslink', the newly re-opened north-south service from Brighton through London, via London Bridge, Blackfriars and King's Cross, then north to Luton and Bedford.

It was highly unlikely that the developers would have paid the whole cost – estimated at a gigantic £1.4 billion – and King's Cross low level had two other major disadvantages. 'At King's Cross we had to dig up the whole of Camden and Islington',

7 These had originally been the enormous depot where freight on the Great Northern Railway from King's Cross to Newcastle and Edinburgh was transferred to road transport.

8 *Sunday Times*, 31 July 1988.

Facing page: in March 1989 BR published its route – which differed from all the four alignments it had published in the previous July. It involved a long tunnel from Swanley, on the outskirts of London, right through to King's Cross – with a sub-surface junction at Peckham, where the Waterloo spur would emerge to join existing tracks.

said a senior engineer, 'put in a station and then fill up the hole'. Although in fact only seven acres (2.8ha) on the borough boundaries were directly affected, the two councils naturally objected. Additionally, as we shall see, it greatly complicated the situation at Warwick Gardens in Peckham – which had turned out, so unexpectedly (to BR at least), to be a NIMBY heartland. The King's Cross bill had already been published because of the need to start work before the 'railway lands' to the north were redeveloped. It provided for a station with eight platforms: four for international, two for commuters, two for Thameslink.

Kent County Council announced in January 1989 that it accepted the necessity for a high speed line – but that it rejected all four BR route options. It again stresssed the need to establish a single transport corridor through the county. Then in early February Mrs Thatcher became personally involved. Like so many of the politicians in this story she had a Kentish connection, since the first constituency she had fought was at Dartford in 1950 – a campaign memorable mainly because it was when she met her Denis[9] – and, in the late 1980s, she bought a retirement home in Dulwich not far from one of BR's four routes. Following a ministerial meeting which decided that public money might have to be involved (a fact not, apparently, conveyed to BR) John Welsby was called in for his 'Thatcher moment', and very typical it was too. Her opening remark, accompanied by the familiar gimlet stare, was simple: 'So you're the man who's going to lose us the Kent local elections' – due three months later. The grilling went on for two hours, and included a searching question about the tunnelling problems associated with the Thanet Sands, a question to which both Welsby and Nicholas Ridley – a former civil engineer, and by then Secretary for Trade and Industry – found it impossible to provide a convincing answer. But after the ordeal she said simply: 'OK; go ahead'.

By March '89 BR had accepted that the 'effects of capacity limitation on the existing routes would be felt within ten years of the Channel Tunnel opening to traffic in 1993',[10] and published its favoured route. This, it turned out, differed from all four of the routes proposed in the previous July, spreading yet a further wave of alarm across Kent and South London. The decision on the route was made by the British Railways Board; there was speculation within the industry that the benefits stemming from property developments at and around Waterloo and King's Cross were foremost in its mind. Mark Bostock of Arup noted the following summer 'indeed it could be concluded that the whole alignment is being driven by the two [property] deals'.

BR's criteria for the fast link now included 'to use existing rail and other transport

9 At the time he was chairman of the local Conservative party and chauffered her around in his Daimler.

10 *Channel Tunnel Rail Link* (British Railways Board, March 1989).

BRITISH RAIL'S MARCH 1989 ROUTE

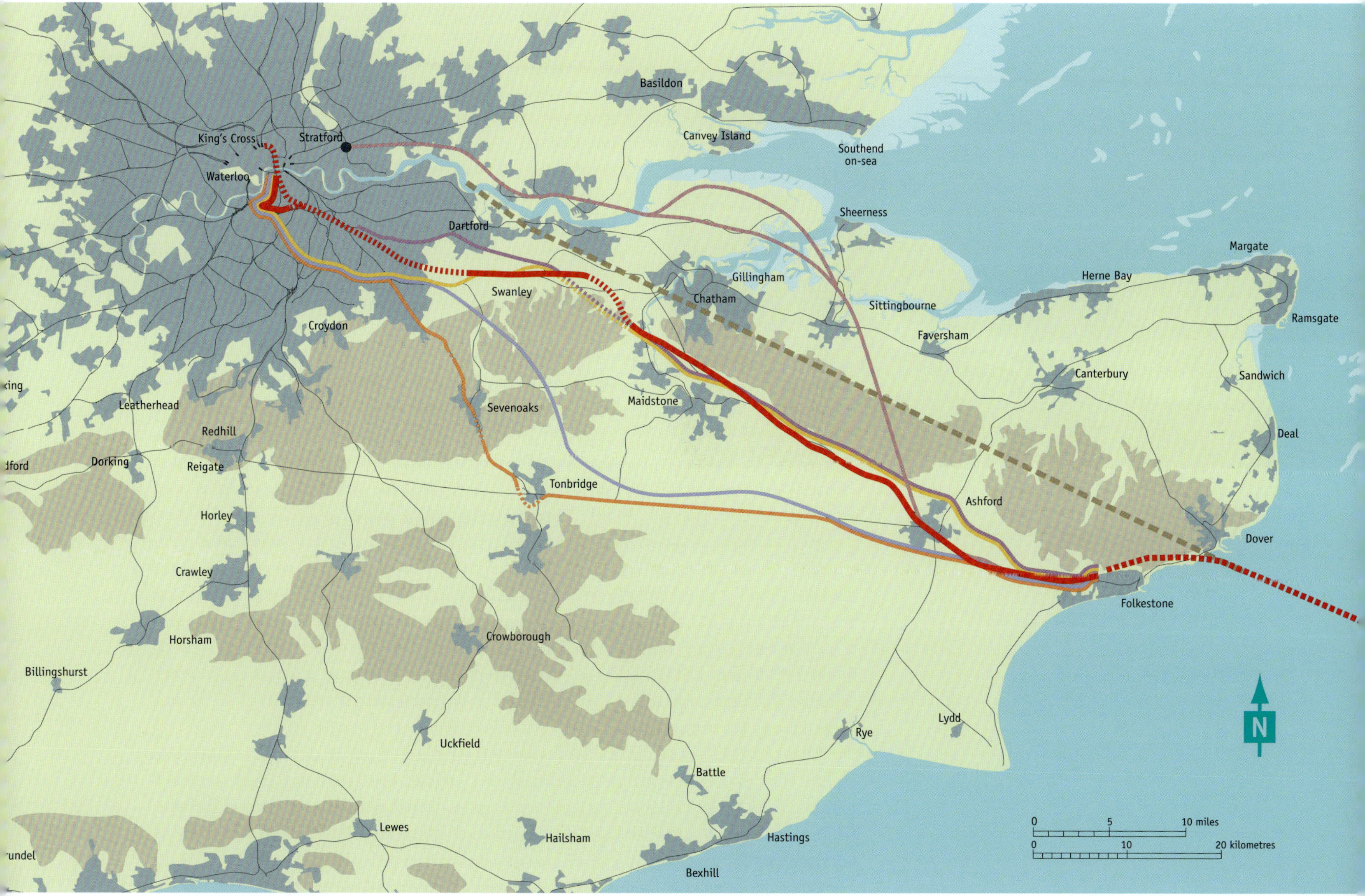

New route — Route 1 — Route 2 — Route 3 — Route 4 — TALIS — RACHEL

Until 2007, the Eurostars had to snake slowly through areas like Clapham on their way to Waterloo: concern over the noise and vibration from the enormous trains led to mass protests at BR's plans

corridors wherever possible' – which involved exploiting the transport corridor already employed by the M20, being extended to the tunnel terminal at the time. Unfortunately the railway demanded more sweeping curves than a new motorway, and so could not follow the route exactly – in one place the motorway had been designed with a series of curves to avoid houses which BR now proposed to pull down. On the other hand, the railway occupied a much narrower corridor than the road. As BR pointed out, 'the average width of the line between fences will be only 20 metres' – compared with 50 for a dual three-lane motorway like the M20. As a result, all the traffic between London and the Channel could be concentrated into one corridor – as Kent County Council had demanded. Most significantly, only 22 per cent of the new route would be in a new transport corridor, and there was to be a new 'Mid-Kent Parkway' Station between Maidstone and the three major towns of North Kent, Chatham, Gillingham and Rochester. Of course this solution could have been arrived at much earlier had BR not published alternative routes.

BR had had to abandon both 'Boat Train' routes because the 'extensive enhancements required … would be unlikely to be cost-effective'. This meant that over a third of the distance from King's Cross to Folkestone was to be in tunnel. To make good its pledge to 'make maximum use of tunnels on the approaches to London' it proposed a long tunnel of 17.5 miles (28km), from the M25 at Swanley right through to King's Cross – taking the line clear under the London suburbs except for a sub-surface junction at Warwick Gardens, Peckham, where the spur to Waterloo would leave the main King's Cross line and join existing surface tracks.

These changes, especially the longer tunnels – including one under the North Downs and another on the western approach to Ashford – added £500 million to the previously-estimated cost of £1.2 billion. One eminent engineer brushes aside a long-standing belief that the terrain in South-East London was unsuitable for tunnelling as 'just an excuse by London Underground because it didn't want to extend the tube network south of the Thames'. Or, as a borough council engineer in South-East London commented at the time 'it just shows: if you have a pot of money you can dig through anything.'

As one engineer put it, the new route involved a 'delicate balance between environmental protection and financial viability … balancing the speed, journey time, cost and environmental impact'. So the maximum speed would be a mere 140mph (225kph) – the same as the original proposal for a modernised West Coast Main Line from Euston to Birmingham and the North. The speed, 75kph slower than France's TGVs, allowed for a shorter viaduct over the Medway and above all would reduce the noise pollution. The result would be a journey time from London to the tunnel of 40 minutes: 30 minutes less than the time taken on the existing Boat Train routes – and 45 quicker than the time in peak periods. The new line would provide for express commuter services, and for 'light parcels and express freight' – not a wholehearted commitment. Pressure from environmental groups was assuaged by assurances that the trains would be less noisy than existing trains elsewhere in Britain, while those directly affected by the plans were offered 'more generous compensation'. BR would undertake to acquire all affected properties within 240 metres of the new line – a far better deal than with new motorways, as well as providing noise insulation where required.

If the BR Board expected a welcome for the new plan it was soon disappointed. MPs in Kent promised to 'fight [BR's] bill all the way through Parliament … if necessary, rallying support to kill the bill' (Jacques Arnold, Tory MP for Gravesham). Kent County Council, while welcoming the lifting of the threat from areas blighted by the four routes, vowed to 'stick together' to monitor BR's plans – especially the freight routes, which would be separate from the new line.

The decision to tunnel under London stemmed from the bruising BR had suffered at the hands of the suburban NIMBYs since the publication of the four routes in July 1988. These had envisaged not just the surface running of the Eurostars – which of course was what happened, without a great deal of complaint, between 1993 and 2007 – but also the widening of existing routes by adding extra tracks alongside them, and by adding flyovers and other junctions. All this was to be shoe-horned into the tightly-knit townscape of South-East London, where the existing railways were a century old and where much marginal land beside the lines had already been developed for housing. 'The preliminary consultation in the London suburban area indicated that there was extreme opposition to building new tracks alongside existing lines', BR reported, showing once again its ability to spend a long time discovering the obvious. 'Given the density of development … any widening would have a severe impact on

1988

April

- Sunday Times reports leak of BR plan for a rail link: three possible routes, one north of Thames

14 July

- BR announces four alternative routes across Kent and four London station options: King's Cross Low Level, St Pancras, White City and Stratford

July

- RACHEL route published

October

- Government announces private-sector participation in Rail Link is vital

November

- BR, advised by merchant bank Lazards, issues formal invitation to tender

December

- House of Commons debates rail link plans

property … and would be very disruptive to train services for a lengthy period.'[11]

BR had also discovered quite how dogged the protestors could be, and how sensitive some locations were. Routes Two and Three ran on an embankment above Dulwich College playing fields, within sight and sound of the semi-rural idyll of Dulwich Village, where the Dulwich Society – which helped pay for the protest campaign – numbered one Denis Thatcher among its committee. Herne Hill, Clapham, Beckenham, Brockley – all were newly on the map for London's growing middle classes, priced out of their traditional heartlands north of the river. All these districts were now threatened by red lines on BR's muddily-printed maps. The NIMBYs set to: 'their money, skills and home computers have shaken BR's bulk', *The Economist* noted gleefully.[12]

By coincidence, BR's four routes were published at the same time as a set of 'Transport Options Assessment Studies', commissioned by the Department of Transport in an attempt to find solutions to London's traffic gridlock. These floated some wildly unpopular plans for urban motorways – through precisely the suburbs now also threatened by British Rail.

The mood of opposition to transport schemes – any transport schemes – was thus intense. Residents' groups, councils, MPs were already geared up for the fight. Into this maelstrom BR wandered unprepared: it did not help that one of the rail lines proposed for the Eurostars was also earmarked by the transport studies for a six-lane toll road. (These schemes came to nothing: as an observer noted at the time, 'there is strong doubt among Whitehall-watchers whether the political will exists to carve new roads through gentrified suburbs'.)[13]

Some aspects of BR's public relations were improving. In February 1989 – at Welsby and Southgate's suggestion – Theo Steel from BR Communications took two groups from Kent across the Channel to see the construction works south-west of Paris on the new LGV Sud-Ouest, returning in November to see (or rather hear) the trains pass by. Even though the plane broke down it was, says Steel, 'amazing what wine does to make a few friends out of foes!' Nevertheless in May 1989 British Rail made matters worse by backtracking on a verbal promise to release to the NIMBYs their brief to the environmental consultants (ERL). Then, apparently, the Railway Inspectorate stuck an oar in, saying that BR needed far more ventilation shafts than planned – another example, it seems, of the haste with which the plans were drawn up: had BR not spoken to the Inspectorate before?

Unfortunately even BR's new proposals attracted less than total acceptance. As the

11 The West Coast Main Line upgrade ran into considerable problems because of the risk and cost of laying new track into a live rail corridor.

12 February 25 1989

13 *London Property Guide 1989* (Mitchell Beazley)

Daily Telegraph put it: the result was 'a text-book case on how not to handle a sensitive issue of local planning'.[14] BR's earlier material had been referred to the Advertising Standards Authority as misleading, and John Welsby had, albeit belatedly, admitted that BR needed external advice. He hired Saatchi & Saatchi – not the most suitable type of propagandists to sell the line to people of Kent, who promptly responded (in the case of one group of protesters) by hiring blue-chip PR and parliamentary lobbying companies of their own....[15]

Other voices were equally dismissive. In May 1989 Tony Gueterbock, public affairs manager for Eurotunnel and thus an active campaigner in favour of a new line, told the *New Civil Engineer* that he was 'grieved and appalled by some of the things I have seen ... there is an urgent need to establish credibility and trust, both corporate and individually'. Consultation, Gueterbock pointed out, 'is not telling and preaching: it includes listening and explaining with a genuine willingness to see another point of view and make changes'.

Gerry Bowden, the MP for Dulwich, said in July 1989, 'the route was designed by the seat of its pants'. He said he was worried by 'the lack of professionalism' he encountered in his dealings with BR, and felt 'there is no firm hand in control. They are particularly inept at dealing with personal problems, causing endless human misery'.[16]

Although Kent still had some reservations, the site which came to symbolise the whole opposition to the March 1989 plan – or indeed any which involved a route through suburban London – was Warwick Gardens, a relatively small green oasis in Peckham with a railway line to one side. It was the nodal point at which BR's planned 'long tunnel' from Swanley would come to the surface and join existing lines to Waterloo, thus in itself guaranteeing immense dislocation and some demolition. But this was multiplied when King's Cross was added to the route, since the Gardens would be the point at which the line would plunge into another tunnel under inner south London.

The Gardens would become a depot as well as the access-point to the tunnel, which would mean it was occupied for six years. Even BR had to admit that there was 'a serious consultation problem with local residents', but it had not helped its case with a parliamentary ruling over the King's Cross Bill that the protesters lived too far from the

WARWICK GARDENS AND COMPENSATION ZONE

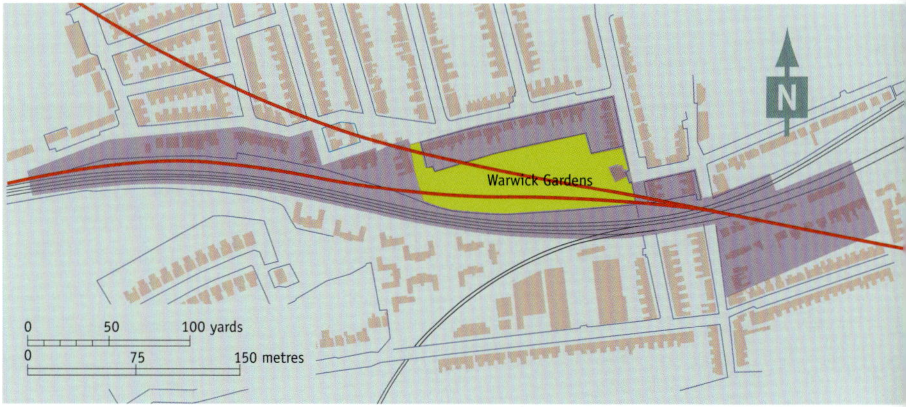

BR's definition of the zone that would qualify homes for compensation at Warwick Gardens in Peckham (in purple) was both irregular and illogical. The red lines show the planned CTRL tunnel and underground junction; the lower spur was to rise to the surface and join existing tracks (shown in black) to Waterloo.

14 March 8 1989

15 In charge of the account at at Saatchi was Michael Dobbs, the creator of TV's fictional politician Francis Urquhart; but even Dobbs couldn't do much for BR's image.

16 *Evening Standard Magazine*, July 1989.

Facing page: the new technology of home computers and photocopiers meant that BR faced an unprecedented deluge of well-orchestrated local opposition. The national press brought no comfort.

station to have the right to object – a ruling which enabled fully half the 288 objections to be disallowed. (Privately BR – sublimely unaware just how much the demography of the area had changed – dismissed the small park as 'Dogshit Gardens'.)

It was left to Harriet Harman, the local MP, to point out to them that this corner was not the North Peckham of Del-Boy Trotter. 'Some years ago', she went on, 'it was run down, but it has regenerated itself by the commitment of those who live there and those who have moved in.' Indeed, its symbolic importance was emphasised by the nature of the inhabitants. The streets surrounding 'Dogshit Gardens', it turned out, had largely been colonised by younger members of the professions – teachers, lawyers, City workers, journalists and doctors from nearby hospitals who had taken advantage of the then relatively low cost of the area's small, but agreeable, early Victorian villas, not far from the open green sweep of Peckham Rye. And although there was a Londoners' Action Group which brought together all the London objectors, among the most vehement, as BR were to discover, was PEARL: Peckham and Camberwell Action on the Rail Link. (Indeed PEARL's founders were well connected enough to give Gil Howarth, then the engineer in charge of the project, lunch at White's in late '91 after the route had at last been diverted away from their back yards.)

PEARL was founded in January 1989, by which time its members had an inkling that, as one local put it 'we are not only on the chosen route but are set to be one of the most seriously affected areas'. In the previous December the *Sunday Times* had published 'a confidential consultants' report' that listed the London areas affected – from Chiselhurst to King's Cross – and the paper further provided a helpful table detailing the 6,100 homes facing a 'visual or noise impact', as well as the 350 that could be demolished. Already, people were pulling out of property deals as the rumours spread.

Then came the March announcement in which BR confirmed the Peckhamites' worst fears. PEARL promptly geared up for a long campaign, with seven working groups to 'research, plan and organise action on specific topics. Eight major events are planned for the summer and autumn'. But there were hints that the line was inevitable; one of the objects was 'to press for full, fair and prompt compensation for all individuals and communities involved'.

They met Michael Portillo, then junior Minister of Transport – who simply referred them to BR. In April John Welsby met PEARL. Welsby tried to quiet the uprising by conceding that BR was examining ways of engineering 'a less disruptive scheme to its present proposals'. Unfortunately he then upset the Peckhamites with his attitude to

ON THE LINE

PECKHAM AND CAMBERWELL ACTION ON THE RAIL LINK

PEARL was set up in January 1989 to co-ordinate the campaign against British Rail's Channel Tunnel Rail link proposals. At that time Peckham and ... areas threatened. We

Over the past six weeks PEARL has been gearing up for a long campaign. Seven working groups have been set up to rese... specific topics. E...

BATTL

BROCKLEY AGAINST THE TUNNEL LINK

President: The Bishop of Woolwich
The Rt. Rev'd Peter Hall MA

RIL 1989

Lewisham SIGNALS

12 May 1989

– keeping the people of Lewisham in the picture ... the Borough – and what you can do to help !

A4 ☆☆

6,500 urban homes face BR blight

by Maurice Chitten...

THE day the Marwood... to exchange contracts f...

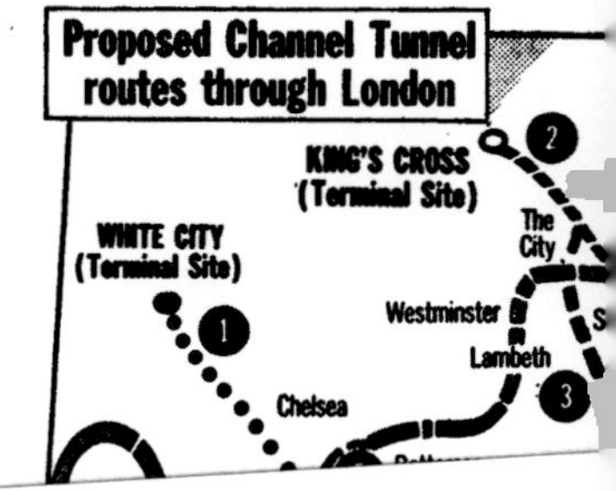

SINK THE LINK

Channel Tunnel Rail Link u...

PECKHAM WHY?

COMPENSATION

The BR announcement has ca... extreme distress throughout ... of Peckham and Camberwell. ... compensation corridor for ... to follow only the line ar... construction site.

- Why is BR only admitting ... a very limited area aroun...

CONSTRUCTION AND ENGINEERING

BR are trying to suggest ... only be 'some disruption ... area ! The truth is:

- BR **do not know** what th... because they have not ... plans, nor have they ... environmental assessme...
- These proposals will ...

☆☆

Channel train threat to Kent

by Cathy Jaskowiak

SCORES of homes and busi- ... homes and 80 businesses and

0 miles 2...

■ MPs ON THE LINE

Members of Parliament, their constituencies and their majorities, in South East London and Kent, in the 1987 Parliament. All MPs are Conservative except where stated. The list starts at Waterloo and ends at the coast.

Stuart Holland (Labour, Vauxhall) 9,019 (replaced by **Kate Hoey**, Labour, in a by-election in June 1989)
Simon Hughes (Liberal: Southwark & Bermondsey) 2,779
Gerry Bowden* (Dulwich) 180
John Fraser (Labour: Norwood) 4,723
William Shelton* (Streatham) 2,407
Harriet Harman (Labour: Peckham) 9,489
John Maples* (Lewisham West) 3,772
Joan Ruddock (Labour: Lewisham Deptford) 6,771
Colin Moynihan* (Lewisham East) 4,846
Rosie Barnes (Social Democrat: Greenwich) 2,141
Sir Philip Goodhart (Beckenham) 13,464
Peter Bottomley (Eltham) 7,500
Roger Sims (Chislehurst) 14,507
Edward Heath (Old Bexley & Sidcup) 16,274
Cyril Townshend (Bexleyheath) 11,687
John Hunt (Ravensbourne) 16,919
Ivor Stanbrook (Orpington) 12,732
Jacques Arnold (Gravesham) 8,792
David Evennett (Erith & Crayford) 6,994
Bob Dunn (Dartford) 14,929
James Couchman (Gillingham) 12,549
Geoffrey Wolfson (Sevenoaks) 17,345
John Stanley (Tonbridge & Malling) 16,429
Andrew Rowe (Mid Kent) 14,768
Sir Patrick Mayhew (Tunbridge Wells) 16,122
Dame Peggy Fenner (Medway) 9,929
Ann Widdecombe (Maidstone) 17,345
Roger Moate (Faversham) 13,978
Jonathan Aitken (Thanet South) 13,683
Roger Gale (Thanet North) 17,480
Julian Brazier (Canterbury) 14,891
Keith Speed (Ashford) 15,480
David Shaw (Dover) 6,541
Michael Howard (Folkestone & Hythe) 9,126

** shows Conservatives who lost their seats in the 1992 General Election, indicating the marginal status of the constituencies*

public consultation: he is quoted by them as saying that 'public meetings are often a dialogue of the deaf', and that as a result he would no longer attend such meetings, and would only meet small deputations from PEARL. His claim that the disruption from what was 'not a massive project' would last only three or four years did not help. He then made matters worse by implying that people were bringing the hardship on themselves. 'I am amazed', he was goaded into saying, 'at the situations people get themselves into financially'. Speaking as he was at the height of the property boom of the late 1980s he had a point: many of the vocal, but inpecunious, incomers had had to stretch themselves to the limit to buy their homes. Not surprisingly the remark resulted in immediate uproar and was much quoted.

Theo Steel, by then BR's Communications Director, also found himself in the thick of it. At a meeting in April 1989 with the residents of Lyndhurst Grove, the epicentre of the problems, it became clear how little BR knew of the details of its own plans, or their likely effect on the locals. He was faced by a full-blown demonstration (right down to flowers representing each of the houses along the line). According to PEARL's newsletter 'Mr Steel admitted that Warwick Gardens had only been chosen as a site weeks before the route was announced. It appears that engineering drawings will not be available until the summer. As the private Bill (the King's Cross bill) is due to be presented to Parliament in November, we asked Mr Steel if he really considered it possible to develop such a large-scale engineering project, with full regard for the technical and environmental implications, in such a short space of time'.

Steel stressed that the DoT had forced them into a ridiculous timescale for planning the link, and commented that in every respect BR was constrained by the Department of Transport. To make matters worse, BR's environmental consultants refused to release their advice, while the Secretary of State, Paul Channon, assured protestors – when buttonholed outside an international rail conference – that he would not allow a link to go through that was environmentally unacceptable to the people of South London.

In the debate in May 1990 Harriet Harman summed up the problem, blaming 'the commercial pressures imposed on British Rail', combining the speed of the project and the ridiculous financial targets, which 'led it into misrepresenting the devastation that would result from its cheapest option.

'British Rail implied that there would be a minor bit of re-turfing in Warwick Gardens and that it would all be all right, resulting in only minor disruption. The equipment that British Rail admits will be used to carry out that work includes two bulldozers, two or three excavators, two bored-pile rigs or two diaphragm wall excavators, one concrete-batching plant, two or three front- and back-end loaders, one bentonite slump production plant, one large soil compactor, one reinforcing-bar bending shed, four mobile cranes, four dumper trucks and numerous site huts – all on Warwick Gardens, one of the few patches of green in an area that is struggling to regenerate itself. Warwick Gardens would, in effect, be turned into a giant construction slum for up to ten years. That would be the effect of trying to do the job on a cheapskate basis.'

PEARL's response was more succinct. 'British Rail claim that there will be little disruption. If they believe that, they are deceiving themselves. And us.'

The exaggerated traffic forecasts – of up to eight passenger trains an hour by day, and up to sixty freight trains each night – merely reinforced the nightmare scenario. As so often, BR's sheer naïvety had made matters worse for itself, in this instance by providing an elaborate model of the works throughout the long construction period. BR also claimed that it would remove spoil from the tunnel by river – having failed once again to do its homework. A multi-storey office block had been built on the proposed wharf on the Thames.

Unfortunately the exact route had still not been decided, and the compensation arrangements ranged trom the inadequate to the chaotic. According to the 1990 edition of the *London Property Guide*, BR had 'offered to buy 170 homes around Warwick Gardens which would have to be demolished, or would be very close to the workings on the junction.' But in a letter sent in April 1989 to one unimpressed local resident with a home in neighbouring Chadwick Road, Theo Steel claimed that BR was hoping 'to limit compulsory purchase to approximately 20-30 properties. Outside that we have offered to purchase another 150' – not including the lady's – though 'we will assess the house purchase area again when we have the detailed plans'. Unfortunately the detailed map of the area provided by British Rail (see page 75) shows that in reality BR's theoretical '240-metre compensation line', designed to compensate above all people who lived within 100 metres of the railway, represented an illogical zig-zag, leaving numbers of very close houses outside the zone, while others much further from the tunnel were inside.

Inevitably the many other homes in the wider area affected by years of work on the junction immediately became unsaleable. In March 1989 BR offered to buy 'any residential property within the 240-metre corridor shown on the map. This offer will

remain open until either the rail link opens or BR decides not to proceed further with the project'. BR would not only purchase affected homes but would also make 'a disturbance payment covering the costs of removal, reasonable conveyancing and removal fees and a home loss payment, all in accordance with normal purchase practice'. Also, in accordance with the law, there would be compensation for loss of value due to noise pollution.

However, the chaos was compounded when, according to one of PEARL's newsletters, 'BR refused to admit any [general] obligation to buy, but talked to householders on an individual basis. Some lucky people got letters from BR agreeing to buy, but then ran into months of red tape, prevarication, lost documents, blank denials that deals had been agreed'. When all her attempts to communicate with BR fell on resolutely deaf ears, the Chadwick Road homeowner wrote direct to its chairman, Sir Bob Reid: 'Dear Sir, I would like you to do three things with this letter: 1. Read and understand it. 2. Reply to it. 3. Answer all the questions....'[17]

In 1990, a year into the saga, Harman reported to the House of Commons that 'many people want to sell their homes but cannot, either because they are just outside the compulsory purchase zone or because they cannot prove severe hardship. They have been left completely stranded because the "compulsory purchase zone" description is completely inadequate. The blight has spread far wider than the ... zone, and people have been unable to take up new jobs or to move for family reasons. They have seen the value of their homes collapse. They cannot sell their homes – they are stuck'.

More permanently, the blight over the entire area spread to Rye Lane, the neighbouring shopping centre. Quite a few businesses, most crucially Marks & Spencer, moved out; they have never returned. To this day, governors of the local primary school say that the flight of middle-class families had a permanent effect on the school, for the disturbance has left a lasting scar over the whole area. In the event BR ended up being forced to buy several hundred homes at the height of the house boom of the late 1980s, at a cost of perhaps £200 million, only to sell them a couple of years later in the depths of the property slump of the early 1990s, losing perhaps a third of their involuntary investment.

However by 1989 BR did not have the field to itself. More imaginative spirits were proposing dramatic alternatives to BR's ideas, all entering London by the east and not the south. BR could easily brush aside the scheme proposed by the famed violinist Sir Yehudi Menuhin in a letter to a national paper, to build an underground monorail between London and the Chunnel as a way of protecting what remains of the Kent countryside. But more serious opposition was emerging from a number of sources.

As Gerry Bowden, the MP for the (very marginal) constituency of Dulwich,[18] pointed out in a House of Commons debate he initiated in May 1990: 'taking the route through north-east Kent is the idea that they all seem to have in common. Thereby, they will take the route through one of the most deprived parts of the South-East, where there is a fair amount of derelict industrial land and the local communities could benefit from an economic uplift. Any such route, with its freight and passenger transport potential, would introduce new jobs and give a boost to the industrial economy. We should consider the issue not only from the benefit to be gained from operation of the route, but from the intrinsic value it will have for the community through which it passes.'

When Bowden raised the point with BR, he was told that Transmark was looking at it. But Transmark was a BR subsidiary and Bowden suspected that 'part of Transmark's job was to point out the speck of dust in the eye of the other proposal, to distract attention from the lump of concrete in its own'.

The first sketch of an easterly alternative had come from Arthur Tansley, a retired civil servant. He studied the geological maps which showed that the chalk that made the Chunnel so relatively easy to dig extended right under Kent. In July 1988 he proposed RACHEL (Rail Alternative to the Channel Tunnel) consisting of a continuation of the Channel Tunnel as far as the Medway. But this was obviously too expensive, and in January 1989 it was superceded by TALIS (Thames Alternative Link to the International rail System).

Originally this had been devised by Tim Bain-Smith, a chartered patent agent living at Charing, plumb in the path of BR's proposed route. In its final form this was a doubly radical proposal. Not only did it propose an eastern approach to London through Stratford, but swung north-west after leaving Ashford, tunnelling under the eastern North Downs to by-pass the Medway towns and cross the Thames east of Tilbury, with a total of 29 miles (47km) in tunnel.[19]

Facing page: 'Community Effects, Route Section 18: one primary school affected': the reality behind BR's consultants' words captured on camera. The school's plight was in addition to the twelve homes that just this two-mile section would demolish. The number of homes directly affected by Section 18 was 683.

17 In the end BR did agree to buy Ms Wilkins's house; despite vigorous attempts it was unable to renege on the offer, having omitted to head its letter 'subject to contract'.

18 Even in the 1987 election with its overwhelming Tory majority his margin of victory was a mere 180 and, not surprisingly, he lost his seat in 1992.

19 With elegant symmetry, the TALIS proposals of January 1989 drew attention to EEC Directive 85/337, which had become effectively British law in July 1988. This demanded that infrastructure projects, including 'lines for long-distance railways', be subject to assessments of their environmental effect 'at the earliest possible stage of all technical planning and decision-making processes.' Furthermore, the public must have access to all these studies before the project is initiated. The existence of this Directive seems to have not registered with BR until early 1989, despite it having stemmed from Geoffrey Howe's work in 1974 (see Chapter 2) on the previous Channel Tunnel plan.

The TALIS idea attracted the attention of Manufacturers Hanover, a major American bank, where its proponent was a vice-president, Angus Dunn, who called it 'the acceptable face of NIMBYness' – by no coincidence his house, too, was on BR's proposed route. Dunn formed a powerful group called RailEurope. He recruited Bechtel, the enormous American construction firm, and SG Warburg, a leading merchant bank. He received backing from British Urban Redevelopment, Margaret Thatcher's favourite regeneration agency, which was promoting a plan for a theme park at Rainham on the north bank of the Thames on the TALIS route – an idea dreamt up by MCA, the powerful American group that had launched Universal City, a highly successful such project in Hollywood. RailEurope's plans changed over time, but involved a long tunnel under much of Kent (utilising the chalk strata), coming out at Rainham and proceeding through Stratford, either stopping there, as proposed by Newham Council, or going on to King's Cross. A major problem was that it went through the middle of Grays, and thus would require the complete rebuilding of the town centre.

Unfortunately for their proponents, Kent dismissed both TALIS and RACHEL. 'They had no virtue', said Odling, largely because the county council had always, and rightly, believed in the use of the M20 corridor. BR was obviously already aware of the 'eastern' alternatives, but announced that its southerly approach was 'superior in business, financial, and economic terms'.

However, BR were unable to dismiss so easily the rival easterly route presented by Arup, the prestigious engineering consultants founded by the extraordinary figure of Ove Arup, who had given his colleagues the confidence and technical skills required to 'stretch the envelope' in every aspect of construction and planning, and to challenge even the most powerful and well-established of orthodoxies – and institutions.

NO ORDINARY ENGINEER

Those engineers who work with good architects in a spirit of harmony and common aims are really a new race; created by, and creating, a new sort of architecture and, thank God, a new sort of architect. The whole situation is almost the invention of one man, yourself.

Sir Alan Harris

Sir Alan Harris, himself a distinguished engineer, understood Ove Arup's contribution to the art and science of engineering creation. But even he could not grasp the complexities of a man who, to begin with, thought of himself primarily as a philosopher. This was what informed his legacy, which lay not so much in buildings as in a unique, and uniquely international, consultancy firm whose scope extended to cover dozens of specialist disciplines – by no means all of them related to engineering. It is worth digressing to look at Arup the man and his creation, Arup the firm – which, in the year its founder died, began the process that would lead to the building of High Speed One.

Throughout his long life – he died in 1988 at the age of 93 – Arup followed his basic intellectual tenet: that an engineer should be the catalyst who could unite architecture, art and philosophy, conforming to his belief that all man-made structures should be classed as 'architecture'. In practice the engineer should be the architect's partner from the genesis of a project, and not a mere, and necessarily subservient, consultant called in only when the architect thought fit. 'Engineering', he once wrote, 'is not a science. Science studies particular events to find general laws. Engineering design makes use of these laws to solve particular practical problems.'

As he repeated throughout his life: 'Total Design is the key to what is built'. In the words of Sir Jack Zunz, a life-long colleague, Ove[1], as he was invariably called, saw his role in trying to stem 'the divergence between architecture and engineering which began with the industrial revolution'. As he wrote much later, when the firm he created embraced dozens of different disciplines: 'only the intimate integration of various parts of the various disciplines will produce a desired result'. For Ove, his apparently ambitious vision was merely part of a yet more wide-ranging dream of breaking down barriers to mutual understanding wherever they existed. Moreover he was a truly Renaissance figure, loving art and collecting omnivorously wherever he travelled.

In real life he was the very model of the absent-minded philosopher, bewildered at other people's incomprehension of his many and invariably individual perceptions: 'I don't know', he would say, 'why it is that things which seem obvious to me are not obvious to everyone else'. He was totally disorganised, his holidays resembling a Jacques Tati film. Congenitally absent-minded, he would forget his spectacles; would claim to have lost the oversized chopsticks he habitually carried (to filch a taste from fellow diners' plates); would then discover he had them in his pocket all the time. Just before she retired, his devoted secretary Ruth Winawar had to remind her boss that 'you are going to *Oxford*. If you change at Didcot and ask someone at the station which platform

1 Invariably pronounced as in 'by Jove' rather than in 'Okay'.

the *Cambridge* train goes from, you may get into difficulties'.

He was typically Danish – and thus the very opposite of what is normally meant by 'Scandinavian', for the Danes are open, pleasure-loving – fans, too, of good food and wine. Indeed Ove appeared to many people as an irrepressible bohemian intellectual with a delight in luxurious living: a truly champagne socialist. Moreover, throughout his life he rather enjoyed and even exploited his position as a double outsider: a foreigner among the British and an engineer among architects and intellectuals. Although his mother was Norwegian by birth he remained truly Danish – speaking the language at home throughout his life. He also spoke fluent German: English was only his third language.

All his life he was a philosopher manqué, leaving behind no fewer than three million words of his musings – many of which, however, were merely attempts to clear his mind: 'how can I tell what I think until I see what I say?' he would exclaim. He invariably said exactly what was passing through his head at the time. As Zunz put it, 'he was always thinking aloud, writing or saying everything that occurred to him'. When designing the staircase to the pulpit of Coventry Cathedral – he started with a ten-inch roll of tracing paper – he 'went on talking and doodling. He generated a mode of thought that was for ever exploratory. His words were always spontaneous, flexible, part of his eternal quest for truths many of which he knew were likely to be disproved upon further reflection'.

The results could be disconcerting, says his long-time Danish colleague Jørgen Nissen. 'He would try ideas out aloud, at times declaring that the idea which he had had ten minutes earlier was no good.... He had this restless intellect – but this was what made him such an inspiring person'. Indeed, the success of the firm that he began was due largely to its founder's self-confidence and the lack of any limits on his intellectual ambitions – qualities that have always permeated the firm. It helped, says Nissen, that he was vain, 'but he was utterly charming'. One associate remembers sitting next to him one day at a lunch during which he spent much of the time carefully peeling an orange so that the peel remained in one piece. He then replaced the flesh of the orange in the case that he had so painstakingly created, a

'How can I tell what I think until I see what I say?' A habit of abstractedly scribbling in the margins of any sheet of paper to hand meant that anything from a quick doodle to a poem or elaborate design might accompany a note from Ove.

beatific smile on his face. And no, he didn't bother to eat it; the satisfaction of a job done to perfection provided him with adequate reward.

In his article on Ove Arup in the *Dictionary of National Biography*, Povl Ahm, his fellow-Dane, long-time collaborator and a subsequent chairman of Arup, provides a brilliant description of this 'tall and lean man' with his 'warm, intelligent and quizzical' face; 'his well-known inability to finish a sentence' marking a constant search for exactness and truth, rather than vagueness. 'This, as well as the strong Danish accent he always retained despite decades of residence in Britain, made any encounter or conversation with him a remarkable experience. He was always a visionary and an idealist who hated compromise.' Zunz said simply that 'he liked to understand things'.

Ove was born – in Newcastle upon Tyne – on 21 March 1895, the first son of Johannes Arup and his second wife. She was Norwegian and had been the much-loved governess to Johannes' three daughters (Astrid, Ellen and Ingeborg, to whom Ove was close throughout his life) by his first wife, who had died young. Johannes led the peripatetic life typical of many well-educated Danes at a period when large numbers of his countrymen left home to work elsewhere, above all in England. A veterinarian employed as a consultant by the Danish government, he was moved to Hamburg when Ove was only a few months old. Intending to retire back home, he sent Ove to the Danish equivalent of a British public school. But it was very different, encouraging its pupils to be independent and to take up in artistic activities including music; throughout his life he was a more than competent pianist – his founding partners gave him a spinet made by Arnold Dolmetsch for his 70th birthday.

While at school Ove first read the works of Charles Darwin, appreciating his 'sober, methodical, scientific approach' and became a disciple of Denmark's greatest philosopher, Kierkegaard, admiring particularly his empirical philosophy and his attacks on official Christianity. He had an abiding hatred of abstract ideologies, on the grounds that they tended to detach their adherents from reality – unlike many of his friends, the intellectually pragmatic Ove was never attracted to communism. And for all his verbal meanderings, his reflections invariably led to a clear decision: to go out and create. As his son Jens put it: 'he always bent the power of his far-ranging mind to the *actual problem* [his italics], the reality before him.' In a sense he was a precursor of Karl Popper, the apostle of the free and flexible philosophy 'The Open Society'. Feeling that he had to think through what he wanted to do, he decided to study philosophy – for, as he wrote at the time, 'it seemed rather absurd to me that the object of life would be to earn a living'.

His second year at university saw the outbreak of the First World War. Denmark remained neutral; but a depressed Ove wrote in his diary that if his country did get involved 'I think I will join the Academic Corps and make sure that I get shot as soon as possible.' His depression, and his conviction that he was never going to be an outstanding philosopher (a friend had got the only vacant lectureship in the subject) led him to study engineering – mainly because, he claimed, he couldn't think of any alternative apart from suicide. This was a piece of self-dramatisation; according to Zunz, he had also considered studying architecture 'but felt unsure of his artistic talents and always said that he would rather be a good engineer than a second-rate architect'.

In Britain, which once led the industrial revolution, engineering has in modern times been considered a second-class intellectual discipline. By contrast, Denmark's remarkable recovery after 1814 (when it had lost Norway, previously a dependent state, and had to declare itself bankrupt) had been greatly helped by the encouragement of engineering as an academic subject, and it continued to be respected as an intellectual discipline. Ove proved to be a talented engineer, with the mathematical background – throughout his life he was a passionate chess player[2] – that was increasingly necessary as buildings grew ever more complex.

Ove Arup in his twenties: still the earnest student. Later his wife would joke that he was 'pre-stressed'.

Many of Denmark's most talented engineers of his generation devoted their careers to the use of reinforced concrete, a material largely developed in France and Germany, and one used at the time above all in the construction of harbours and in coastal protection – both vital in a country like Denmark with an inordinately long coastline relative to its size. It was probably this experience that underpinned Ove's conviction of the legitimacy of what has been called 'the Brunel approach' to engineering, where engineers develop their own ideas to solve specific problems. As Jack Zunz points out, when the Institution of Civil Engineers was founded in 1812 it included architects, who only set up their own organisation some decades later. More recently, such outstanding architects as Frank Lloyd Wright and Renzo Piano initially trained as engineers.

In the 1920s Danish firms, particularly Christiani & Nielsen and JL Kier, were considered as the leaders in the design and development of concrete structures – a speciality where Ove's mathematical training was vital, since so much of the work consisted in calculating the stresses involved in this new form of construction. In particular Christiani, whom he joined, employed the best engineering graduates as a matter of course – as Ove himself was to do half a century later. Ove was lucky: his new

2 In his retirement he designed and tried to market increasingly intricate chess sets, a sure-fire money-loser.

employers, although they were constructors, also preferred to do their own design on their own projects, a combination which appealed to his instinctive feelings – and throughout his life Ove would never do anything he didn't believe in.

The young engineer was first sent to Hamburg. He tried to transfer to Paris but instead was sent to London, where he was faced with the deep anti-intellectualism of the British engineering profession and a society which avoided serious discussion. But, put in charge of a project in Southampton Docks, he demonstrated to himself that he had 'a specific field where I can show what I'm worth and which I can take an interest in'. Unfortunately the British tradition separated the – often rather gentlemanly – breed of consulting engineers from the construction companies responsible for the actual work: a division which Ove found unnatural and limiting. For throughout his long working life he was obsessed with the need to integrate design and construction to form 'total architecture'.

Fortunately his first ten years in Britain were mostly concerned with docks and jetties, where the civil engineer was the responsible person. From the first Ove was clear, as he neatly summed it up during a lecture that he gave in America at Harvard University, that 'the aim of the structural engineer is to provide the necessary stability of the building at as low a cost as possible consistent with the preservation or creation of commodity and delight'.

For years, starting with his student days, Ove had agonised over his relationships with successive girlfriends – relationships which, in most cases, he took more seriously than they did. In this aspect at least the epitome of the brooding Dane, his lengthy letters were typical of someone who took himself all too seriously. But within two years of his arrival in London he had found a wife: Ruth Sorensen.

'Li' (as he and everyone else always called her) was the daughter of a distinguished Danish engineer and his half-Jewish[3] wife. Unfortunately Li's parents had separated when she was still a schoolgirl – an experience which gave her an obsession with family stability, a lifelong horror of divorce and absolute moral standards as well as a continuing absorption with the lives of her Danish relatives. She was beautiful, with a sense of style and elegance that extended to their house and its furnishings; she also had a natural talent for cooking – it was said that she never bought a single tin of food.

Indeed, before her marriage Li had taught domestic science to members of Women's Institutes; but Ove discouraged her from sharing her often unique recipes through writing articles, or indeed indulging in any activities outside the home: his attitude to

3 Li's much-loved grandfather was a respected rabbi deeply involved in the evacuation of Danish Jews to Sweden during World War II.

women remained pretty reactionary throughout his life. Nevertheless Li was by no means a subservient wife; although she herself was no great lover of social gatherings, she was perfectly capable of rebuking her husband sharply for his rudeness and social gaffes – traits due, fundamentally, to his lifelong self-absorption. She and her son appropriated the term 'pre-stressed' to describe anyone like Ove 'who is possibly admirable as a husband, father and engineer, but a dead loss as an ordinary dinner companion or for the ordinary social occasion'. For 60 years they were a devoted couple, even though she was not greatly interested in his work; and when he invited people home his intellectual snobbery still led him to retreat to his den rather than make the effort to chat to his colleagues' wives.

During his early years in London Ove was greatly influenced by the two leading architectural theorists of the time: Le Corbusier, the most outstanding of France's unequalled crop of architects, with his emphasis on the creative capacity of engineering, and Walter Gropius with his holistic, supposedly democratic, vision of bringing together craftsmen and artists to create a better world. Professionally Ove was making rapid progress, and so started writing the first of the thousands of articles he published over the following half-century.

Throughout his life he remained shocked by the anti-intellectualism of his British colleagues, but in the 1930s he did find his own world. In 1932 he, Li and their two oldest children, Anja and Jens, moved to a house in Hampstead Garden Suburb, which he decorated himself. The Suburb was an oasis of intellectual enlightenment, and Ove moved there in time to meet the increasing number of refugees, most but not all Jewish, fleeing from the growing Nazi menace. They provided Ove with a stimulating intellectual environment, naturally centred on the architects. They included Gropius, the appalling Erno Goldfinger and Berthold Lubetkin, a brilliant charmer, a networker, a Marxist, who taught Ove that good architecture involves taking infinite care over every detail. It was Lubetkin who brought him into MARS,[4] a group which brought together the few architects and designers in London interested in modern architecture.

Ove was thus in an ideal position to work with the newcomers. But when Lubetkin wanted to use reinforced concrete in building Highpoint, the famous block of flats on Highgate Hill, Christiani & Nielsen would not take on the contract. So in 1934 Ove moved to JL Kier, another well-respected contractor where, as chief designer, he worked closely with Tecton – the practice that included Lubetkin and other leading modernists – on many of the most famous structures in pre-war Britain. Among these were

4 Modern Architectural ReS.

the still-iconic Penguin Pool at the London Zoo, and a number of projects in the Socialist-run borough of Finsbury, including flats and a famous health centre.

Although he enjoyed the technical challenges presented by the material, he believed that the modernists often used reinforced concrete wrongly, for, as he said, it 'could be an unsuitable material for housing'. Although they knew next to nothing about the material the architects used it 'to do things that could be done better and more cheaply in another material'. Later in life he wrote how 'Lubetkin would tell any lie to the client': a wall like the one at Highpoint would have been much cheaper to build with bricks, but Lubetkin claimed that concrete was functional and economic. But 'it wasn't "functional" at all: it just had to be "modern"'.

Functionalism really became a farce. 'What is wrong with a sloping roof? They can't afford to pay what it costs to make a flat roof really waterproof. Lubetkin didn't care. He just cared for the picture in the architectural magazines.' The cheapness of their construction, 'as with all these modern Corb-inspired buildings', sighed Ove, greatly annoyed him and provided opponents of modernism with legitimate grievances. Unfortunately, as he admitted, 'I could only work with Lubetkin because as an engineer he provided me with what was at that time an unusual experience in the design and construction of reinforced concrete'.

In 1935 Ove published a definitive statement of his views on the material, declaring that its 'monolithic' character meant that it could be moulded into any shape, and permitted a 'structural' approach which satisfied three conditions: economy, simplicity and freedom of architectural planning. By then he had acquired 'a reputation for doing tricks with reinforced concrete'. Despite his profit-sharing arrangement with Kier – by 1937 he enjoyed the then enormous income of £6,000 a year – in early 1938 he and his cousin Arne, an engineering entrepreneur, set up their own firm: 'Arup & Arup, Civil Engineers and Contractors'. At the same time he established his own personal engineering design consultancy. One year later, war broke out.

Although some members of his and Li's families did manage to escape to the United States, most were trapped in occupied Denmark. Ove himself felt largely excluded from the war effort. Although he did design some communal – and for the partnership extremely profitable – bomb shelters in Finsbury, and others for such varied clients as the Air Ministry and the firm of Gestetner, his obvious foreignness and his close links with communists and communist-friendly organisations prevented his ideas from being

Facing Page: Arup at the still-iconic Penguin Pool at London Zoo, designed by Berthold Lubetkin and one of Ove's first exercises in complex concrete constructs

taken seriously. He was, however, commissioned to design a large number of installations – oil tanks, hangars, pill boxes and the like – where solidity was an absolute necessity.

Ove Arup was also responsible for the secret underground headquarters of Coastal Command at Northwood in Middlesex (still a major command centre today), as well as devising the concrete fenders designed to protect the pierheads of the Mulberry harbours that sheltered ships landing men and equipment in the first weeks after D-Day. Ove enjoyed the intensity of the work – but the result was a burst blood vessel, neuritis and a six-week stay in hospital. The enforced rest provided him with time to contemplate his future after the war.

Ove's doodles enlivened agendas and reports in Arup meetings

AN ORGANISM NOT AN ORGANISATION

A firm held together by an idea, not by management

Sir Duncan Michael, chairman of Arup 1995-2000

The elegant Kingsgate concrete footbridge at Durham University

At the end of the war, Arup made a half-hearted application for the professorship in concrete engineering at Imperial College – a role which would have greatly restricted his professional activities. His first major post-war commission was for a new bus station in Dublin, a site which he visited regularly for three years. But it was only in April 1946, when he was already 50, that he went it alone by dissolving the partnership with his cousin – a far from amicable split not finally settled for six years, largely because of Ove's bickering. The firm he then founded has never been an orthodox organisation, for its progenitor entirely lacked any organisational or managerial skills. It has never had anything approaching a 'business plan' of any description, yet its turnover has increased every year from £12,700 in 1946 to nearly £500 million in 2006, and is now growing faster than ever before.

In the same period, the number of employees – none of them paid generously, to say the least – has grown from a handful to nearly 9,000, and five of them, headed by Ove himself, have received knighthoods. Ove himself claimed to be dismayed by its growth but, as his Danish-born colleague Jørgen Nissen pointed out, 'he may have been horrified by the expansion, but his character encouraged it'. From its foundation, it was very different from other engineering firms – significantly the head office has always been not in Victoria Street, like the more orthodox consultants, but in Fitzroy Street on the edge of Bloomsbury. 'Fitzrovia' was famous in the immediate post-war period as the haunt of London's louche artistic community. Ove's team promptly became known as the 'Bloomsbury engineers', to emphasise their intellectual pretensions.

Ove himself did little actual design work by then – he was proudest of a minor project, a bridge across a deep valley connecting two parts of Durham University: a design, in Zunz's words, in which 'essentially simple structural concepts were elegantly expressed'. But Ove was the crucial front man, deploying his charm among his wide network of friends. He said that one architectural conference 'provided me with a unique opportunity to meet interesting people from all over the world in beautiful surroundings'. He personified the unique style and capabilities of his firm, which he established as the only consultancy that could work as an equal partner with architects. 'Yes he was opportunistic', says one old-timer, 'but he never abandoned his principles'. As Sir Jack Zunz put it, 'he was a dreamer – inspirational, not a manager'.

He exercised his exceptional gift to inspire people by what Zunz describes as 'a mixture of example, encouragement and detachment, never direction or instruction, according to a recipe which came naturally to him and was unique'. He was able to transmit his own 'divine dissatisfaction', his perpetual quest for a better answer to any problem, to form an atmosphere that could be daunting. His combination of self-confidence and high standards made life difficult, especially for young newcomers unused to the stress involved. Not surprisingly Arup has always had an attrition rate of around ten per cent: but they usually lose people only in their first year. As Zunz puts it 'we were kindred spirits operating in a pragmatic liberal environment – though there was plenty of competition, especially among the younger engineers – and the policy of throwing youngsters in at the deep end, providing them with their own challenges at an early stage in their career'.

One key result of the founder's open self-doubt (an attitude which belied his underlying self-belief) was the openness of the firm, which retains what one senior figure calls 'the innate, unspoken knowledge that an idea from any employee, however unbidden, will be taken seriously. Very few institutions gain this status (and deserve it)'.

'He taught us that the client is number one', said Sir Nigel Thompson, Arup's deputy chairman, 'but that the best way to serve the client might mean that you don't always do what they want.... We have this spirit in Arup of questioning and trying to do what's right'.

The sheer flexibility of the set-up was crucial in enabling the firm to develop over the decades into an ever more multi-disciplinary establishment without too many institutional problems; one that combined techical excellence, fair dealings, and reasonable prosperity. To an outsider the recipe appears to be obstinacy with more than a touch of arrogance, summed up by one director: 'if we can do a job we will be proud of afterwards, well and good – but we will do it our way. In the long run this attitude pays'. But within this elite regiment democracy prevailed, for the object was: 'to eliminate the psychological barriers to teamwork, to create a kind of composite brain for each job'. 'He had an open mind: that's why we stayed', says Zunz simply. In the words of another old-timer: 'All of us were given space; [we] were trusted' – at least within their own specialities.

The way Zunz was hired was typical of the firm since its inception and tells a lot about the method in Ove's apparent madness. Zunz was Jewish, from a family that had fled from Berlin to South Africa; after war service and taking a degree he moved to London. The young immigrant had written to a dozen or more potential employers, but only Arup responded. At the interview he and Ove talked for an hour about 'anything and everything' before Ove told him there was no job for him. Next day he found a letter offering him a job. Cynical observers suggest that this was partly because the mean-minded Arup could recruit refugees like Zunz on the cheap, but this is unfair;

even today staff have continued to be hired by their seniors (it would be ridiculous to call them managers) because they filled a need – or even in anticipation of future requirements. Quite frequently, even today the decision is made on the grounds that 'this guy will come in handy'. After all, as the founder put it, 'to do work of quality we must have people of quality … it is up to us … to create an organisation which will allow gifted individuals to unfold'. 'No man is an island', quoted Ove, with the hope of Arup becoming 'a small-scale experiment in how to live and work happily together'.

To begin with growth was gradual, and during the 1950s and '60s it was very largely concerned with industrial buildings and the public sector, through the growth of Britain's universities and the expanding world of municipal housing (Arup had some novel – and efficient – ideas about how to build tower blocks). Later Arup steadily moved away from relying on the public sector, or indeed on Britain, but remained susceptible to the general construction cycle: the only times the number of employees fell was at the end of the 1970s and the 1980s.

In the early years, when money was indeed tight and clients slow to pay, Ove relied on an overdraft and his handful of employees were paid a pittance: the top salary was £7 a week. His own finances depended very largely on income from family investments in Denmark. He was also taking ten times the money out of the firm as his colleagues; by the mid-1950s this amounted to nearly £20,000. He could be extremely mean, showing a distinct lack of understanding of his employees' financial problems. 'You only need two meals a day', he would say, ignoring the fact that many of his own were consumed in London's finest restaurants. Ove's meanness – towards other people anyway – has continued to this day. Michael Somers, the long-serving chief accountant and, more recently, finance director, observes 'you don't stay in Arup to get rich; there's a relatively small salary range. There are no external shareholders, so no-one is taking money out of Arup'. Employees were, and are, less interested in financial rewards than in what Nigel Thompson describes as 'the excitement of the project'. Ove himself underlined: 'if we let [money] divide us we are sunk as an organisation – at least as a source for good'. This does not imply financial incompetence. As one senior engineer puts it 'we were judged on the billability of any given project', i.e. was there money in it for Arup? This canniness means that invoices are issued monthly on continuing projects.

Jørgen Nissen points to the way that much of the firm's development 'was of course done by [Ove's] partners, inspired by him. Ove chose wisely when he chose his partners – or perhaps they chose him!' For Ove clearly depended on a handful of key associates, most of whom had been his colleagues in Christiani or Kier's. Probably the closest to Ove himself – intellectually anyway – was Ronald Jenkins, a man who struck his collaborators as a 'strange, aloof' figure. He was by far the firm's best mathematician, bringing the same intellectual rigour to engineering analysis as did Ove himself; he was the man who enabled Arup to tackle complex technical projects. Of the others, Geoffrey Wood had had vital experience of working with architects in India during the war. Peter Dunican, the head of the drawing office, who had worked with Ove since 1943, became a partner in 1956 and effectively ran the business for many years. For a long time, indeed, all the incoming letters passed through his office and he received copies of all outgoing correspondence.

Dunican, the son of a policeman, had risen through studying at a lowly technical college and was the practical opposite to Arup: 'he got things done', says Zunz. In 1977 Dunican succeeded Arup as chairman although, typically, Ove had never shown any real acknowledgement of his importance. For years Ove had impressed on his colleagues that the firm was supposed to be a proper partnership, but he treated even his partners as his inferiors, assuming that he had a special position as the founder, an attitude which naturally aroused a rumbling sense of resentment. As early as 1947 Ove had to be rebuked – by Peter Dunican – for substituting 'I' for 'we'.

Although Ove's inner circle was mostly British, the firm was always truly international. Nissen, who became a world-famous bridge engineer, worked in an office with only two British-born workers out of fifty, and one of those was Irish. 'It was a wonderful place to work', he recalls; it helped that 'everyone was so young', with people in their thirties taking on major projects. As a result the 'first generation' employed in the late 1940s and 1950s continued to dominate the firm until the end of the century. They all had the self-confidence that was the hallmark of the firm from the very beginning – that, and a feeling that, as Nissen says, 'the rules were unwritten; the feeling for even the most ambitious projects was "why not do it?"' Ove himself said, 'we succeeded initially because we were structural engineers with a civil engineering outlook, or philosophy'. But he went further. 'You cannot tack architectural advice onto an engineering scheme'.

Thanks partly to his reputation and to the contacts he had made before the war, Ove could – and did – ignore professional rules by actively seeking work. His contact list was enlarged as a founder-member of the Institute of Contemporary Arts, enhancing the uniqueness of his situation – a reputation recognised by the award of the CBE in 1953. He naturally got a lot of commissions through the MARS group – by the time it dissolved in 1957 he was working with the post-war generation of modernist architects like Denys

The iconic shells of the Sydney Opera House, **above**, and seen under construction on the **facing page**. Arup's structural design 'permitted their realisation', in the carefully-chosen words of a reference book.

Lasdun and Basil Spence, the architect of the rebuilt Coventry Cathedral. As early as 1950 Arup could list projects as varied as schools, flats, offices and factories – including an iconic one at Brynmawr in South Wales, for which Ove and Ronald Jenkins received a major prize thanks to its large span and concrete shell roofs. Outside Britain and Ireland Arup was also working in the Gold Coast, Nigeria and Southern Africa. In 1947 Ove visited Kuwait and produced a detailed technical report on proposals to build two new towns. By the mid-1950s Arup, like its older-established competitors, had offices throughout the British Empire, which the ever-restless Ove loved visiting.

Arup's worldwide reputation, however, was gained in the 1960s, through its painful involvement in building the Sydney Opera House – one of the greatest architectural and engineering achievements of the 20th century. Within days of the news that a young Dane, Jørn Utzon, had won the competition for the Opera House Ove had written what even he described later as a 'cheeky' letter to his fellow-countryman. Even the practical Jack Zunz found Utzon 'immensely imaginative; he made me see things I had never seen before'. But although Utzon dreamed up and sketched the breathtakingly original shape of the roof as a series of sails billowing over the harbour, he found it almost impossible to face the task of transforming his ideas into reality. In other words, the Opera House happened both because of him and despite him.

Utzon's dream involved an amazing series of concrete shells which however, according to at least one expert, 'were not self-sustaining' (engineer-speak for 'will collapse'). Arup's specialists soon realised that they were faced with 'an extremely complicated and difficult job', and that its realisation 'will call for the development of new techniques for the calculation, testing and construction'. Not only were the shells large and their shape unique; the structure of each shell had to be designed separately. It took four years of intensive calculations to implement Utzon's essential ideas. The Opera House was one of the first projects to use computers on a large scale.[1]

After Ronald Jenkins had resigned from the Sydney job following some bitter arguments about the approach to the design of the shells, Ove handed over most of the work to Zunz and his fellow South African colleague Michael Lewis. Unfortunately, for political reasons, building work had to start before adequate drawings were available. Moreover everything about the interior was vague in the extreme. Eventually Utzon

1 Over the last thirty years the development of computers, and above all computer networks and the internet, has greatly simplified the firm's ability to exploit specialist skills from the whole world on individual projects. For instance, work on a transportation project in Bangkok was shared between the Hong Kong and London offices.

formulated the final design, with a roof in which each main shell was a part of a sphere.

But by this time Utzon's attitude was becoming clear. 'I don't care what it costs' he told Zunz, 'I don't care how long it takes. I don't care what scandal it causes. That is what I want'. He went further, telling Lewis that the number of seats in the auditorium and even the acoustics didn't matter – provided that the audience was overcome by the beauty of an edifice without a defined interior. Ove felt betrayed by Utzon, and in 1963 he suffered one of his regular periods of depression. The strain led to a suspected heart attack involving weeks in hospital and a period of convalescence at home. Nevertheless, he flew to Australia to persuade the state government to continue with the second stage of the project and accept a budget raised to £12.5 million – nearly four times the original estimate. The overruns continued to mount – the 1957 estimate of £3.6 million had soared to £25 million by 1965 before doubling again.

During 1963 things went from bad to worse. The visionary Utzon had become famous by winning many competitions before he had been responsible for any major project – a success that resulted in inner insecurities. By 1964 Utzon was insisting that Michael Lewis, who had taken over the project, be kept out of the negotiations with any of the supervising bodies.

Unfortunately for Utzon, at the beginning of May 1965 a new minister had taken over responsibility for the Opera House. Ove himself tried to resign, to bring the arguments into the open. Utzon refused to allow him to do so but then resigned himself, receiving the unexpected and immortal reply from the minister, 'I accept your resignation. Thank you very much. Goodbye'. If Arup was left to sort matters so that Sydney got the opera house that it wanted and was paying for, the firm also had to put up with the blame for all the earlier problems. Nevertheless this prolonged and Byzantine affair made the reputation of the firm. 'People started to take notice of us', says Zunz.

In the words of his biographer Peter Jones, 'the scale and complexity of the project transformed Ove's firm in many ways'. But Utzon's behaviour had a profound, and profoundly destructive, effect on Ove himself. He retired to Portugal exhausted and heart-broken: a septuagenarian realising that Utzon had shattered a lifelong dream that had sustained him for nearly 50 years. 'In the judgement of his family and close colleagues, he never regained his uninhibited enthusiasm for architects, nor did he risk complete trust in any of them outside his own team'. He lost his delight in architecture and steadily withdrew from the company to concentrate on larger themes, human and political matters.

But Ove's suffering had not been in vain, for the Opera House had ensured that Arup was the structural engineer of choice for most of the world's 'signature' architects in the last third of the 20th century, such as Richard Rogers in iconic buildings like the Pompidou Centre and Lloyds of London, Norman Foster in the Hong Kong & Shanghai Bank.

The 2008 Olympic Games in Beijing will be housed in a number of Arup-engineered buildings – most prominently the 'Water Cube', its design based on the natural shape of soap bubbles, and naturally used for aquatic events. Probably the best illustration of the way Arup's technical competence could create a major opening came in Hong Kong. The firm was called in by the Hong Kong & Shanghai Bank to investigate the collapse of a building on one of the colony's steepest slopes, on which they had lent a lot of money. Arup found a solution – draining the hill. In doing so it gained so much credibility it has ended up with an office of over 1,000 engineers in a city everlastingly building ever-taller towers – including HSBC's spectacular headquarters and many more.

With such a charismatic founder, the key problem for the firm in the 1960s was life after the 'Founding Partner'. Surprisingly, a sensible transition was effected despite Ove's initial opposition and the increasing complexity of the 'corporate structure' – there were separate partnerships in each country, with a London partner involved in each one. In the end Zunz and Stanley Berwin, an imaginative lawyer, came up with an plan implemented by Peter Dunican.

Over the eleven years from 1966 the partners gave away the firm's equity: by 1977 employee and charitable trusts owned the whole of it. Arup's underlying concept was, and remains, very similar to that of the John Lewis Partnership: all the partners have a say in major decisions within a structure that ensures permanent independence. Ove himself was happy. 'He knew', says one insider, 'that his son wouldn't take over but that the new scheme ensured that his name would be immortal – and it is'. The firm celebrated its 60th year in 2006, of which 37 had been in beneficial employee trust ownership.

Even before his retirement much of Ove's thinking had been prophetic. Already by the mid-1960s he was sketching as future concerns population explosion, conservation of the world's resources, spoilation of nature – he was an early member of Friends of the Earth – the division of the world into rich and poor, the adverse effects of new inventions on traditions and civilisations, the world's over-reliance on fossil fuels. As he once said: 'the worst thing you can do with oil and gas is to burn it'. But as far as his firm was concerned, its ethos was summed up in what is still known today as 'the key speech'.

In the speech, which he gave to the partners in July 1970, he set out his key beliefs for the firm – despite his disclaimer that it would be better called 'musings of an old man

Ove's doodles from the 1960s show that the Opera House was ever on his mind

Facing page: From Arup's portfolio, clockwise from top left: the Pompidou Centre; Hong Kong & Shanghai Bank; Lloyds Building, City of London; the Oresund Bridge; Stuttgart's museum complex

in a garden'. They were based, he said, on his version of 'Western Humanism', imbued with the moral qualities he deemed essential. The essence was his lifelong belief in 'total design' combined with a 'relentless pursuit of quality' which set the ethical atmosphere for the firm in line with everything he had thought and written in the last 40 years. His boldest ambition was to create a 'model fraternity' with the emphasis on the quality of the firm's work.

In doing so, he said, 'we make a contribution to what is almost the central problem of our time: how to overcome the social friction and strife which threatens to overcome mankind'. For the difference between the key speech and equivalent 'mission statements' issued by so many major organisations over the years is not just the sincerity and simplicity of Ove's words, but their practicality and good sense. And, above all, the way that they are taken perhaps even more seriously today than they were when the speech was made 37 years ago. The words of 'the key speech' still pervade the Arup atmosphere the world over; some Chinese employees know it by heart.

After the Utzon disaster, Ove increasingly objected to 'architectural reputations built on art', but foresaw that, thanks to Arup's architectural wing, they would become increasingly concerned with briefing the client 'because the right decision on what to build is usually more important than how we build it' – and if they disapproved of a client's intentions they should refuse the contract. Above all came the credo learnt before the war from Le Corbusier and Gropius: 'everything built is architecture'. His essential pragmatism emerged in the belief that 'anything is right which leads to the right result.... Sound engineering is the only way to make architectural excellence so competitive'.

By then the firm's activities affected everything around us. Ove's intellectual restlessness and self-confidence ensured that his firm could never remain 'small-scale', that it would spread far beyond the increasing specialisms involved in modern structural engineering and indeed beyond providing the 'total architecture' which had been the fundamental theme of his whole life's work through a partnership of equals between engineers and architects. For the firm's first quarter-century, Arup had concentrated almost exclusively on individual buildings. As Ove himself put it, 'they have succeeded in this attempt to eliminate the psychological barriers to teamwork, to create a kind of composite brain for each job' and through their influence aim at 'a reform of the whole building industry'.

But the architectural historian Robert Thorne had spotted that 'Ove was forced to acknowledge that total design or total architecture were as likely to be achieved through diversification within the practice as though collaboration with other firms, even if that meant growing to a size which alarmed him ... he saw diversification spread far wider

than he had dreamt of earlier on, with far more of an emphasis on civil engineering, building services and other specialisations than the practice had originally had' – as well as a burgeoning number of overseas offices.

As early as 1958 Ove had accepted an invitation to design and build a new students' residence at Somerville College in Oxford – the design-and-build approach had been previously confined to industrial buildings. Five years later he formalised Arup's 'Building Group' as a separate organisation, Arup Associates, headed by a young architect, Philip (now Sir Philip) Dowson. He put its *raison d'être* as 'the conviction that close-knit, multi-disciplinary design teams are necessary to confront the scale and complexity of modern buildings if an architecture is to survive which embodies humane ideas'.[2] The team, originally housed in the basement of the firm's offices, naturally upset the architects with whom they would be competing – including some of Arup's best friends like Denys Lasdun and Jane Drew. Like so many of Arup's groups it grew and spread: 80 major buildings were designed between 1955 and 1981.

The existence of Arup Associates enabled the firm to cope with the ever-increasing complexity of large commercial and industrial buildings, like air-conditioning and, later, the facilities required for computers, all of which played straight into Arup's strengths and developed them. It was not surprising that they were called in by Tim Smit, creator of the Eden Project in Cornwall. As he put it, the job of Arup's engineers 'was to design the basic services like heating, climate control and lighting systems throughout the project … if they failed, our plant collections would die and so would they. No pressure there, then'.[3]

Ove's own background was in civil engineering, but only a handful of his partners were civil engineers. It was Povl Ahm who, in 1965, won their first road project in the UK and set up a highways and bridges group in London; this was followed by roads through virgin jungle in Malaysia and across deserts in Saudi Arabia. The first bridges in Britain were mostly in sensitive locations, so it was natural that Arup was one of the first consultants to involve architects in its design team. With the help of a 60-strong Road Construction Unit spun off from the Department of Transport in 1980, Arup could plan and engineer major roads. The geo-technical engineering[4] group was set up in 1970 under a leading academic, David Henkel. He introduced aerial photography for studying land forms and geology, and brought in other experts in such esoteric specialities as geomorphology and seismic engineering – the latter in response to project work in earthquake zones. Even an archaeologist was hired to advise on the safe passage of projects located in historical sites such as in the City of London.

2 Michael Brawne *Arup Associates – the biography of an architectural practice* (Lund Humphries, 1983).

3 Tim Smit *Eden* (Corgi Books, 2002).

4 A core engineering discipline defined as 'the art and science of designing structures in the ground including design using soil as a construction material'.

Ove's legacy can be summed up in the extraordinary variety of skills his firm had accumulated by the time he died, a business armed simply with the vision expressed in the key speech. By 1988 the firm was divided into three loosely-defined business areas: Buildings, Industrial Engineering and Civil Engineering – although any specific project could involve people from any sector or geographical region. Zunz's statement that 'we steadily broadened the skill base' is totally inadequate to describe the almost uncountable sprawl of its activities by the time of the founder's death, which ranged from fire engineering, the speciality of one of the firm's few senior women, Margaret Law,[5] to academic analysis of the earth on which its buildings were based.

The Building Group itself could boast skills ranging from mechanical and public health engineering to refurbishment and restoration. Civil engineering – now labelled Infrastructure – provided a world-wide network of engineers and covered highways and bridges, airports, energy, major projects, maritime, rail, site development and regeneration, tunnels and water engineering. Planners include the environmental specialists required for routing motorways, environmental assessments and audits, land-use planning, pollution assessment and control, contaminated land reclamation and waste management – as well as the Research and Development Group established in 1964.

The specialist consulting business also involved an absurdly complex sprawl of specialities including acoustics, lighting, logistics, project management, research and development, risk and security consulting, transport consulting, vehicle design, venue consulting. The Arup definition of economics involved a broad range of development issues in economics and rural and urban planning and design, and all stages of project development. It was through this development that in 1980 Lewis hired Arup's first economist, Mark Bostock. In his book Smit describes Bostock's impact and style graphically, if rather over-dramatically. It was, he said, rather 'like meeting a buffalo on a narrow street … A big man with glasses, City-issue suits and a limp, the result of a nasty accident playing squash … His playful terseness implied that any disagreement with him could only be the result of woeful ignorance on your part'.

Bostock had been born in Nairobi, where his father was a missionary – and one of Nelson Mandela's few life-long white supporters. He had been educated there, and then at Edinburgh University where he studied economics. A variety of projects throughout East and Southern Africa kept him occupied for nearly fifteen years. Then, in 1980, he came across Arup when an engineering team led by one Terry Hill – today Arup's chairman – was working on a feeder road in Botswana: an experience which so

5 *Engineeering News Record* (USA) made her 'Man of the Year' in 1979.

intrigued Hill that he embarked on a degree in economics at Birkbeck College.

Michael Lewis was looking to broaden Arup's range even further, and also saw that Bostock could gain entry into the bosses' offices in his old stamping-ground and elsewhere. Bostock – who, as someone said, 'has only to see a box to start thinking outside it' – took his first step by rejecting the five-strong group of engineers sent out to work on a project in the newly-independent Zimbabwe, and further ensured his independence through heading a separate group, Arup Economic Consultants, which would not, however, be a department, but effectively the vehicle for the projects in which he and Arup would be involved.

The breakthrough came in 1984 when Ernie Irwin, head of Arup's engineering office in Birmingham, asked Bostock to help work on Birmingham's application to host the 1992 Olympic Games. Irwin and Bostock acted as the 'joint-venture' leaders of the multidisciplinary team which did the initial feasibility appraisal and prepared the subsequent IOC application sent to the Olympic Committee's headquarters in Lausanne by Arup on behalf of Birmingham and the UK. It was this bid which formed the springboard – and provided the boiler-plate – for later Olympic bids inspired by Arup.

Ove did not live to see his firm's new ambitions. Even after 'retiring' in 1977 he retained an office and came to work three days a week, spending most of his energy on general philosophical work. 'I am', as he wrote in the last year of his life, 'no longer the engineer-ingenious who created the famous Arup firm, but rather a philosopher, philosophising about Art and Quality, Good and Bad, Existence and the Meaning of Life'. At the age of 90 his last piece of self-analysis and testament had hardly changed from his student efforts seventy years earlier. In the last months of his life he drifted in and out of consciousness and on 5 February 1988 he suddenly woke up; sat up; looked around; and died. Eighteen months later Li followed him, having never told him of the cancer from which she had suffered.

It was left to Jørgen Nissen to sum up the result of Ove's inspirational leadership – or should it have been 'guidance' – which not only gave his colleagues the confidence to aim for any sky that happened to be around but also equipped the firm with an unrivalled range of precisely the sort of skills required for any new project, even one in a sector in which the firm had little or no previous experience. In the light of all that experience it is easy to understand why the emergence of a strategic project such as the Channel Tunnel Rail Link saw Arup prepared to enter the fray, not only with its actual design and project management, but much earlier in the project's conception and planning.

DAVID AND ALL THE GOLIATHS

It is rare for a consulting engineer to go out on a limb and promote a massive scheme on its own and to spend what must have been a considerable sum of money upfront

Professor Tony Ridley, The Times 10 October 1991

■ It was the unusual figure of one Colin Stannard who sparked off Arup's involvement in the fast line. Stannard, the very epitome of a cheerful Cockney chancer, had joined the then Westminster Bank[1] as a 16-year-old – largely because his sister was already working there. Always, he says 'a stroppy and confident lad', he became deeply involved in computerising the bank's systems – where 'I upset even more people'. He was then recruited, largely by accident, by a fellow spirit: one Mr Hitchcock, manager at the St Mary Axe branch in the City of London.

This branch was in a street packed with the offices of shipbrokers and other agents – the heart of the international shipping business. Hitchcock had built up the branch's international department, and had become the banker of choice for Greek shipowners. Stannard then ran the budding projects department of the newly-merged NatWest, providing finance for developing North Sea oilfields, thus gaining valuable experience in organising 'off-balance sheet' transactions.

As one of the handful of British experts in the field, in 1985 Stannard was asked by the Department of Transport to evaluate the bids for construction of the Channel Tunnel – where 'a computer analysis of cost and revenues made it totally obvious that only a double-bore railway tunnel could be viable'. He first came across Arup when the firm applied for the job – which it didn't get – of performing the 'due diligence' study on the finances of the projected Tunnel. A natural progression led to Stannard's role as the chief fundraiser for the winning Channel Tunnel group, as joint chief executive before the arrival of Alastair Morton. But once the first funding exercise had been completed Morton, as is the way of dictatorial new brooms, saw no place for Stannard, so he accepted 'a profitable redundancy' and set up his own consultancy working from his London home – 'it never occurred to me that I couldn't find some odd jobs', he says.

Arup's actual involvement in the saga of the fast link was sparked off at a meeting of the Major Projects Association, when Stannard described his experiences in helping to launch the Channel Tunnel. In response to his talk he received an encouraging letter from Michael Lewis of Arup, who felt he was 'speaking Arup speak' in his holistic approach to the project. This, combined with the announcement by the Secretary of State for Transport Paul Channon in October '88 that the new railway would be privately financed, led Stannard to the proposal of a partnership with Arup, bringing together Arup's technical and his financial skills in a Design, Build, Finance and Operate venture to bid for the link to Waterloo. (The government formally asked for pre-qualification

1 Subsequently the National Westminster, now a subsidiary of the Royal Bank of Scotland.

applications from interested parties in November.) He received a positive response from both Lewis and Povl Ahm, who took over as chairman in April 1989. The two were personally by no means close but, as the only civil engineers apart from Jørgen Nissen on Arup's board, both were outsiders so far as the Arup 'establishment' of structural engineers was concerned.

Stannard found an enthusiastic ally in Mark Bostock's assistant John Couch who, in Bostock's words 'very quickly picked up the Stannard thinking'. Couch was an academic, had spent twenty years teaching government at Birmingham University, and had been asked to help with the Birmingham's Olympic bid. Bostock's reaction after the bid was characteristic of Arup's hiring methods. He simply told Couch: 'it looks to me as if you've got a job'.

Colin Stannard recognised two crucial points: first, that Arup could bring along its involvement in the plans of the London Regeneration Consortium (a partnership between the Rosehaugh and Stanhope property companies and the National Freight Corporation) to regenerate the 135 acres (55ha) of 'railway lands' north of King's Cross, which 'put Arup in an extremely strong position with BR'. Second – a *leitmotiv* picked up by Arup – that after the experience of the way the contractors promoting the Channel Tunnel had estimated their costs, 'a contractor-oriented consortium is unlikely to be favoured by either BR or the financial markets'. As Stannard pointed out, the ten contractors involved in the Chunnel, being both owners and operators, devised for themselves a building contract that would have been unacceptable to any truly independent owner.[2] Conveniently for them, other clauses provided for very low penalties for any delays. As Nicholas Comfort wrote,[3] 'the contractors' final act was to write the contract under which they would build the Tunnel, a balance of risk that Eurotunnel's subsequent chiefs were to rue'.

Stannard could also have pointed to the inadequacies revealed in the construction

The empty 135-acre site stretching northward from between the two stations, St Pancras and King's Cross, had tantalised developers for years; but it took the arrival of the CTRL in the 21st century to assure its regeneration. The new line curves across to enter the extended and restored St Pancras.

2 Since then the idea of a 'contractors' cartel' has been abandoned even by the contractors themselves. In early 2007 the Metronet contractors' consortium responsible for the upgrade of two-thirds of London's Underground system was faced by delays and overruns of such an extent that it put out all its work to open tender – the practice of the far more successsful consortium working on the rest of the network. Metronet subsequently went into receivership.

3 *The Channel Tunnel and its High-Speed Links* (Oakwood 2006).

Waterloo, with Nicholas Grimshaw's Eurotunnel terminus curving sinuously alongside the main station

of the Channel Tunnel by the contractors' ignorance of railway engineering, as opposed to digging holes. This delayed the project by up to two years because they didn't start work early enough on fitting out the Tunnel, and pushed up the bill because they had no real idea of the cost of the rail infrastructure. Morton himself excused a 250 per cent increase in the cost of the rolling stock: 'nobody had any idea what they would cost in 1986–7'.[4]

Ove Arup himself had always objected to the 'contractors' package-deal, which could so easily develop into a menace to good architecture'. Not surprisingly both Stannard and the Arup partnership felt that the dominance of the contractors had been the fundamental problem with the costs and delivery of the Channel Tunnel. Stannard was – rightly – anticipating that all the other bids for the fast rail link would be 'teams of contractors put together in much the same way as the Eurotunnel consortium'.

The outcome of this thinking was a response to BR (which had invited firms to tender for the rail link to Waterloo on a Build-Own-Transfer basis) that suggested instead a joint venture with BR to select the most appropriate route and then to deliver it. The group, led by Arup and involving County NatWest, was called Kent Rail. However, its creation disguised a fundamental gulf between the partners. Stannard believed that Arup should 'project create', to design, finance, build, own and operate a rail link from Dover to King's Cross. In his mind this meant promoting a proposition which was deliverable and affordable, would earn big fees and of which he would be the boss. As he stated in a letter in February 1989: 'my intention is to control and direct all aspects of Kent Rail's development'.

A few months earlier he had already made his attitude clear in a letter to John Martin (who became Arup's chairman in 1992): 'the real question is, should Arup be involved in project promotion? My answer to this is "yes", because the nature of the market has changed. Therefore new projects have to be promoted by the private sector. A firm the size of Arup requires large project involvement in order to maintain continuity of work. The most certain way of obtaining such involvement is to participate in promotion of the project'.

Stannard was hoping to persuade Arup to follow the policy of placing some of their

4 Quoted in *The Economist*, 7 October 1989.

profits into an 'equity fund', to enable it to take a substantial slice of equity in any future project. But his hopes were completely unrealistic, given Arup's corporate culture and its ingrained concern about the firm's reputation. For Arup has always been run, financially, very conservatively: never going into debt.

Moreover, although by the late 1980s the Arup name had a far higher profile than ever before, nevertheless, as one observer put it, Arup 'was afraid of its own shadow … they didn't even take the credit due for the Sydney Opera House'. By putting forward their own ideas, they were coming out of the closet. For even a more modest version of Stannard's proposals would mean that for the first time in the firm's history Arup would initiate a project – after all, even the plans for the Birmingham Olympics had been drawn up at the request of a client. As the deeply-respected Jørgen Nissen said of Arup's involvement in the fast link: 'we have no sponsor and would need to meet our own costs until we have a project … What are these costs, and what are the risks?' Merely developing an alternative route to that proposed by BR was an unprecedented step – and one deemed a step too far by many of Arup's directors of the day.

It is not surprising that the unprecedented, and – by Arup's standards, anyway – costly, leap into the dark involved in even putting forward their own proposals encountered ferocious internal opposition. It came from the structural engineers who formed the company's backbone, and were used to playing a subsidiary role to the architects rather than acting independently. The key was that both Ahm and Lewis were looking for additional work for the civil side of the business. To the financially-minded Stannard they were all 'aesthetic engineers' rather than businessmen.

Nevertheless in February 1989 Arup's management board gave an – obviously reluctant – go-ahead to the idea, including the expenditure of £1 million for this specific initiative as a sort of 'virility symbol'. Stannard had already sent a fully-fledged proposition to Lazards, the merchant bank advising the government, which had demanded responses before the end of January in order to draw up a short-list of pre-qualified bidders. Its handful of proponents within Arup emphasised that the submission would 'give us the opportunity to exercise our skills and extend our capabilities – not because we want to "break out" of consulting engineering. We would have to provide resources for strategic planning, coordination of design and project management'. The board was genuinely split, and not just financially. Although Arup had traditionally served architects, yet another aspect of its inheritance was the founder's entrepreneurial instincts, his self-awarded freedom from the disciplines

1988

April

- Sunday Times reports leak of BR plan for a rail link: three possible routes, one north of Thames

14 July

- BR announces four alternative routes across Kent and four London station options: King's Cross Low Level, St Pancras, White City and Stratford

July

- RACHEL route published

October

- Government announces private-sector participation in Rail Link is vital

November

- BR, advised by merchant bank Lazards; issues formal invitation to tender

December

- House of Commons debates rail link plans

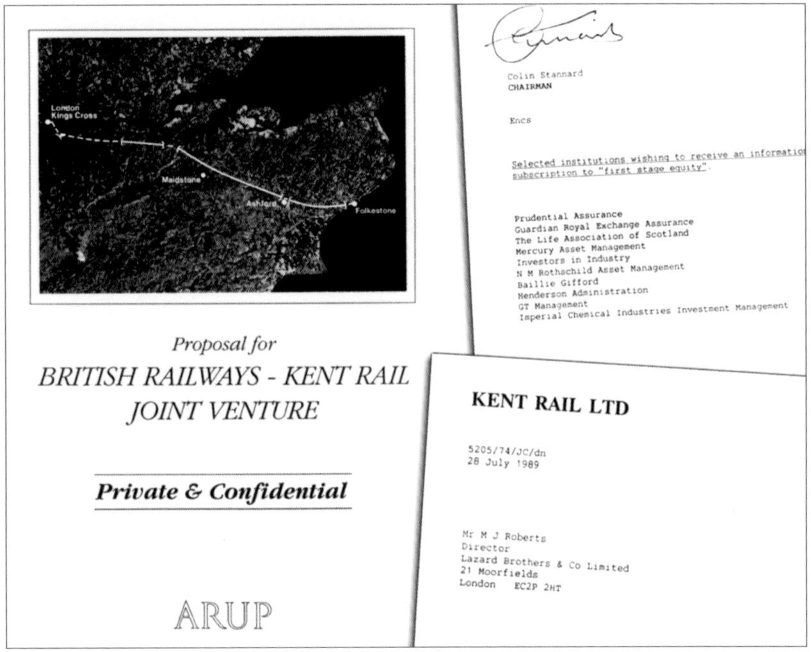

Kent Rail was the vehicle devised by Colin Stannard and Arup to bid for the building of the Channel Tunnel rail link

normally imposed on the engineering profession.

While Arup was cautiously entering new territory, British Rail – since announcing the 'four routes' in July 1988 – was stuck with the same set of problems it had faced in the early 1970s. Establishing the alignment was just one issue. Financing it, under the terms dictated by the government (Paul Channon had set these out in October '88), was quite another. BR had to find a private-sector partner – in which case it would get some government support unobtainable if it went it alone.

This was hard: British Rail was already haunted by the prospect of privatisation, and, above all, in trying to ensure (as it turned out, unsuccessfully) that the process would not involve its breakup. Unfortunately for British Rail, the earlier privatisation of British Gas had left that organisation a largely untouched monopoly; the Treasury was now determined not to repeat what they saw as a mistake with the railways. So BR felt that even one joint venture would be a precedent for fragmentation – especially as, before he left office in July 1989, the Secretary of State Paul Channon made it clear that he favoured breaking up the network into smaller regional companies. In a letter to Channon, BR and Lazard stated that they viewed a joint venture or 'private-sector involvement … as an incursion into their single-entity objective'.

Six bidders emerged from the pre-qualification process – all contractor-dominated but one: the Arup-led Kent Rail. By July 1989 five of the groups had submitted formal bids to British Rail, including Arup.

Meanwhile, John Welsby – BR's director in charge – had waited to bring in a proper project director until he was sure that the new link would go ahead, but by May 1989 he was confident enough to employ an outsider to manage the job. He was Gil Howarth, one of the brightest young project directors in the country. Howarth had made his name at British Nuclear Fuels, where he had been responsible for the design and construction of a £262-million plant for treating metallic radioactive waste at Sellafield. It was completed both on time and on budget. After he started work for them, he and his future wife sensibly checked on BR's kitchen-table planning by spending ten days walking the whole CTRL route. It also helped that, notably unlike Welsby, Howarth rather enjoyed the public consultation process. Unfortunately, in May John Welsby went off sick with a back problem; by the time he returned he had already been appointed as Chief Executive-designate of BR, which meant that the project was left slightly in mid-air.

Soon after his return to work in September, Welsby recruited his old Department of Transport colleague John Palmer, who had just retired, to take charge not only of the construction of the CTRL and its associated stations but also of European Passenger Services, which was going to run the trains. Apparently John Palmer found a rather unsatisfactory situation in which even Gil Howarth did not have adequate authority as project director – BR not being in the habit of encouraging autonomy. Also, in John Welsby's absence the Treasury had been playing up rough and refusing funds to start construction of the terminal at Waterloo. Having privatised most of the major nationalised industries, the Treasury now had the time and inclination to look more closely at BR – especially as the costs of the link kept increasing.

BR would have liked to submit the Bill to enable the project to go ahead (as opposed to the one already put forward for the terminal at King's Cross) in the spring of 1990, with the target of Royal Assent in early 1992. This would have allowed for a two-year lead-in period for ordering major items like tunnel-boring machines, a start of work in 1994 and completion in 1999. But the timetable imposed by the government had been further foreshortened by the likelihood of an election in June 1991: suddenly the Bill needed parliamentary approval within 18 months.

British Rail was by now taking freight more seriously, despite its chairman's warning that 'nobody yet has run a fast line mixed with freight. It may work on a train-set, but it doesn't work in real life'.[5] BR had abandoned its previous idea, of centralising all freight shipments through its major depot in Willesden in North-West London, and was sensibly planning twelve regional centres – although not all of them on routes up to the normal UIC loading gauge. But, as Stannard and others pointed out: 'without a UIC line [right through to the trains' final destination] BR would not be able to attract its due share of the freight traffic, simply because customers on the Continent would not be willing to confine themselves to the relatively small wheels and small containers available on the BR loading gauge'. As in its plans for passenger trains in the 1970s, BR was relying on sending heavy freight trains west along the line through the Surrey Tory heartland (see map on page 39), which naturally created squeals of protest – though, as BR pointed out, those routes were already used for freight.

5 But in 2007 SCNF proposed to carry urgent parcels traffic over its precious LGV tracks.

1989

January

- TALIS proposal published
- Newham Borough Council publishes report 'The case for a Channel Tunnel Terminal at Stratford'
- Six thousand protestors march through Maidstone, Kent
- Protest groups begin to form in South-East London
- BR announce that a low-level station at King's Cross is their preferred choice for the second London terminal

End January

- Deadline for pre-qualification of private sector proposals for Rail Link: six bidders qualify

March

- BR announces single route corridor (different from all four July 88 routes) with a sub-surface junction at Warwick Gardens, Peckham; lines into King's Cross low level and Waterloo

July

- Five private-sector bids in, including Kent Rail, the Arup-led team proposing a joint venture with BR

Meanwhile, back at Arup Bostock and his allies concealed the ever-mounting expenditure by dividing it under a selection of job-numbers, so that no-one could add up the total spend. It obviously helped that, at a board meeting held on 25 May 1989, 'Michael Lewis confirmed that he would be taking ultimate responsibility on all matters concerning Kent Rail Ltd and the Channel Rail Link'. Nevertheless the responsibility and the insecurity remained. Bostock was fully aware that he was 'ducking and weaving... stretching the space' allowed to Arup executives.

Lewis made one of his regular reports to the board on 1 June, with a final decision on 'continuation or otherwise of the venture' due at a board meeting on 17 July. In the meantime Duncan Michael, a future chairman and spokesman for the hard-core structural engineers on the board, requested that the project be presented to a full partnership meeting the next month to decide whether it 'is dead or alive'. It was finally decided that Arup's aim was merely to be 'the engineer' to the Kent Rail consortium, and 'provide consulting engineering services which are design-led and care for the environment, rather than money-led'. This decision ended Stannard's original dream.

Stannard was fully aware that Mrs Thatcher 'won't believe any scheme that doesn't have overwhelming backing from the private sector'. By the time the Kent Rail bid document went to Lazards in July 1989 Stannard had assembled an impressive list of financial backers. Ten blue-chip institutions, including 3i, then Britain's leading provider of venture capital, Prudential, NM Rothschild and the ICI pension fund were on the list of first-stage equity investors. Stannard's old employers NatWest were prepared to act as stockbrokers to the Kent Rail consortium.

But British Rail was apparently stalling, and meetings with Bob Reid and Lazards didn't appear to lead to much progress. Arup were not alone; press reports said that their TALIS rivals Manufacturers Hanover (now working under the project name RailEurope, and also to find themselves left off the BR shortlist) 'also complained that it had great difficulty in arranging top-level negotiations with BR, necessary to develop a detailed feasibility study'. Right through 1989 BR was said to be 'prevaricating', and that it 'would only talk to engineers'.

By then BR was working on an 'accelerated timetable', with the choice of a preferred route due by the end of June '89 and approval by the BR board by mid-October – the King's Cross Bill was already before Parliament. Indeed, at a meeting with BR, Howarth told Arup that the route 'was virtually settled', and without blinking said that the report on TALIS by Transmark was due in early July, not troubling to mention that Transmark was a BR subsidiary and therefore unlikely to support an alternative. Not surprisingly Bostock reported his 'feeling that BR are *continuing* [his emphasis] to prevaricate … In order to secure the Bill deposition in November, there is going to be little or no time to have any influence on the physical nature of the project'.

Things were getting desperate for Arup, who realised that they were not in the frame: they had not even been called to interview by British Rail. 'There was no traction at all between us and our potential client', remembers Bostock. 'BR wanted a railway that simply met their criteria and was an extension to their network.'

And then, in July, Arup's Kent Rail bid was thrown out – deemed to be 'non-conforming'. The reasons exposed a clear rift in thinking and approach between Arup and BR. Kent Rail was told that its bid did not meet the November 1988 project specification issued by BR and Lazards, in that it proposed a joint venture between BR and Kent Rail as the basis for first developing the rail investment and then delivering it, after deciding the best strategy for getting value for money out of the contractors and their supply chain – all of whom would be selected by competitive tender. While the original bid specification stipulated that BR reserved the right 'to treat as valid any pre-qualification application which is not entirely in order' (as Bostock noted at the time), it was clear that they were reverting to their preferred Build-Own-Transfer model to deliver their March 1989 route – very firmly under their direct control.

Behind this was a change in emphasis at government level. Paul Channon was replaced as Secretary of State for Transport by Cecil Parkinson in August. Parkinson made it very clear to BR that the private sector must be central to the rail link process. Michael Lewis appealed to Parkinson for an early meeting, attacking 'BR's blinkered approach' which would 'certainly result in a very substantial volume of petitions' and undoubtedly delay the Bill. But it was no use; it seemed highly improbable that BR would reopen the competition.

Arup had wanted to examine alternative alignments jointly with BR, and select the best route. They and Stannard had argued that if private-sector financing was to get involved in this major project, then reviewing the route alignment would have to be a pre-condition. Indeed, as Mark Bostock reported to an Arup meeting in September 1990, 'I am sure each of the six groups that submitted pre-qualification information … by end January 1989 … thought that the selected group would be directly involved in selecting the route in order to minimize engineering costs and maximize revenue … Then to our astonishment in March 1989 BR published its route' (see chapter 5).

As he further pointed out, BR's route was a passenger-only high speed railway.

1989

July

- Kent Rail bid rejected as 'non-conforming'

August

- Cecil Parkinson is Secretary of State for Transport

October

- Eurorail consortium (Trafalgar House/Balfour Beatty) announced as BR's private-sector partner

November

- Rail Link estimated cost now £3.35 billion: Eurorail scales back London tunnel plans and announces further studies into London end of the route

Sir Nigel Broackes of Trafalgar House

Arup maintained that 'to our knowledge no new railway could finance itself from operating revenues alone. Other income sources had to be found. A new high-speed railway for passenger services could not realistically be divorced from freight services'. Nor indeed from property development: 'the ability to raise future income from ... developments directly associated with the stations [and from] property developments in Kent which gain from their connection with the ... Link' as Stannard put it in Kent Rail's July '89 submission.

So another interesting and innovative aspect was Arup's plan to set up a parallel joint venture with Kent County Council. This partnership enterprise company was to identify development zones that could maximise the benefits from any new railway – clearly an attempt to integrate rail investment with land development.

By September BR was down to a short-list of two consortia. The winner, formally announced in October, was Eurorail, a consortium created to build the line in which the British Rail Board held half the shares, with Trafalgar House – owners of Cementation – and BICC, which owned Balfour Beatty, a quarter each. Not only was Sir Nigel Broackes, Trafalgar House's chairman, a favourite of Mrs Thatcher, but the firm's loyalty had been shown when it rallied round during the Falklands war by sending one of its ships, the *Atlantic Conveyor*, with the fleet; unfortunately, it was sunk. The venture was clearly a pilot scheme for partnerships beween the public sector and private capital – boosted by the claim that the return would be eighteen per cent, against the eight per cent which BR had been unable to achieve. Essentially the BR/Eurorail venture was given the Channel Tunnel Railway mandate, subject to them demonstrating that they had a financially viable proposition in terms of Government policy at that time.

Arup's answer to BR's decision was a defiant one: a pledge, backed by Povl Ahm, to commit enough resources to identify the best route from the Channel Tunnel to London and beyond. Arup remained committed to the need for a 'skill-based approach' – i.e., one that was not led by contractors – unlike the other bidders.

Arup's team had one major advantage: their acceptance, unlike BR, that 'the future would be different from the past'. Like BR they realised that the M20 corridor proposed by the Men of Kent was the ideal route from Ashford to the North Downs. But there – after the rejection of the Kent Rail bid forced a radical rethink – they parted ways. Arup did not want to approach London from the south.

EASTERN PROMISE

We have found the PIMBYs – Please In My Back Yard

Colin Stannard, interviewed in the Evening Standard

Arup had realised that East London was full of empty 'brownfield sites', in contrast to the congested, built-up, NIMBY-packed south-eastern suburbs. As a result, the Arup team abandoned its idea of simply providing a better way of building the line on the route proposed by BR, and began thinking of an easterly approach – though one very different from that proposed by RailEurope. Terry Hill, a future chairman of Arup, was one of the trio from Arup's team who finally decided on the route through East London. Since, ironically, British Rail was having one of its regular weekly strikes, he and two colleagues met in the home of one of their number and drew it up. Hill says simply: 'the route designed itself'.

Hill had the inestimable advantage of knowing East London very well from the five years he had just spent on the East London [Traffic] Assessment Scheme, one of a clutch of government-financed studies into London's transport problems (an exercise which had finally put paid to the building of new motorways in the capital[1]). This meant, too, that he was in a perfect position to consult the local inhabitants, as well as businesses like Ford and the local authorities – not just Newham, but others like Havering and Thurrock, all equally keen on the rail link. His experience helped him: 'you can improve relationships if you relax and just listen and don't behave like the then DoT, which was simply going through the motions'.

But Arup's success was not primarily due to the team's interviewing skills. It was, says Hill, the fact that 'BR kept to their brief, whereas Arup never accepts anything; it's always asking the next question'. Since he, like every other Arup person, saw no bounds, he was asking a fundamental question: 'how do you make the line as useful as possible? BR had swallowed the limited French TGV brief … we didn't want a clone of the TGV lines' – which were designed exclusively for fast passenger trains. Arup wanted to 'serve multiple stakeholders' by including provision for freight and commuter traffic – and also for development and regeneration along the route.

For the Arup team and Stannard were thinking big. Stannard went along with the idea of a route through south Essex – it was he who coined the term 'Thames Gateway' – to King's Cross. He and the Arup team proposed a largely four-track railway, with two tracks devoted to slower freight and commuter trains, that could allow stops at any station along the route without obstructing the Eurostars.

The tracks would run through an immersed tube tunnel underneath the Thames to the north bank, near Dagenham Dock. Here the freight trains would join the London–Southend line, while the passenger trains would enter a tunnel to King's Cross;

1 See Chapter 5, page 74.

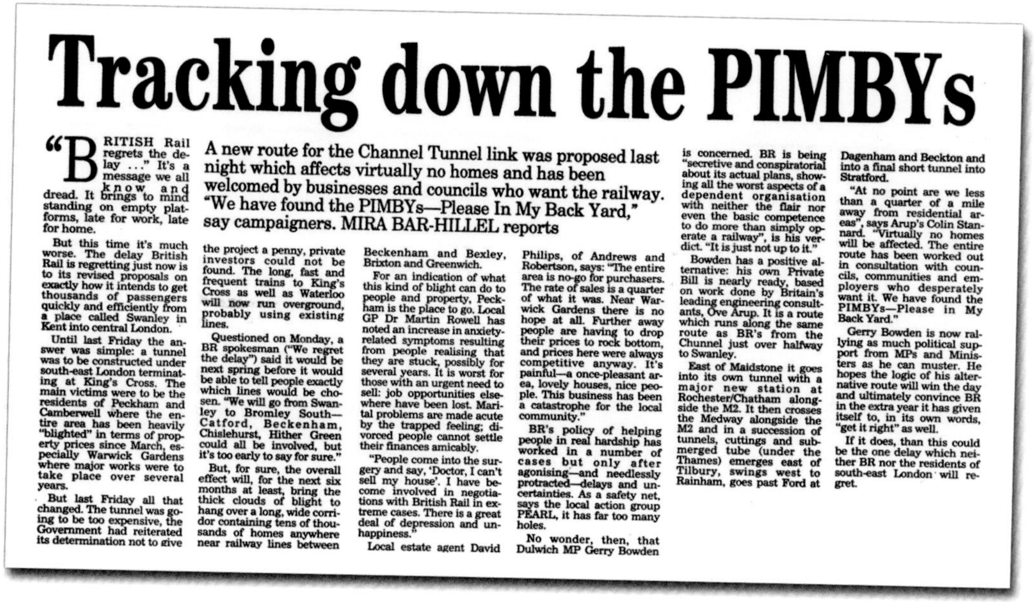

Tracking down the PIMBYs

A new route for the Channel Tunnel link was proposed last night which affects virtually no homes and has been welcomed by businesses and councils who want the railway. "We have found the PIMBYs—Please In My Back Yard," say campaigners. MIRA BAR-HILLEL reports

"BRITISH Rail regrets the delay ..." It's a message we all know and dread. It brings to mind standing on empty platforms, late for work, late for home.

But this time it's much worse. The delay British Rail is regretting just now is to its revised proposals on exactly how it intends to get thousands of passengers quickly and efficiently from a place called Swanley in Kent into central London.

Until last Friday the answer was simple: a tunnel was to be constructed under south-east London terminating at King's Cross. The main victims were to be the residents of Peckham and Camberwell where the entire area has been heavily "blighted" in terms of property prices since March, especially Warwick Gardens where major works were to take place over several years.

But last Friday all that changed. The tunnel was going to be too expensive, the Government had reiterated its determination not to give the project a penny, private investors could not be found. The long, fast and frequent trains to King's Cross as well as Waterloo will now run overground, probably using existing lines.

Questioned on Monday, a BR spokesman ("We regret the delay") said it would be next spring before it would be able to tell people exactly which lines would be chosen. "We will go from Swanley to Bromley South—Catford, Beckenham, Chislehurst, Hither Green could all be involved, but it's too early to say for sure."

But, for sure, the overall effect will, for the next six months at least, bring the thick clouds of blight to hang over a long, wide corridor containing tens of thousands of homes anywhere near railway lines between Beckenham and Bexley, Brixton and Greenwich.

For an indication of what this kind of blight can do to people and property, Peckham is the place to go. Local GP Dr Martin Rowell has noted an increase in anxiety-related symptoms resulting from people realising that they are stuck, possibly for several years. It is worst for those with an urgent need to sell: job opportunities elsewhere have been lost. Marital problems are made acute by the trapped feeling; divorced people cannot settle their finances amicably.

"People come into the surgery and say, 'Doctor, I can't sell my house'. I have become involved in negotiations with British Rail in extreme cases. There is a great deal of depression and unhappiness."

Local estate agent David Philips, of Andrews and Robertson, says: "The entire area is no-go for purchasers. The rate of sales is a quarter of what it was. Near Warwick Gardens there is no hope at all. Further away people are having to drop their prices to rock bottom, and prices here were always competitive anyway. It's painful—a once-pleasant area, lovely houses, nice people. This business has been a catastrophe for the local community."

BR's policy of helping people in real hardship has worked in a number of cases but only after agonising—and needlessly protracted—delays and uncertainties. As a safety net, says the local action group PEARL, it has far too many holes.

No wonder, then, that Dulwich MP Gerry Bowden is concerned. BR is being "secretive and conspiratorial about its actual plans, showing all the worst aspects of a dependent organisation with neither the flair nor even the basic competence to do more than simply operate a railway", is his verdict. "It is just not up to it."

Bowden has a positive alternative: his own Private Bill is nearly ready, based on work done by Britain's leading engineering consultants, Ove Arup. It is a route which runs along the same route as BR's from the Chunnel just over halfway to Swanley.

East of Maidstone it goes into its own tunnel with a major new station at Rochester/Chatham alongside the M2. It then crosses the Medway alongside the M2 and in a succession of tunnels, cuttings and submerged tube (under the Thames) emerges east of Tilbury, swings west to Rainham, goes past Ford at Dagenham and Beckton and into a final short tunnel into Stratford.

"At no point are we less than a quarter of a mile away from residential areas", says Arup's Colin Stannard. "Virtually no homes will be affected. The entire route has been worked out in consultation with councils, communities and employers who desperately want it. We have found the PIMBYs—Please in My Back Yard."

Gerry Bowden is now rallying as much political support from MPs and Ministers as he can muster. He hopes the logic of his alternative route will win the day and ultimately convince BR in the extra year it has given itself to, in its own words, "get it right" as well.

If it does, than this could be the one delay which neither BR nor the residents of south-east London will regret.

The article in London's *Evening Standard*, 8 November 1989

there would also be a connection to the North London Line at Custom House.

Even more ambitiously, Arup also proposed that a major part of Britain's main-line rail system should be upgraded to UIC B+ gauge, the size employed for the link itself, for the benefit of Continental-size freight trains – as well as assuming that Crossrail, the planned east–west fast route under London, would be built.

Arup and Stannard went public with their eastern route in early November 1989, four months after the rejection of Kent Rail's proposal to BR – and just as BR finally admitted that, due to cost increases, its grand London tunnel plan had unravelled and that the Eurostars would be back on the surface: thus reigniting all the fights with the NIMBYs of Dulwich. 'We have found the PIMBYs – Please In My Back Yard', Stannard was able to tell the *Evening Standard*. 'At no point are we less than a quarter of a mile away from any residential areas. Virtually no homes would be affected. The entire route has been worked out in consultation with councils, communities and employers who desperately want it.'

Stannard's interview with the London newspaper came in the week when BR and the government had announced the virtual collapse of the rail link plan. After a year in which, to quote one observer, 'the cost seemed to rise regularly in £500-million jumps' it was revealed that the private Bill – and thus the entire project – was 'shelved' for a year (see Chapter 10). Suddenly, the BR/Trafalgar House deal was in question; the field was open for Arup, and anyone else, to come up with a better plan.

Because of the limitations imposed by the King's Cross Bill, then in preparation, Arup and everyone else had to accept one of the most contentious (and expensive) elements in BR's plans, the idea of a King's Cross low-level station – although approaching it from the east at least ended the threat to the Bankside power station (now the Tate Modern) and Peckham. To retain any credibility, Arup had to demonstrate to BR that its

ARUP'S PROPOSED LONDON CONNECTIONS

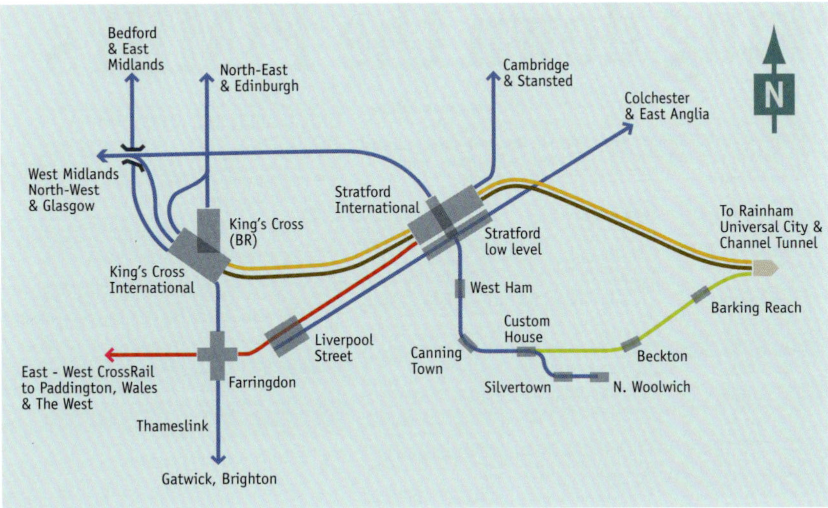

- International passenger traffic
- Outer commuter traffic
- Inner commuter traffic
- Proposed East-West Crossrail
- Existing BR traffic

In Arup's vision, Stratford International would be a major hub, with links to Crossrail, the North-West main line (via the North London Line) and Eastern England. King's Cross International would link to both north and (via Thameslink) south. A freight spur would link with the Gospel Oak–Barking line, connecting it to the rest of the BR network.

Facing page: Arup's March 1990 proposal was for a four-track railway built to UIC gauge, with six intermediate stations – Ashford, Medway Parkway, Blue Water, Dartford, Rainham Universal City and Stratford. Tunnels would run under the North Downs, the Thames and East London.

alignment for King's Cross low level fell within the 'lines of deviation' as set out in the Bill. As the proposals were developed Arup 'had to keep adding tunnels', and were obviously looking for a suitable point at which to bore under the Thames. They were fully aware that the financial viability of their route depended on the possible revenue from commuter traffic, though they were confident that their proposed stations were even more convenient for commuters than BR's. BR wouldn't provide any traffic figures, so Richard Foster on the Arup team had to work them out for himself (and was naturally proud when it transpired that his figures were parallel to theirs).

Once Arup had devised a robust technical solution, they realised that the project had to secure the approval of government and the wider world of politics, in particular backbench MPs. A key player was the feisty, obsessive figure of Maureen Tomison who, hired by Arup as a public affairs consultant, was to play an important role in ensuring that the firm's proposals had backing from MPs, above all those representing constituencies north of London. Scottish (Orcadian) by birth, she was a natural Tory but, even more so, a fanatical supporter of British involvement in Europe.[3] As a member of the committee of University Young Conservatives – then a powerful body – she had already got to know a whole generation of youthful activists destined for high office, above all those from Cambridge like Kenneth Clarke, John Selwyn Gummer and Kenneth Baker. As a young journalist she became one of the first women to be admitted to the parliamentary lobby, where, she says, 'sexual harassment was compulsory'. (She learnt even more about the structure of power when she sat in on numerous meetings as a researcher for a Granada television programme on the State of the Nation, an experience she describes as 'a great apprenticeship in understanding power'.)

Headhunted by Jim Sherwood of Sea Containers, owners of a major fleet of ferries, she had travelled all round Kent lobbying for his opposition to a Channel Tunnel on behalf of Flexilink, and then as part of the 'Sink the Link' campaign. So she already knew BR's route (and indeed most of Kent) as well as the county's key MPs – many in marginal Tory seats (see page 78). But she also insisted that Arup 'go wider and deal with

3 In 1961 as a student at St Andrews she had proposed the first motion supporting our entry into the Common Market; in the 2005 General Election she stood for Labour against Michael Howard because of his anti-European policies.

ARUP'S ROUTE, MARCH 1990

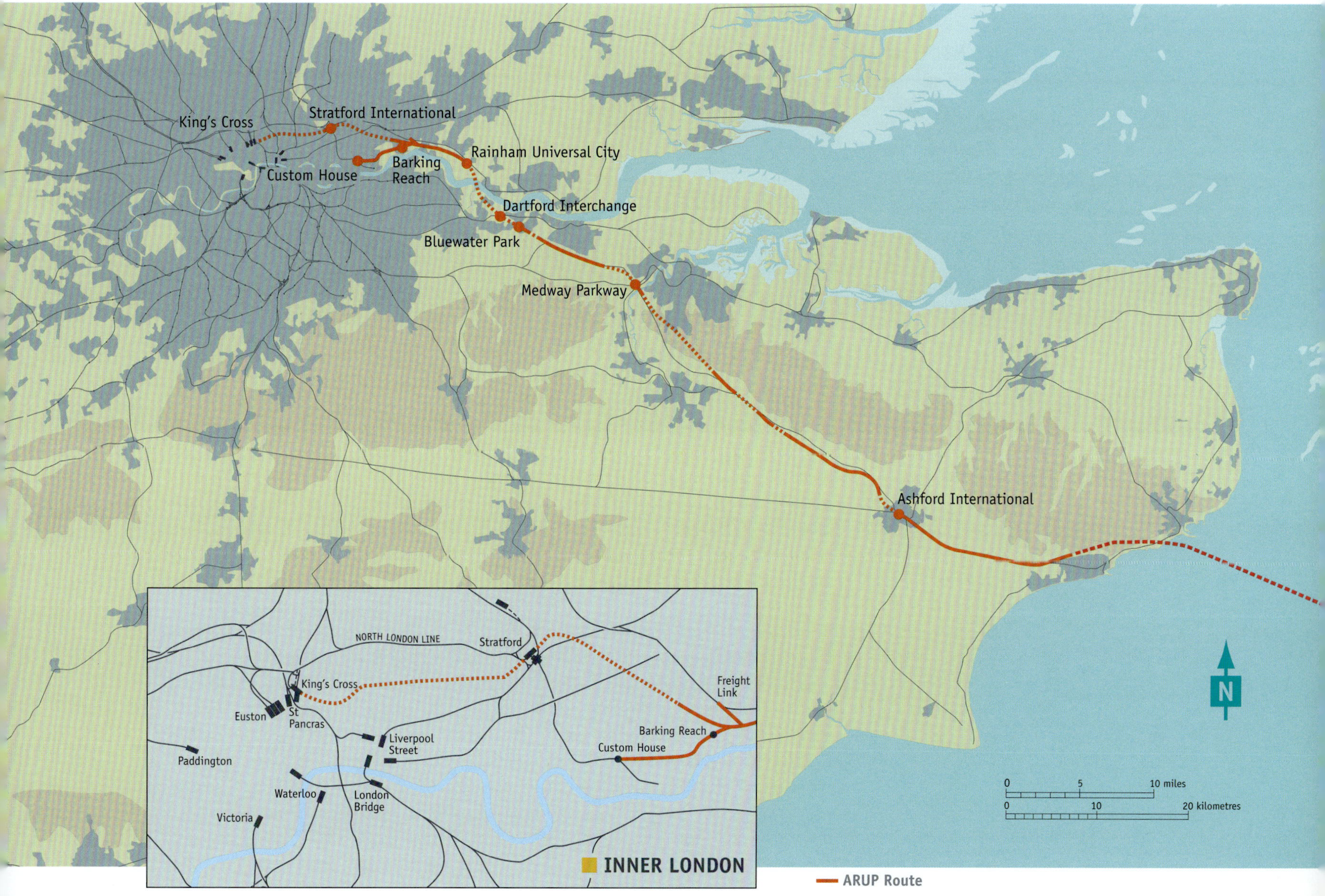

Stratford and the Lea Valley – only a mile or two from the gleaming towers of Canary Wharf and the City – were in 1990 languishing in semi-dereliction

politicians and pressure groups on a national basis'. She believes that she found the solution to one key route problem – how to align the stretch from the North Downs tunnel to the Thames – on a rainy Sunday afternoon walk. Looking down from the top of Bluebell Hill just north of Maidstone,[4] she saw the possibility of a route running under the North Downs and reaching the Thames east of Dartford across the enormous tract of redundant chalk pits dug out by Blue Circle cement. These pits, a whitefield if not a brownfield site, have provided the more than 500 acres required for the Ebbsfleet International station complex; also a home for the giant Bluewater shopping centre.[5]

But Tomison's main role was straightforward lobbying, a skill Arup learned about from Colin Stannard. As Mark Bostock recalls, 'this was a new world to Arup. We were learning our way around'. Tomison's first contribution was to attend up to 90 meetings, mostly at weekends, with small groups of locals; she also claimed to have contacted 27 MPs in July 1989 alone. 'She was crucial' says Malcolm Noyce of Arup's team, 'in getting us access to MPs and enabled us to network with them in an informal setting at her many parties'. (These were monthly affairs – all, allegedly, celebrating her 50th birthday.) 'There was always a member of the cabinet or shadow cabinet there', remembers Mark

4 She was accompanied on her walk by Malcolm Noyce of Arup, who remembers having to carry her shoes on the climb.

5 She was not the first to spot them: Lupin Pooter was a century ahead: 'I give you a tip, chalk pits are as safe as consols, and pay six per cent at par.' *Diary of a Nobody* (1894).

Bostock. 'Never before had Arup's name been so much before the public'. One party in May 1991 was enjoyed by dignitaries ranging from the former Prime Minister, Edward Heath (MP for Old Bexley and Sidcup – which was on the BR route) and current ministers, through sundry MPs and peers to a diplomat from the Russian Embassy. The effect worked. At a House of Commons Christmas party in December 1991 – after the Arup route had been chosen – Malcolm Rifkind, the Secretary of State for Transport who announced Government approval of Arup's route, turned to Bostock and said 'that man there was responsible for getting the support of 331 MPs'. In fact of course it was Tomison whose work had undermined the otherwise implacable opposition of the DoT.

The combination of lobbying, attendance at party conferences and 'birthday parties' ensured that the argument emerged on the radar-screens of several hundred MPs, not only those who were directly affected by the BR route. As she said, 'ordinary MPs had been totally out of the loop' – and from 1989 on, Arup's name cropped up whenever the CTRL was being discussed. As Kenneth Warren, chairman of the important Trade and Industry Select Committee, commented 'we would have known very little about the Channel Tunnel Rail Link without Decision Makers'.[6] Tomison's terrier-like attitude extended to journalists; Nicholas Comfort, then working as a political correspondent, recalls how she 'lobbied me relentlessly for the Arup route'.

To some extent, Maureen Tomison was pushing at an open door. The mass grass-roots indignation had scared the Kent MPs, and she was able to report to Povl Ahm in December 1989 that 'the BR/Trafalgar House route is immensely unpopular among MPs. We find very few supporters'. She also made the prescient comment that 'Arup has made many friends for the future among politicians'.

Arup was not alone: other people too had refused to give up. Among the most prominent of these was Newham Council. Even after BR's refusal to consider Stratford,[7] Stephen Timms and his council colleagues continued to campaign through the other groups which had emerged, and which were backing an easterly approach, via Stratford. 'Our six months' campaign may have been unsuccessful', he says, 'but it drew attention to the site ... for me the proposals became an obsession'. Although the neighbouring borough of Hackney never showed any enthusiasm,[8] he was encouraged by the unprecedented backing of the local business community, and by the fact that an opinion poll within the borough had shown an 80 per cent majority in favour, acknowledging that 'we need the jobs'.

Newham became a serious opponent of the King's Cross Bill, and in November 1989

1989

8 November

- Arup goes public with first outline of an alternative, Eastern, route

November

- Newham Council organizes conference 'A National Focus on the Channel Tunnel'

1990

February

- Amended proposals presented to government by BR/Eurorail, with the cost now down to £2.6 billion: London tunnel drastically shortened, public fears re-ignite
- Michael Portillo, Minister of State for public transport, rules out direct subsidy for Rail Link

March

- Arup Eastern Route proposal published, with detailed map and strategic overview

6 The name of her small lobbying company.

7 'We have taken heed of the strong and vociferous Stratford lobby', wrote BR's consultants Transmark. 'The second terminal is represented as a prize to be awarded to the most disadvantaged London borough. But viewed as a straightforward business proposition concerned with the conveyance of people, different criteria apply.' (TALIS report, July 1989).

8 After the easterly route had been chosen, Brian Sedgemore, the maverick Labour MP for Hackney South, made an hysterical speech in Parliament attacking the whole notion that the new route could provide any benefits to the people of East London.

organised a conference, 'A National Focus on the Channel Tunnel', as part of its efforts to promote an easterly approach with (naturally enough) a station rather than a terminus at Stratford – an idea supported by John Prescott, the Labour shadow Secretary of State for Transport. They were already aware of the Arup easterly approach, which included a station at Stratford: this they eagerly embraced.

By the end of the year the position was becoming clearer. In early December the DoT was able to announce that: 'the investments on the passenger side are worth about £175 million. I can also announce that we have just approved investment of about £80 million on electric freight locomotives and on electrification of the line between Tonbridge and Redhill. That forms part of British Rail's core investments of a further £175 million in Channel tunnel freight. The Government have now approved the great majority of British Rail's investment plans for 1990.'

To which the answer was, so what? Missing from the list was a clear plan, and a solid, signed-up joint venture partner, for the CTRL. But at least Arup knew where they were: in Bostock's words, 'once BR had turned us down and we were alone, was the crucial moment of standing up to be counted' – a totally unprecedented experience.

Encouragement came from an unlikely source: in September 1989 the *New Civil Engineer* concluded that, having committed £1 million to the project, 'Arup's hat is now seen by bankers and potential clients to be in the ring for anything similar in the future'.

STALEMATE

You [BR] are told to look for ways of building a self-financing fast railway to the Channel Tunnel. The government then bows to political pressure to make it environmentally friendly and therefore too expensive to pay for itself, but offers no subsidy. Bidders for the Channel Tunnel Rail Link found it hard to cope with shifting rules and rumours about how much subsidy they might get and what conditions would be set by British Rail.

The Economist, 11 November 1989

■ The whole of 1990 was spent in attempts, inevitably futile, to square the circle: to devise an answer to the CTRL riddle which would satisfy all Whitehall's many, and usually contradictory, interests – as represented most obviously by 10 Downing Street, the Department of Transport and the Treasury. Not to mention the restive natives in Kent and South-East London and their vociferous spokespersons.

By this time BR's Gil Howarth had 340 people working with him. Arup were competing with a team of five or six, headed by two people, Ken Cole and Richard Foster, neither of whom were specialist railway engineers. Cole proved absolutely crucial: he combined enormous technical knowledge – which included his speciality, earth science – brilliant draughtsmanship, and a great capacity for clear explanation. These qualities were shown to the full at vital moments when Arup's technical credibility was at stake, thus neutering the attacks by Whitehall and BR on Arup's capacity. Despite their scant resources Arup produced a 1:10,000 route map, while BR spent about 300,000 man-hours for a more detailed 1:1,250 map.[1] Both Cole and Foster were fully aware of the likelihood of failure and, while Cole was nearing retirement (and in the event was forced to retire early for medical reasons), the much younger Foster felt that he was liable to be sacked if their plans didn't work. What is more, both of them had to keep working at their previous 'day jobs' – Foster spent two days a week working on a possible tram link in Leeds. All the team, says Malcolm Noyce, another of the select group, were doing the work 'out of hours'.

'Arup didn't have a formal investment budget', says Bostock, 'we had to play the system'. Through it all 'it was the team's [belief and] professionalism that gave me confidence in the project. I was totally dependent on their technical competences'.

The one rail specialist involved, Fraser Smith, had been brought in to the firm because light rail was thought to be a promising development – and in any case his contribution was on the political, rather than the engineering, side. Cole, the senior engineer, later proved vital when tackling two of the biggest problems involved in the eastern route soon chosen by Arup: tunnelling under the Thames Estuary and coping with the marshes north of the river – where he knew they would need a viaduct built on piling to cope with the marshy and unreliable ground which had no strength to support a railway. On the rest of the route he was confident of the terrain – clay in Essex and chalk in northern Kent – for tunnelling purposes. Foster had been hired in 1987 as a water engineer, but had always been a railway fanatic: in his spare time he had compiled a three-volume history of New Street Station in Birmingham and a history of

1 In all, BR was estimated to have spent £40 million on the project – not including the amount spent on property.

the signalling systems used on the London & North Western, the railway linking London with Birmingham, Manchester and Liverpool.

Thanks to Mark Bostock's tactics, it was only when they had spent an unprecedented £750,000 – without being able to allocate the expenditure to a specific client – that they had to approach the board. But, says Malcolm Noyce, 'it was possible only in Arup where it was all very fluid, with no formal managerial structure, no real lines of responsibility'. The rail link team felt that they 'knew more about the subject than anyone else in Arup' (which, however, wasn't saying a great deal), and were haunted the whole time by the feeling that, as Foster says, 'we were going to be found out. The trick was to do enough to know that the proposals would work. No part of the engineering or operational proposals were ever successfully challenged. It was this that gave Bostock the confidence to promote the scheme'. When BR was derided for revealing that they had plotted the route on tracing paper over an out-of-date map the Arup team had that 'there but for the grace of God' feeling, though they – like BR's Howarth – had already walked every inch of their entire route.

Top: Michael Lewis (left) and the late Povl Ahm, the two Arup directors who fought the internal battle over the route
Bottom: Richard Foster and the late Ken Cole, key members of Arup's tiny design team

Meanwhile BR was pushing ahead itself – partly by hiring consultants. During 1989 and 1990 it employed Sir Alexander Gibb & Partners as coordinating engineering consultants. At the time, no fewer than sixteen consultancies were also involved, covering everything from the environment to 'validating BR's project methodology', at a total cost which has never been revealed.[2] (In fact, BR recruited most of Britain's major engineering firms – who were obviously going to oppose any initiative Arup put forward. As Bostock put it: 'the DoT set up the engineering profession against us'. Not surprisingly Jack Zunz, co-chairman from 1984 to 1989, later told Bostock: 'Mark, do you realise you are taking on over half of our client base?')

At last, in early November 1989, just as Arup went public with its own plans, BR had to make its embarassing U-turn. The Eurorail partnership, only recently formed between BR and Trafalgar House/Balfour Beatty, had to lower its sights, responding to cost increases which had taken the construction bill from £1.2 billion to £3.35 billion in a year. BR was forced to announce a change of plan. 'We regret the delay…' said a spokesman. It became clear to the astonished NIMBYs, and an equally nonplussed Eurotunnel, that the whole London end of the line – the long tunnel from Swanley to King's Cross, the Peckham junction – had been scrapped. Chunnel trains would now use existing tracks from the edge of London into Waterloo. But which tracks? BR confessed

2 One Labour Shadow Cabinet member put it at £350 million by 1995 (Michael Meacher MP).

it had no idea – but perhaps it might have 'by next spring'. The spectre of blight lifted from Warwick Gardens, but hovered over a great swathe from Bromley South to Waterloo. It was as if eleven months of 1989, with all its accompanying sound and fury, had never happened. As an MP pointed out in the House of Commons, 'there will be a link, of course, but [at the London end] it will be the same as the South Eastern & Chatham Railway a century ago'. As the *New Civil Engineer* commented, once the conundrum had finally been solved, 'it was a national disgrace that this superb new transport link [the Tunnel] had to be spliced onto an overloaded south-eastern railway network that was built on the cheap in the 19th century and not much improved since'.

The partners in the Eurorail joint venture made it clear that, while the Channel Tunnel to Swanley section was confirmed, there was no agreement between them on a 'bankable' route – one that could be funded – from Swanley into London: thus the abandonment of the 'long tunnel'. The government gave the joint venture an extra five months to work on the problem. As Mark Bostock commented a few months later, 'a strange decision, in many ways, because the problems of securing a financially attractive route either overland across heavily populated South London or underground, tunnelling through variable and inconsistent ground conditions, were daunting'.

To save money, the Eurorail consortium shortened the London tunnel to run from Hither Green and not from Swanley. This was after Sir Alexander Gibb & Partners, the engineering consultancy appointed by BR, confirmed that 'the long tunnel made the project unfundable'. Shortening the tunnel reduced the estimated cost from £3.35 billion to £2.6 billion but, with other changes (most crucially the lowering of the maximum speed on the whole line to 140 mph) increased the journey time to Paris by half an hour… right back again to three hours.

It was clear in retrospect that, given the real financial position, the Eurorail partnership was doomed from the start, a result of the government's refusal to admit that substantial sums of public money would inevitably be involved. The Parliamentary Bill was to be postponed by a year, largely because the exact route was still undecided – with up to ten variations being considered.

Despite this delay, BR and Eurorail were still linked in a joint venture. However, this unravelled fairly fast as the private side did the sums, and demanded the subsidy that the government had firmly ruled out. February 1990 saw the amended, and somewhat cheaper, proposals formally presented to government by BR/Eurorail. All the while both RailEurope (the former TALIS plan) and Arup were developing their alternative, eastern route, schemes. Bostock's interpretation of the BR/Eurorail deal was that although BR could not talk to any other party, nevertheless 'there was no reason why they cannot adopt the Arup route!' Though he added the rider that, unfortunately, 'we cannot secure the copyright': to do so they would have to have accepted Stannard's vision and mounted a major bid of their own – an unthinkable option. Nevertheless Stannard remained defiant, declaring that: 'we believe that BR always wanted the project to be publicly funded and controlled by itself. That is the only conclusion from the way that it has gone about things. It has suddenly gone over to supporting the idea of contracting-based partners and rejected the skills-based approach which we promoted.'

Arup had made valiant efforts to counter the attacks mounted by Trafalgar House in a public relations contest that was becoming distinctly unpleasant. One battleground was parliamentary lobbying (notably by Maureen Tomison), but both sides enlisted Press support. At one point in November 1989 Bostock received a tip-off that a story was about to appear in the *Financial Times* which alleged a split between Arup and Stannard. Much late-night phoning went on to calm Arup directors' nerves in advance of publication. The attacks included claims, as one Arup source puts it, 'that we were a small, unquoted, insignificant Danish company', and that as a result Arup could not possibly find the funds to compete with the £20 million Trafalgar House had said that it was prepared to spend as a show of strength. At that point Stannard came up trumps, inviting ten of his influential and well-heeled friends to a lunch where they were addressed by Bostock. They agreed to find £1 million apiece while Arup would do the same, albeit in man-hours rather than cash – a sign that, like Mrs Thatcher, 'they were not for turning'

In his announcement to Parliament in February 1990 Michael Portillo, the Minister of State for public transport, said that the government aimed to introduce a bill for a line from Swanley to King's Cross in November, emphasising that it was a 'partnership', as £1 billion of public money was being spent on improving rail links, offering three million seats from outside London to Paris and Brussels and a 'comprehensive system of freight services from every part of the country' – but he 'did not foresee any need for a public-sector subsidy' for the fast line itself.

It was the publication by Arup of its alternative, entitled: 'Proposal for a Channel Tunnel Rail Link leading to an integrated, international rail system for passengers and rail freight serving the whole of Britain' which at last set off the great row between Arup and the entire British transport and civil engineering establishment, backed by the

1990

April

- Sir Bob Reid II takes over as Chairman of BR

18 May

- Parliamentary debate on Channel Tunnel rail link

June

- Eurorail consortium dissolves as government refuses further subsidy, saying that the consortium wanted up to £2 billion

14 July

- Secretary of State Cecil Parkinson announces that BR will study routes to King's Cross via Stratford: the Arup and RailEurope (formerly TALIS) plans

August

- RailEurope consortium formed to develop RACHEL/TALIS concepts for an eastern approach
- BR commissions Arup to develop its route to allow a study into both eastern alternatives, and comparison with southern approach

Two of the many ministers in charge of the railways: Michael Portillo, who tried to avoid the battle and Roger (now Lord) Freeman, who was pitched into the heart of the row

Department of Transport and British Rail. Arup's proposal, published with a full set of maps at the end of March 1990 (shown on pages 120 and 121), went far beyond a plan for a faster journey with improved capacity. The document, produced in collaboration with Colin Stannard and Alastair Dick[3], was a veritable manifesto, bringing together the national interest, environmental concerns, commercial objectives and development along the railway. 'Every effort has been made to meet the requirements … for a joint public/private sector owning company,' noted Arup. 'Unfortunately, this has had to be undertaken without collaboration with British Rail.'

The war was essentially political. When Arup's plans became public knowledge, BR suffered from what can only be described as a nervous breakdown. Although both sides were agreed over the route between the Tunnel and Detling, at the foot of the North Downs, the two schemes embodied two totally different philosophies: the one broad and strategic, addressing social, economic and environmental concerns; the other narrow, providing a link at minimal cost, embodying what Arup called 'a reliance on precedent, and a culture of maintenance rather than innovation and technical advancement'.

Arup's ideas (fine-tuned through extensive and intensive consultation with councils, local people and business), embraced the environment, development and regeneration along the route. The Arup plan also allowed for direct connection between the Continent and the UK north of London, much of it through Stratford – impossible with BR's route. Moreover their 'easterly' approach, unlike BR's 'southerly' plans, passed through existing transport corridors as well as through derelict and landfill sites crying out for regeneration, avoided built-up areas as far as possible and people's homes almost entirely. 'In 63km the [Arup] Detling–King's Cross route will pass within 100 metres of five homes; the BR route will pass within 100 metres of 1,900 homes' noted Arup. Later, Arup pointed out with pride that 'we consider that to identify a 63km route at 225kph speeds in the south-east of England without the demolition of any homes is a major positive factor of the eastern approach'.

By this time a new chairman had taken over at British Rail. Like his predecessor he was called Robert Reid (hence the immediate adoption of the shorthand Bob Reids I and II). He was not a career railwayman, but a senior executive from the oil industry. The son of a butcher in a little town near St Andrews, at the age of nine he lost part of his right arm while cleaning a meat grinder. But he learnt to play golf with his remaining arm, went to the local university and, through a blend of charm, energy and determination rose through

3 Alastair Dick was Sir Alastair Morton's adviser on traffic forecasts for Eurotunnel and the CTRL and was deeply involved with Arup in preparing its bid. Later, when working for the National Express Group, he became a director of LCR.

the ranks at Shell, to end his career as head of Shell's UK operations – a post just below main-board level. On his arrival at BR in April 1990 he took personal charge of the CTRL project, shocking everyone by arranging fortnightly meetings to report progress – and, to make matters worse, starting them at 7.30 in the morning. He seemed more open-minded than his predecessor and was at least prepared to meet delegations both from Arup people and RailEurope.

By May 1990 both Trafalgar House and the government were finally happy to abandon their Eurorail partnership. The catalyst for the decision was Eurorail's request for a government subsidy of up to £2 billion: a capital grant of £500 million, a low-interest loan of £1 billion and investment of £400 million by British Rail for terminal developments for the commuter route – an essential element in the scheme to qualify the project for public-sector support. It was also said that Trafalgar House lobbied the government to try and get tax advantages for the project. As the official history puts it, the Treasury 'agreed that the level of risk transfer was insufficient to justify the "overt and covert subsidies" which the private sector required to earn a return (12.5 per cent) on their small equity investment' of the total (14 per cent).

But at the same time Cecil Parkinson could dismiss as overly ambitious the plans proposed by Stannard, standing by the official line that the Arup scheme would be 'hugely expensive' because it was a totally different concept. Whitehall calculated that to get the full benefit of the scheme – including the four tracks and upgrading lines beyond London – would cost between £10 and £15 billion. The Eurorail consortium was dissolved, with the government paying the partners about £5 million to compensate them for the studies they had made. Nevertheless ministers allowed BR to safeguard the – by now accepted – route from Folkestone to the North Downs at Detling.

The willingness of Trafalgar House to abandon the scheme had a lot to do with the intensifying slump now under way in the property and construction sector. This also was to lead to the collapse of Rosehaugh, the prime mover of the plan to regenerate the railway lands at King's Cross. At the time Arup depended on British work for four-fifths of its income, so it too was badly affected, with around a thousand employees leaving during the slump – a near-disaster intensified because the government had just ripped up the fee scales applied to public-sector projects. The result was a significant reduction in profitability for that year.

But by 1990, public interest in the rail link project was not confined to pressure-groups and furious home-owners. Early that year Newham Council set up an all-party

The opponents: Sir Bob Reid II, the chairman of BR, arguing for the southern route and Stephen Timms, in the forefront of the PIMBYs fighting for the line to go through Stratford

Channel Tunnel group of ten boroughs: it opposed the King's Cross Bill and supported alternatives including Stratford, although it adopted the route set by its consultants, Malcolm Buchanan Associates, which followed BR's to South London but terminated at Stratford rather than King's Cross. By contrast Stephen Timms of Newham Council had always made it clear that it did not really matter if Stratford were not to be the terminus as long as there was provision for an international station on the site. Newham also brought up that perpetual chestnut by asking for better environmental mitigation to reduce noise from freight.

May witnessed the only full parliamentary debate on the scheme. It was held on the morning of Friday 18th – a day and time when most MPs, especally those from outside London and the Home Counties, had left for their constituencies for the weekend. Moreover it was held only because Gerald Bowden was lucky enough to be drawn first in the ballot for Private Members' Bills. The Tory MP for Dulwich, urged not only by his much-afflicted constituents but also by the ubiquitous Maureen Tomison, had no difficulty deciding which subject to bring forward. A number of speakers made clear their support for Arup's proposal, involving as it did an easterly approach, a station at Stratford and provision for both freight and commuters. As Bowden put it with some delicacy: 'the Stratford alternative would offer similar opportunities [and] would go through land that does not enjoy the benefit of the prosperity that is found elsewhere'. The arguments for the easterly route were further boosted by Universal Studios' desire to put a theme park, similar to the one they had built in Hollywood, on the easterly route just north of the Thames on the Rainham Marshes.

Bowden's proposition, developed in conjunction with Arup, was simplicity itself: that 'this House urges British Rail to give full and thorough consideration to proposals for a Channel Tunnel Rail Link based on a junction at Stratford, and to enter into professional discussions with those proposing the Stratford alternative before presenting their Private Bill to Parliament for a decision'. The debate showed the frustration felt – especially, but not exclusively, by MPs with constituencies directly affected by BR's proposals – over the refusal of the government to take responsibility, by the lack of any 'joined-up thinking' (or indeed the acceptance of any notion of planning). The debate also exposed the curious mix of narrow reality and larger scale pie-in-the-sky which characterised the whole story. 'Many of us', pointed out Bowden, 'came to the issue because of the need to protect our constituencies from the threat – but the more that we looked at the proposals the more we realised their inadequacy.'

While there were the usual bleats from far-flung consituencies about the 'inadequate links with Wales', it was Joan Ruddock, the Labour MP for Lewisham in South-East London, who put the case most cogently: 'It is extraordinary', she said, 'that we should be debating what is arguably the most significant engineering project of our time, with potentially the most profound impact on our nation's economy, on a Private Member's motion in a half-empty House.

'Why has that happened? It is because the Government have adopted an entirely cavalier approach. They have chosen to ignore the nation's economic needs, and the railway revolution across the Channel. They have chosen to stand aloof while alarm and despondency have spread through public and private institutions alike.'

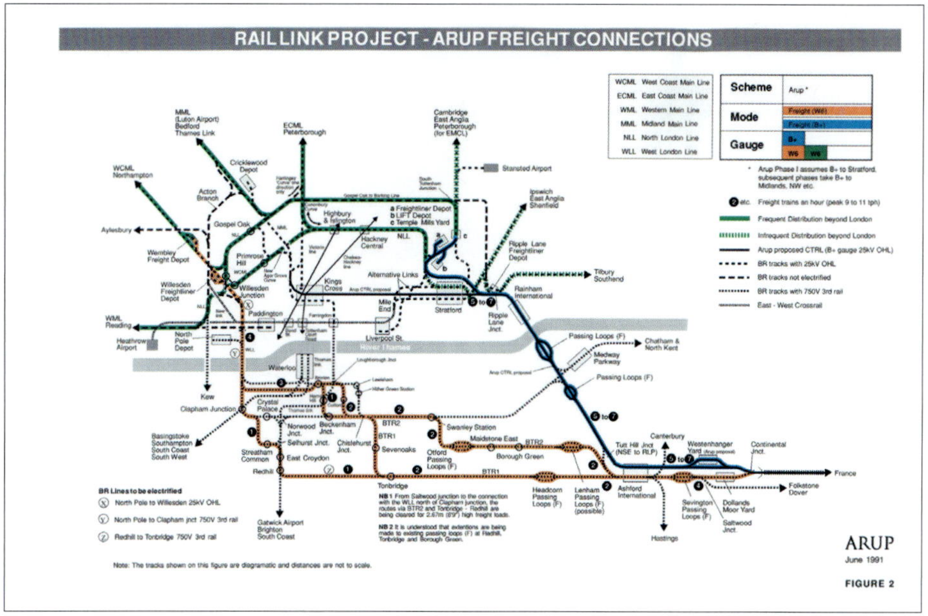

Arup put great stress on freight links between their proposed new line and the rest of the UK rail network

The refusal of the government to take the debate seriously was emphasised by the way its case was presented by Roger Freeman, the newly-appointed junior Minister for Public Transport. He agreed with Tony Banks, the Labour member for Newham North-West, and thus a fully-paid-up member of the PIMBY brigade, who had 'described the debate as being, in effect, a five-hour tutorial for a new Minister – and he is right.'

The pressure on the government from Labour was not confined to back-benchers, for it was spearheaded by John Prescott, then the Opposition spokesperson for transport. On 15 June the *Daily Telegraph* regretted that 'it is dismaying to notice that Mr John Prescott … has sounded considerably more convincing than his government counterpart in his analysis of the transport issue'. The Labour party had already pinned its colours to the mast in declaring that 'we want a high-speed, dedicated railway network, together with good roads to link the regions to the rest of Europe'. As Prescott put it in a policy document entitled Moving Britain into Europe: 'the opening of the Channel Tunnel … offers Britain a unique opportunity to transport more goods and people by rail', envisaging a 'private–public sector partnership in the

As Shadow Transport Minister in 1990, Labour's John Prescott was virtually the only senior politician to understand Britain's transport needs

Facing page: by December 1990 Arup had refined their March 1990 route (see page 121) to allow a direct comparison with the other eastern route and BR's southern alignment. The main changes were a reduction from four tracks to two, fewer intermediate stations, removal of links to other rail lines and the removal of the connection to Crossrail at Stratford. This was to lead to the present situation where the Stratford International station is sited at a distance from the existing BR station, not alongside it as in Arup's original proposal.

high-speed link' based on an analysis that 'takes full account of economic, social and environmental benefits'. Prescott had already written to the then Secretary of State for Transport, Paul Channon, in February 1989 to express the (prescient) fear that 'without public investment in the project, British Rail will take the "least-cost approach" in choosing the route, causing major environmental problems'.

In theory the collapse of the Trafalgar House partnership had left the field open to Arup, for Cecil Parkinson was seemingly more sympathetic to the firm than his predecessor. Indeed in January 1990 he had declared that 'I know a number of people who like the alternative Ove Arup Partnership proposal' (though he was not exactly active on their behalf, falling asleep during one major meeting). But then the Eurorail partners knew, as the *Independent on Sunday* said, 'that were they to fail, Mr Parkinson would consider himself free to send for Ove Arup'. Cecil Parkinson himself declared that the collapse of the Trafalgar House bid left five options: to kill the project; to choose the route but do no more; to commit to the line/obtain statutory powers; to commit to the line and consult on the routes; and to commit to the line and its construction. The Treasury would have liked to abandon the scheme, as would the Policy Unit in Number 10 Downing Street. Nevetheless the project was kept alive, largely because of fear over the reaction of the French – and of the shareholders in Eurotunnel.

The result was a compromise: the possibility of a fast link was to be 'kept in play'; the route from Folkestone to the North Downs was safeguarded but the route for the final stretch, including the London terminus, was left open for 'further study'. This was one of the first occasions on which what might be called the 'TGV solution' was even considered. This would have involved building a new fast line to the North Downs – a route which subsequently emerged as CTRL1 – and then copying the French by running the final stretch on existing tracks. In theory this was a perfectly viable solution; indeed this was what was used from 2003 to 2007. It bypassed the most crowded stretches of the route – the lines east of Swanley where every international train would of necessity displace a domestic one – and provided far more reliable and speedier services from London to Paris.

Nevertheless, the use of existing track into the capital was impractical in the long term, because the London end of the route was hopelessly and increasingly crowded. While speed and thus journey times were the focus of public attention throughout the

ARUP'S AMENDED EASTERN ROUTE, DECEMBER 1990

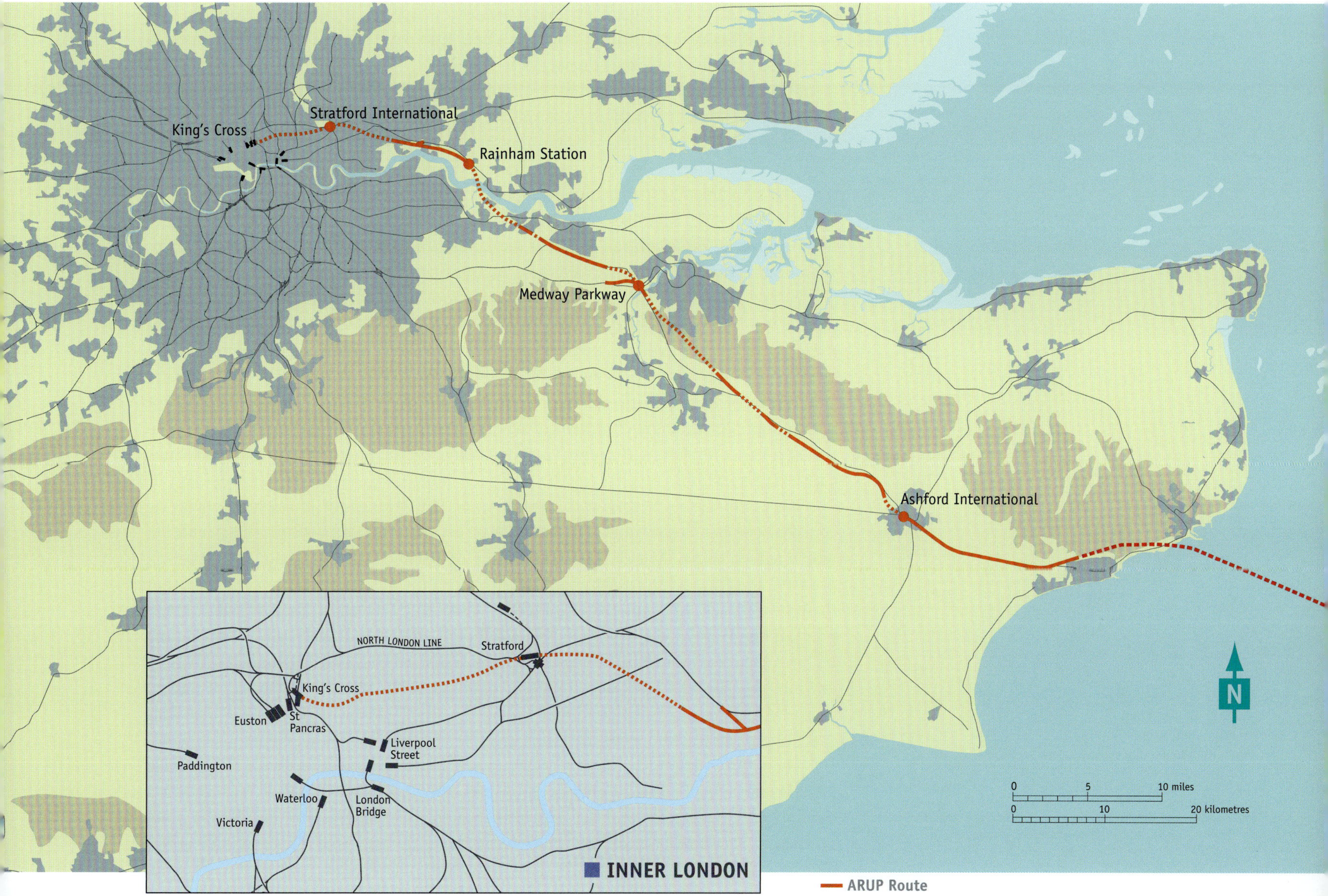

CTRL saga, the railwaymen knew that it was extra capacity, especially in London, that was the real issue. Paris did not have the same problem: thus the quizzical attitude to the British travails sometimes displayed by SNCF.

In the meantime, studies were continuing from BR's raft of consultants. As David Shaw, the MP for Dover had put it in the May debate 'my constituents and I are fed up with continuing delay during which numerous rumours of alternative routes have been bandied about. There is hardly a square kilometre of my constituency that has not been the subject of splendidly disruptive proposals. It seems that every civil engineer in the country has made a bid not only for a railway line but to gain the reputation of an up-and-coming expert on the prospect for a grand renaissance of our railways. Locally, we resent being the guinea pigs for these no doubt stimulating exercises'.

By this point Parkinson was clearly playing for time. On 14 July he told Parliament that he was 'not yet satisfied … that they [BR] have found the best solution, and I am therefore asking British Rail to complete its studies with the aim of maximising the benefits to international passengers and commuters alike.' The alternative routes were 'unlikely to be better financially than the Eurorail proposal or to offer a better deal for commuters. But the new chairman of British Rail is determined to satisfy himself on that and has commissioned a report by consultants on the proposals for routes to King's Cross via Stratford'.

The comparative exercise was carried out by WS Atkins, one of the few enginering consultancies not already engaged by BR.[4] Arup became involved with meetings with BR, which agreed to pay Arup £50,000 to do the necessary work. To make a comparison possible, the Arup 'Eastern Approach' was reduced for this study to a two-track, rather than a four-track, line, for passengers only. Unfortunately, as Richard Foster of Arup pointed out, 'Atkins was being asked to compare apples and pears' since, to simplify matters, the route was to be decided purely on transport criteria and would not include any intermediate stations to accommodate other uses. The scales were heavily weighted against Arup, since Howarth had retained all the other leading engineering consultants – although, as he acknowledged: 'Arup had forced government to have another look'.

The process did at least finally get Arup into a series of meetings with British Rail's key people, where signs of change could be detected. Mark Bostock reported in a memo to his colleagues that 'Gil Howarth hinted that the [eastern route] was more politically acceptable than any southern approach', and that BR's environmental manager 'stated quite categorically that the [eastern route] was more acceptable from

4 By that time virtually every reputable engineering consultant was involved, so much so that when Terry Hill asked for an independent review Bob Reid II said that 'he knew a couple of Nigerian engineers who could do the job'. This was not entirely a joke since he had been head of Shell's operations in Nigeria, (where, by a weird coincidence, Bostock's first wife had been his secretary).

5 23 July 1990.

an environmental viewpoint'.[5]

In fact, financially the two routes were competitive, when put on the same basis, with two tracks and no intermediate stations. 'The cost of the routes', said Howarth, 'was much the same; not more than ten per cent between them'. Arup's route had 24 miles (38km) in tunnel as against 16 (25km) for BR's scheme – but only two homes acquired as against 127 for BR, and none demolished as against 24. BR, however, liked Atkins' work, pointing out that the consultants had 'carried out its work in a sound and professional manner' so the British Railways Board could now 'make its recommendation to government with confidence that the comparison has been fair and that the requirements of our methodology have been met'.

By November Bob Reid II had shown that he understood the wider picture – and his increased room for manoeuvre as the pattern shifted at Westminster. He was asking for the scrapping of the rules that prevented the environmental and social benefits from being taken into account when deciding on railway planning and funding. The political tide was clearly turning: late November saw the sudden resignation of Mrs Thatcher and her replacement by the more pragmatic John Major. The BR report comparing the two eastern approaches with theirs was delivered in December, just in time to form part of the workload of the new Secretary of State in the Major government. Nevertheless by that time it was also clear that Arup was going to have to part with Stannard – and indeed with Maureen Tomison. 'We had ferocious internal discussions about her', says Bostock; 'was she going to lead us into areas where we would be uncomfortable? Would she affect Arup's "virginity", its immaculate professional reputation?' For their part both she and Stannard – who had become a director of her public affairs company – had come to believe that Arup were 'patsies'.

As Malcolm Noyce sees it, 'the Arup culture made it inconceivable that Colin Stannard could succeed' in his attempt to transform the firm into an orthodox project engineer, with all the risks that this implied. As a result he left during 1990. 'Stannard was hugely upset when we and he parted company', says Bostock. 'He had put a lot of his emotional energy into Kent Rail. He has to be given credit for taking us into the "adult" world of prime agency work and providing us with a lot of intellectual leadership in the early days of the Arup promotion'. Indeed Bostock describes Stannard's November 1988 report to Arup, in which he outlined his 'Private Project Promoter' concept, as 'seminal. It had a huge impact on our thinking'[6].

Couch was directly employed by Arup, but there was no longer any role for him.

IF IT WASN'T FOR THE HOUSES IN BETWEEN*

Effects of the competing routes on homes

Houses	BR's final southern alignment	Arup's eastern route
Demolished	24	0
Acquired	127	2
Within a 100m corridor	1,900	5
Within a 200m corridor	5,900	115

Source: Malcolm Rifkind MP, Secretary of State for Transport, Hansard 14 October 1991

* *'Wiv a ladder and some glasses/You could see to Hackney marshes/If it wasn't for the houses in between' – music hall song by Gus Elen, 1891*

6 It was in many ways a precursor to the government's policy on Public–Private Partnerships introduced in the mid-1990s.

So he left too – and went straight off to WS Atkins, a major rival of Arup's. At much the same time Maureen Tomison was told that her services would no longer be required, a decision that Bostock found 'personally very painful'. But in her different way she had gone too far for Arup to be able to follow her – her fees, which were a large part of the £1.5 million spent internally in preparing the bid, were also clearly not affordable in a year dominated by the unprecedented sacking of hundreds of Arup employees.

Not surprisingly both men were disgusted. 'Fear dominated', says Stannard. 'Not even Michael Lewis understood what I was about'. For Stannard the worst outcome was that Arup had handed over its material to the government in return for a small stake in any future venture. In a note to the Board before he left, Couch warned that 'if we fail it will be a long time before the City or government takes us seriously again, rather than as excellent engineers for other people's ideas and entrepreneurship'.

But the events of the next year were to prove him wrong.

1 2 3 4 5 6 7 8 9 10 **11** 12

DECISION TIME!

I didn't agree with what you did, but I respect the way you did it

Michael Portillo to **Mark Bostock**, 9 October 1991

■ Less than a year after the coup which removed Mrs Thatcher, the Gordian Knot was severed. John Major's arrival at 10 Downing Street in November 1990 led to the return of Michael Heseltine to the Department of the Environment (DoE), which he had run for four years following Mrs Thatcher's victory in the 1979 election. Heseltine was never an orthodox politician – indeed is the only senior politician in modern British history to have made a seriously large fortune before he entered the House of Commons. Today the estimated value of Haymarket, the magazine empire owned by his family, is £200 million, putting him in the top 300 of the *Sunday Times*' Rich List. Indeed throughout his political career he had behaved more like a – sometime temperamental, aways decisive, often visionary – tycoon than a politician.

Superficially his managerial style, based on groups sitting around in armchairs, resembled that later adopted by Tony Blair; but Heseltine's decisions, made largely by himself, were usually better thought through. 'Everyone who worked with Heseltine', says one close observer, realised that he 'was a heavyweight who took his own decisions'. The reaction of his civil servants was revealed in a light-hearted summary following his departure from the DoE in 1983, how he 'once again inspired his civil servants to follow him towards the sunlit uplands, which however for some were obscured by the smoke and heat of battle'.

In November 1990 Heseltine had wanted to go to the Department of Trade and Industry (to which he did move after the 1992 election), but John Major insisted he take over at Environment, for a very simple reason. The biggest albatross hanging over the new administration was the wildly unpopular and unworkable local tax, the Community Charge, universally known as the Poll Tax. Heseltine, who had been out of office since he had stormed out of a Cabinet meeting in 1986, was the only senior Conservative not associated with the tax. By the end of April the outline of an escape route – what was to become the Council Tax – was in place, and he could turn his attention to other matters.

Heseltine was never short of visionary ideas, which had most obviously been shown in his first spell at the DoE. These had been inspired by helicopter flights when, as a junior minister with a planning brief in the Heath administration, he flew to Maplin Sands, an island off the Essex coast being considered as the site for a third London airport. On that flight he could clearly see the great stretches of wasteland around the redundant docks on both banks of the Thames east of the City of London. His first idea was for a Development Corporation for the south bank of the Thames; this would balance the over-developed M4 corridor to the west of London with a similar stretch to the east. For until then, says Mike Ash, a dedicated DoE planner who was involved in the South-East planning office after August 1990, the East End 'was London's back-yard; we'd turned our backs on the east'.

Michael Heseltine: back at the DoE with a dream to fulfill

In the early 1980s Heseltine realised the first part of his dream by the regeneration of Docklands, both north and south banks, through an independent Corporation. Everyone was against the idea – including his officials, who saw themselves as custodians of the local authorities that would be overridden by Heseltine's plans. But he pushed on with the foundation of the London Docklands Development Corporation, including a pioneer tax-exempt Enterprise Zone in the Isle of Dogs. He had a vision of 'public investment leading to huge private investment' for, unlike Mrs Thatcher and her disciples, he was always aware of the need for public money as a pump-primer for major projects – indeed had warned, unavailingly, that it would be needed for the construction of the Channel Tunnel. Docklands was a resounding if controversial success, epicentre of all the symbols of the 1980s – property speculation, brash new homes and office towers, bankers in Porsches. And by any measure it was a triumph: nearly £8 billion of private money was invested in the years 1981-88, and the population of the LDDC zone doubled in the seventeen years of the corporation's life.

So it was quite natural that on Heseltine's return to the DoE he revisited the next step in his dream: the regeneration of the whole 'Thames Gateway' from Tower Bridge to the North Sea. In his more ambitious moments, this staunch pro-European also thought of it as a gateway to the Continent. His dream was indeed grandiose, for the Gateway, at 215,000 acres (87,000 hectares) with a population of 1.75 million, was far bigger and more varied than the relatively compact area covered by the Docklands Corporation. As one DoE document put it the Gateway divides into two: 'London's back-yard'– with all that description implies in terms of industrial dereliction – and beyond, to the east, 'historic towns and villages', green belt and sites of scientific interest. As Heseltine said in early 1991 'the East End Corridor down the Thames Estuary from Docklands to the sea … forms an under-used asset which needs to be developed to its full potential'.

By then the role of transport improvements in regeneration – in the case of Docklands the DLR, the City Airport, the extension of the Jubilee Line, the Limehouse Link and other roads, plus the new Dartford Bridge over the Thames – had already been accepted. Heseltine was keen to allow the rail link to play a similar role in the ambitious

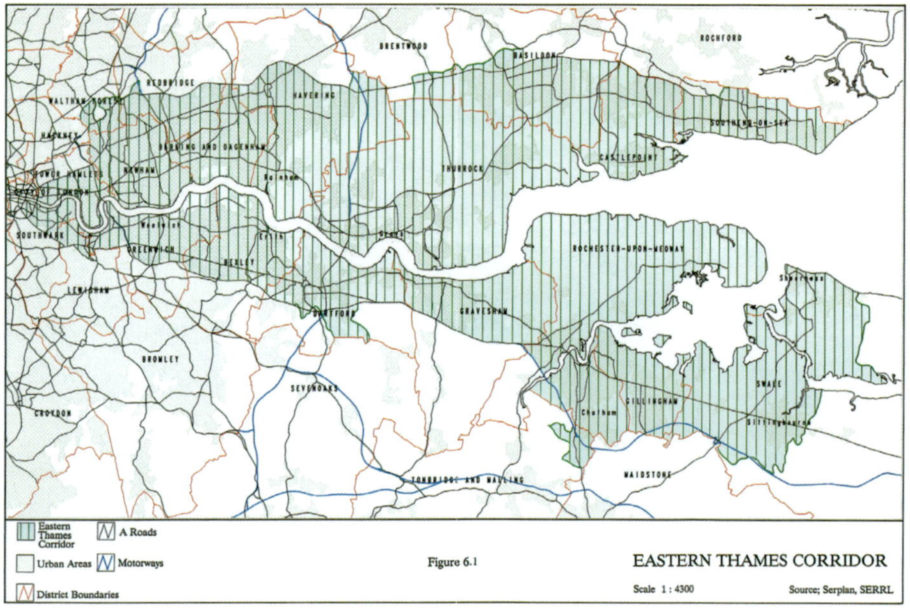

From London to the North Sea: the Thames Gateway, as it became known, from a report published in 1991

regeneration of the whole Thames Corridor: not just through Stratford, but also in impoverished North Kent through appropriate stations.

To achieve his object, which was basically to ensure that broader, above all enviromental, consderations would be taken into account when deciding on the route of the CTRL, Heseltine did not surround himself with consultants. He only needed a single, recognised external adviser. With the backing of Sir Terry Heiser, the Permanent Secretary at the DoE, Paul Mcquail, one of his senior officials, decided to recruit a 'heavyweight academic' and naturally approached Professor Peter (now Sir Peter) Hall, one of Britain's leading experts in urban planning and regeneration.

Hall duly took the summer of 1991 off from his academic job[1]. His attitude was simple: 'I regarded this as a non-political job and tried to identify with the civil servants, not to be isolated in a ministerial ivory tower.' His political antennae – unusual in an academic – ensured that he was able to stay as a Special Advisor in the Department for three years. He soon grasped that 'the East Thames Corridor was one of those rare political decisions that had everybody salivating … Labour boroughs were offered development that they thought they'd been cheated of'.

Hall had long been an advocate of an eastward surge, and had already spelled out a vision involving Stratford, with its ever-improving transport links, as the focal point for such development. Indeed to him, one of the most important elements in the final decision was the choice of stations at Stratford and on the Kent side of the Thames – a site offering transport links and enormous development possibilities thanks to the worked-out chalk pits in the area. As he puts it: 'by the summer of 1991 it was clear that cost-benefit analysis was not enough'. The problem was that the benefits were indefinable: 'they're simply as long as a piece of string'.

But Hall was not alone. Even before his arrival SERPLAN[2] had produced a formal strategy document to try and tilt development away from the M4 corridor. Indeed one

1 As the Director of the Institute of Urban and Regional Development at the University of California at Berkeley.

2 South-East Regional Planning Council: it had long been worried that the main beneficiaries of the economic growth spurred by the Chunnel would be the French.

of the first indications of Heseltine's interest came at a planning meeting regarding the site of a former mental hospital at Darenth. At the end of the meeting he asked 'what should we do about East Thames?' A few months after he had taken over his department he had been 'making noises' in an attempt to be involved in the decision-making process over the fast rail link, trying to introduce the wider perspective which had previously been totally lacking.

As one civil servant put it, 'no single individual played the pivotal role. Ministers were influenced by Arup and others lobbying from outside' – like the local authorities in East London, Essex, and indeed North Kent – as well as 'Peter Hall, Tom Burke [another adviser] and officials working within Government … The fact is that this was one of those occasions where a number of interests came together and a solution presented itself which met a variety of objectives (international connectivity together with competitiveness, domestic rail improvement, economic and housing growth and regeneration in the South-East, environmental protection and improvement, etc)'.

Right through March and April 1991, Arup was in intense and detailed discussions with BR about every aspect of the CTRL as part of the Atkins comparative route study. By that time BR – like RailEurope which was still, seemingly, in contention – was taking freight very seriously, discussing how to thread the trains either through its existing tracks – round London and on the old Boat Train route – or trying to alternate the relatively slow freight trains with the high-speed TGVs. BR had become far more optimistic about freight, requiring paths for 10–20 trains a day. On the other hand peak-time passenger-train numbers were being reduced from nine to eight an hour with three going into Waterloo, and a minimum total of four an hour off-peak.

John Palmer, by now managing director of the Channel Tunnel team at BR, appears to have been convinced by the 'robustness of the Eastern approach' – though not necessarily of its superiority. For his part Bostock was, naturally, insisting on the scope for 'development gain to offset capital costs', and trying to persuade Palmer that in terms of both construction costs and revenues there was not much difference between the eastern and southerly routes – a matter of opinion or at least of rather vague estimates of the costs of stations.

British Rail was, however, obstinately refusing to give way – largely because it was terrified of any split in a business which it was determined should stay intact through the privatisation process. Moreover it was still looking at the new route purely in transport terms even though Bob Reid II was in a hurry (wanting work to start before

1990

November

- Margaret Thatcher resigns as Prime Minister, and is replaced by John Major
- Michael Heseltine is Secretary of State at the Department of the Environment (DoE)
- Malcolm Rifkind is Secretary of State for Transport (DoT)

Malcolm Rifkind, Secretary of State for Transport in John Major's new government (**left**), had to contend with opposition to investment in the CTRL from the Treasury, led by the Chancellor of the Exchequer, Norman Lamont

1995, the end of his five-year term as chairman). He was, however, still urging that the criteria for railway investment should be changed to include 'the wider economic, environmental, social and safety benefits'.

Nevertheless, as one minister puts it, 'they had got the whole thing out of proportion' and remained firmly attached to the southern route as offering the best financial return – albeit only 4.2 per cent. Bostock was also amazed to discover that BR considered that the environmental impact of the two schemes would be similar, even though thousands of homes would be affected by building new lines by the side of old ones in South London (see page 137).This decision was confirmed at a special BR board meeting held on 2 May. Their consultants, Pieda, found only £100 million of benefits for the eastern route. And of course Reid shared BR's bitter opposition to Arup, emphasising support from the north of England for King's Cross, ignoring the fact that Arup – whose route was at least adjudged the best of the easterly routes – also supported it.[3]

By then Michael Heseltine had heard on the Whitehall grapevine of the way that consideration of the project had been confined purely to the DoT – the total lack of any semblance of 'joined-up government' emphasised by the fact that he, the Environment Secretary, had never been officially consulted about this enormous project. As he relates in his autobiography,[4] he then 'asked to be invited to the meeting at the Department of Transport at which these plans were unfolded'. But the rail link was still low on the Whitehall list of priorities: when Malcolm Rifkind, who had become the Secretary of State for Transport in November 1990 met John Major in early May '91, the official history tells us 'privatisation was the main item of business, but the rail link was also discussed'.

As a result an inter-ministerial 'steering group' was established: this immediately asked BR for further information to add to the mountain of paper that it had already presented to the department. The battle-lines were clear. Heseltine was obviously in favour of the easterly route for environmental and regeneration reasons; Norman Lamont, the Chancellor, was against the whole project, while acknowledging that the eight per cent profit requirement was 'not absolute'. The Treasury had started to interest itself in BR, its attention drawn by the considerable sums it was already spending on the project. It was acknowledged that the previous year Thatcher and Parkinson – both of whom had conveniently disappeared from the scene – had 'failed to bite the bullet' and rule the CTRL out. The gap between political and economic reality was brutally exposed – and the decision was postponed until after the summer break.

3 This attitude was clearly shared by Dr Gourvish, who barely mentions Arup in his official history – the name is not even in the index! Gourvish was clearly reflecting Whitehall's continuing attempts to eliminate Arup from the story.

4 *Life in the Jungle* (Hodder & Stoughton 2000).

Bostock got wind in late May of a decision within government to give Arup the chance to present its route to ministers. Bostock's Treasury contact revealed that both the Department of Transport and the Treasury were 'pissed off' with BR: the Treasury because the costs did not seem to them to have been properly calculated. The British Railways Board's Comparison of Routes report to government of 2 May 'lacked quality', the Treasury man felt. 'He is far from convinced by the arguments which have been put forward', summarised Bostock.

The key meeting – unmentioned in the official history – was on 19 June. Bostock, Terry Hill and Michael Lewis made a presentation to the two secretaries of state, Rifkind at Transport and Heseltine at Environment, and three junior ministers – Michael Portillo, Roger Freeman, the minister for public transport, and Sir George Young. Also there were Peter Hall, Povl Ahm, Arup's chairman, and Bob Reid II. According to Mark Bostock this meeting 'appears to be the turning-point in favour of our easterly route … it was the first time ministers had understood our proposition'.

Terry Hill and Mark Bostock present Arup's final plan to Whitehall – including Michael Heseltine and Malcolm Rifkind – at the crucial meeting in June 1991

In the words of one civil servant quoted by Michael Crick,[5] 'Heseltine just ran the whole meeting and ran roughshod over Rifkind; and he had this mania' – a pure Sir-Humphrey attitude towards any show of enthusiasm by a minister – 'over the East Thames Corridor and regeneration. Rifkind just let him run it'.

But the key intervention came during the discussion of the respective costs of the BR and Arup proposals. Michael Lewis of Arup brought up the whole question of risk analysis. He naturally raised the £500 million benefits to be expected from regeneration, but focused mainly on the problem of deep-level tunnelling on the BR route through South London – difficulties which had stopped many underground lines continuing south of the Thames. He argued that to apply plausible risk contingencies to the figures for both routes showed Arup's route to be, in fact, better value, a view fully supported by Povl Ahm from the floor. Bob Reid II was 'incandescent', Bostock recalls, 'but Heseltine told him, "shut up – I want to hear this".'

5 Michael Crick, *Michael Heseltine* (Hamish Hamilton, 1997).

Professor Peter Hall, the eminent planner, who was Special Advisor to Heseltine at the Department of the Environment

Facing page: the Promised Land – the Thames Gateway stretches eastwards from Canary Wharf all the way to the sea

At the meeting, according to Bostock, Heseltine took a deep interest. 'He got more out of us', says Terry Hill – whereas Rifkind had asked routine, prepared questions, like a barrister simply doing his duty. Indeed throughout the summer Rifkind's opposition to Arup was never all that ferocious. For a start he was only too aware of Heseltine's power and the effect of any rift on his future career; and, in a theme which was present in the background in the whole story, his main concern was to ensure that British Rail would be privatised as an integrated operation, not fragmented with the track separated from the rail services, as the Treasury wanted.[6]

Two days after the June meeting Freeman pointed out in a radio broadcast that a further year would be needed 'to study the environmental impact of the route into central London … and then a period, it could be two or three years, of obtaining planning permission for the line'. This put back a serious start on construction to 1995, which exacerbated the division between Heseltine and Rifkind.

Throughout the summer the battle continued over the line, which had been renamed New Kent Main Line, dissassociating it from the Tunnel and presumably making it possible to attract public funding. According to one insider, 'there was still pressure from the Treasury asking "do we need it at all? And if so what's the cheapest option?"' Moreover the Treasury was alleging an element of double-counting in the assessment of the benefits – to which Peter Hall replied simply: 'Jobs'.[7] The battle was by no means over. 'The decision was not resolved when I returned to Berkeley at the end of August', says Hall.

Indeed the decision was only reached, at long last, in September. Jonathan Hill, Major's Political Secretary, had 'taken soundings' and discovered that Rifkind 'would not die in the last ditch' over BR's proposals, leading Heseltine to declare that he 'would not allow the Treasury to drive a wedge between us on this issue'. Chancellor of the Exchequer Norman Lamont was still, however, expressing a preference for the cheapest alternative, Newham's southerly route to Stratford – although ideally he would have preferred 'to kill the scheme now'. Hill produced a compromise: that the easterly route would be safeguarded, but finance left to the private sector.

By now the pressure was building up for the government to say something at the Conservative party conference in early October, and on 27 September John Major convened a 'brass tacks' meeting with Rifkind and Heseltine. Michael Hesletine recalls 'I said, "look, this is an incredible regeneration opportunity and we've got to try to make

6 Sadly for Britain's rail system his successor John McGregor took the opposite view, and remains one of the handful of people who still defends the way BR was privatised.

7 Unemployment, high and climbing, was a government priority at the time.

HSBC

it work." John Major said "I think Michael's right".' Heseltine remembers that he was always confident of the outcome: 'I relied on the PM's overview … I'd fought the machine and other colleagues before'.[8]

In the words of one senior civil servant, 'Michael Heseltine went into the meeting a minority of one, but got the Thames Corridor'. At the time the civil servants at the DoE were growing increasingly pessimistic over the outcome, but Peter Hall provided crucial backing. In fact John Major, a new, insecure prime minister, 'was looking to find a grand, ambitious gesture'. He was also fully aware, as one minister put it, that at the time 'Michael could do no wrong, if only because he could have made life so difficult for John' if he showed any sign of disloyalty. The unique combination worked. 'We didn't think we'd get it until the cabinet meeting', says one Arup insider – although in reality the decision had been made, as Heseltine told me, at the earlier meeting between Major, Heseltine and Rifkind; as so often, the cabinet merely rubber-stamped the proposal.

Even after the supposedly decisive meeting, the exact phrasing of the announcement had to be a delicate balance: as positive as Heseltine wanted, but without any financial commitment to which Lamont would never have agreed. This meant that Rifkind only reached some sort of truce with Norman Lamont the day before his announcement – in itself inevitable, but nevertheless Rifkind had to frame his statement exceedingly carefully to avoid any definite financial commitment to the scheme by the government.

According to Sarah (now Lady) Hogg and Jonathan Hill,[9] the battle between the two was 'the longest-running conference battle of 1991'. Such fights were 'a traditional horror of conference week, because ministers want to brighten up their speeches with little news-breaking nuggets that have neither been cleared with colleagues nor underwritten by the Treasury' – none more so than the CTRL. As a result 'Jonathan had flogged backwards and forwards most of Wednesday, trying to get agreement on the words Malcolm Rifkind could use. Eventually, at 2 a.m. on Thursday 9 October, he and Sarah clinched a deal between Lamont and Rifkind; the Prime Minister's precious sleep was saved'.

The previous evening Rifkind had summoned the top brass of BR – which had been kept totally in the dark – to Blackpool, and told them of the planned announcement 'in the basement of a seedy hotel', in the words of one embittered participant. 'We took the decision like a kick in the balls', he says, the pain exacerbated by the fact that BR believed that 'Arup had not behaved professionally but politically . . . we had no confidence in

8 When recounting this meeting, Heseltine recalled a similar one at which he persuaded colleagues of the need to create the LDDC to develop Docklands. 'Geoffrey Howe [Chancellor of the Exchequer] told me it could not happen because it involved spending money. Keith Joseph [Secretary of State for Industry] said it was doctrinally unacceptable as it involved state intervention. I called a meeting with Margaret Thatcher, Geoffrey and Keith and persuaded them to go with the LDDC.'

9 In *Too Close to Call* (Little Brown, 1995). At the time she was head of the Number 10 Policy Unit; he was John Major's Political Secretary.

Arup's work which presented enormous difficulties and, frankly, Lamont would have objected to any other route just as vociferously'. This did not stop Rifkind, whose carefully phrased statement at the Conference on Thursday simply said that the route would be 'on the lines put forward by Ove Arup … BR were quite properly looking at it from a transport point of view; but we have had to look at the wider implications'. He had decided, he said, that the route must 'not only satisfy our transport objectives, but greatly minimise the impact of the line on the environment and on residential property. It also offers substantial development along the East Thames corridor … Government has also taken into account the long-term requirements for rail freight that might use the Channel Tunnel'. Rifkind went into more detail in Parliament on the following Monday (as the next chapter relates), but it was his Conference speech which made waves.

Thanks to Maureen Tomison's contacts with London MPs – and her continuing belief in the Arup plan – Bostock had become aware of the likely contents of the announcement the previous evening: knowledge backed by the fact that Rifkind's office had tried to get hold of Povl Ahm, the then chairman of Arup, to tell him. The announcement was rapturously received – above all by the many MPs of constituencies blighted by BR's plans. As one cynic put it 'the conference was not interested in urban regeneration – but *was* interested in the problems posed by the BR route to the many marginal seats in Kent and South-East London that it would have affected'. 'Michael Heseltine's political instincts helped', said one Tory – though Heseltine himself says he took no heed of back-bench *angst*. 'This was all about a vision – for the East End. I didn't do it just to save Dulwich'. But the announcement came as a shock to almost everyone.

British Rail was naturally stunned. So confident was it that its own plan was assured, that it had already printed the voluminous documents to send to property owners along the route: the mounds of paper were sitting in a warehouse ready for despatch. At a bitter press conference after the statement Bob Reid II said 'a golden opportunity has been missed here … this decision has been taken for political not transport reasons.' He claimed that all the government wanted was to avoid six Tory marginals in South-East London and that the whole saga was a 'pantomime … the route chosen will take commuters where they didn't want to go and add up to twenty minutes to their overall journeys to work compared with the southerly route … its net financial effect will be at least £750 million worse and international passengers will take longer to get to Central London.' When asked whether he was going to resign in

1991

2 May

- BR Board rejects easterly routes in favour of southern approach

May

- Inter-departmental steering group set up in Whitehall to monitor Rail Link plans

Summer

- Professor Peter Hall appointed advisor to the DoE

19 June

- Arup makes presentation to Heseltine and Rifkind

27 September

- Prime Minister John Major convenes meeting with Rifkind and Heseltine to thrash out Rail Link decision

9 October

- Malcolm Rifkind announces to the Conservative Party Conference that the route will be 'on the lines put forward by Ove Arup'

14 October

- Malcolm Rifkind announces the decision in the House of Commons

protest he said bitterly 'Oh no. For heaven's sake if you're in the middle of a pantomime you want to stay with it'.

Reid had reason to be bitter, having accepted the Thatcherite terms and conditions which had now, he must have felt, been set aside. 'BR's job' he once said, 'is to provide a service that is profitable, not what is desirable'.

Palmer and Howarth seemed at times that they would choke on their words, such was their rage. Howarth, drawn with fury, blurted out that 'it will be seen as a victory for Arup, but the true test is if it is ever built.' He was especially bitter at the way the government had moved the goalposts: in 1988 there was great pressure for a route; in 1989 'the government wanted the private sector involved; in 1990 it was commuter benefits – and now it's urban regeneration'. At every stage 'we delivered the remit we were given', providing what the Secretary of State for Transport agreed was 'the best transport solution'.

The DoE's reaction was simple: 'we got what we wanted', says one insider. And why did Arup win? One anonymous answer was straightforward: 'salesmanship – and the fact that we got it right'. After the announcement 'Arup had a mere half-an-hour to take the project over', remembers Bostock. 'We couldn't do it. We didn't know what the next step was. I thought my heart would stop'. The only mistake he will admit to was taking over a bar at the conference and offering drinks to all comers. But already some people had seen the opportunities offered by the decision. That day Jenny Sandrock of Arup's Business Development Unit received 600 telephone calls and 150 faxes from interested parties, including residents' associations and some very abusive property owners, as well as estate agents – and steel welders offering to lay the tracks.

But they were to have a long wait – nearly seven years – to get any work on the project.

1 2 3 4 5 6 7 8 9 10 11 **12**

CHOICES AND CONSEQUENCES

It was the investment of money and effort by Arup in effective promotion of the scheme which unlocked the vital government support that had been absent before. Now, thanks to a small group of engineers who saw the best way ahead and pushed for it, the industry is engaged on a project which will be an enormous benefit to the nation as a whole.

New Civil Engineer, 7 March 1996

■ Rifkind told Parliament of his decision to adopt the Arup route on the following Monday. It resulted, he said, from allowing for 'all the relevant considerations, including regional planning, the environmental impact, and the effect on property as well as transport objectives'. But on the question of financing, Rifkind could go no further than he had the previous week. The decision set off a stately process lasting nearly seven years before construction actually began. For Arup, its triumph provided two wholly novel challenges: one immediate, the other longer-term. First it had to establish its own team within BR's Channel Tunnel Link team and its band of sceptical consultants, then it had to provide an unprecedented range of services in the actual construction of the route. Not surprisingly Bostock was worried by the challenge, asking himself 'have we got the capacity to do it?' They had.

But this is the story not just of a project, but of the opportunities it offers for the future, and the lessons to be learnt from its lengthy and convoluted progress. Arup's involvement was far greater than on any previous project, and demonstrated the extraordinary breadth of the services it could provide. Perhaps even more important in the long run, the CTRL had proved – to Arup itself and to the outside world – the firm's capacity to dream the impossible... and then to make the dream come to fruition against the odds. This gave Arup the extra assurance which has enabled it to initiate other, equally imaginative, projects – like the entire 'eco-city' it is currently planning for China. The CTRL triumph is today embedded in the firm's internal psyche. It was the step that made the difference, Arup people tell you – amongst whom are some who were still at school in 1991.

The story of Britain's first high-speed railway also demonstrated that a broader vision, a joined-up approach taking in the (often unquantifiable) economic, social and environmental aspects, is the only way to tackle the country's major infrastructure projects. The success of the CTRL seems set to have a considerable influence as the British government, not before time, reappraises the planning of schemes of national significance.

But, such is the timespan involved that we will not know for years, if not decades, after the whole route is in use what the full consequences of High Speed One will be. Already two accidental, totally unplanned gains have become apparent: the opportunity the route provided for London's Olympic bid, and the rebuilding of St Pancras into the world's finest station, while at the same time making a major contribution to the renewal of a formerly seedy corner of Central London. Both these gains were not only unforeseeable, they were also unquantifiable: yet further proof that an appraisal like that used by the British Treasury, based solely on financial and transport criteria, is totally inappropriate when dealing with a major project that involves so many and varied opportunities. And many benefits, of course, turn out to be profitable in financial terms as well – albeit often in the long term.

To take one aspect: the contribution made to North and East Kent by the far shorter journey times on the commuter service to Stratford, Ebbsfleet and Ashford will become apparent only years after that service is opened in 2009 (see chart page 158). It will take just as long for European passenger traffic beyond Paris and Brussels to develop to its full potential as new high-speed lines are opened in France, the Netherlands and Germany. By then, thanks to improvement in mobile phone, wi-fi and other services, passengers will increasingly be prepared to take the train, rather than fly, for longer than the three-hour limit now accepted as normal. Nearer to home, while the line will certainly act as a major impetus to regeneration not only in East London but in North Kent as well, the full results will not become clear for even longer.

The Victorian Gothic grandeur of St Pancras Station: in the 1960s it was narrowly saved from demolition; in the '90s it emerged as the ideal terminus for the fast line; in the new century it has been extended and restored to become 'the finest station in Europe'

To return to 1991 – and the immediate consequences of the government's decision to adopt the Arup route. Poor BR had to dispose of the hundreds of South-East London and Kent houses that it had bought at the very top of the property market in 1988 and 1989. When they came to sell, a mere couple of years later, the market was in depression: extrapolating from specific case histories, they lost at least a third of their 'investment'.[1] But the biggest trauma was for Gil Howarth and the hundreds of engineers he had assembled at the Rail Link Project's offices in Croydon, including a sizeable number from half a dozen major consulting engineers[2]. Arup was simply added to the

1 It was claimed in the January 1995 Parliamentary debate that the figure was £140 million.

2 The official history states that BR hired 40 consultants, 'among them Arup'. In fact there were six others.

team, with Hill as Arup's chief engineer. They were now all working for Union Railways, a separate, initially BR-owned, agency company which replaced the previous British Rail subsidiary in early 1992. John Palmer was suceeded as chairman by Dr John Prideaux, formerly the chairman of BR's InterCity business, with Gil Howarth as managing director.

The fast link decision marked a major shift in British public life: a new way to finance major infrastructure projects. The biggest innovation was the reliance on private capital through the 'transfer of risk' on projects where the private sector was deemed to be better than publicly-owned organisations. This involved the creation of what were called Private Finance Initiatives or Public/Private Partnerships. After the abolition of the old Ryrie rules,[3] which had prevented any commitment longer than a year, successive Chancellors of the Exchequer Norman Lamont and Kenneth Clarke could map out a new financial landscape for such projects. In December 1991 Samuel Montagu, then a leading independent merchant bank, was appointed together with the Bank of England and engineers WS Atkins to advise the government. By January 1994 John McGregor, who had replaced Rifkind as Secretary of State for Transport in early 1992, was able to announce that the fast link would be the 'flagship of the Private-Finance Initiative'.

The cut in international journey times and – equally important – the extra capacity for international trains, are the key justification for the investment. Most of the Arup route, as far as Ebbsfleet, is designed for TGV speeds of 300kph (186mph), and even the approaches to London are to be at 230kph (143mph)[4]; commuter trains will travel at 225kph (140mph). The trains will then take seven minutes for the remaining six miles (9.3km) into St Pancras. But the sheer magnitude of the leap in service for commuters – from the slow, uncomfortable, slam-door, essentially 1940s trains then still in use on the Kent lines, to the prospect of a truly modern service – is still sinking in. Journeys now too long, on routes far too congested, for a daily commute will from 2009 become practicable, and new hubs for development – Ebbsfleet, Stratford – will be served by them.

Merely eliminating Arup's four tracks over much of the route brought the cost down nearly to BR's estimates. John Prideaux's suggestion that the route from Stratford to St Pancras should not be in tunnel but on the surface was rejected, but his proposal that St Pancras should replace King's Cross as the terminal was welcomed. By January 1993 a final route had been established, the costs varying from £2–3 billion depending largely on the number and location of the stations, of which from £1.1–1.6 billion would come from the government.

Two months later John McGregor confirmed the route, and in January the following year the choice of St Pancras as the terminus. (This at last meant the renovation of its splendid Gothic buildings, which Sir John Betjeman had fought so hard to save from demolition in the 1960s.) The project would receive 'substantial public-sector support' – thanks to the inclusion of commuter services. In February 1994, as part of the CTRL concession, Union Railways' finances were reorganised and it was guided into the private sector under the leadership of its new chief executive, John Armitt. (Armitt was later to go on to become chief executive of Railtrack, then of Network Rail and, in 1997, chairman of the London Olympic Delivery Authority.)

Two major, and interlinked, questions remained: the pattern of commuter routes and the stations. Domestic passengers from the whole of east Kent would have first to get to Ashford before using the CTRL, thus reducing its benefits to some of southern England's most isolated corners. The Channel Tunnel Act had required only 'provision for a station' at Ashford; it did not demand that one be built. Political pressure now ensured that Ashford would have its station, serving both domestic and international traffic. By contrast Stratford still had to fight. In January 1994 McGregor announced that he wanted two stations between Ashford and St Pancras: a battle began between Ebbsfleet in North Kent, Rainham east of Dagenham, and Stratford. Rainham was abandoned when the idea of a proposed theme park on Rainham marshes failed to materialise. Even if Stratford won, there was only to be a 'short box' at the station which could not take the long international trains. The newly-formed Stratford Promoter Group battled away under the slogan 'Change at Stratford'. Nevertheless, the issue was still undecided when the Bill establishing the route went before Parliament in November 1994.[5]

Select Committees of both Houses of Parliament studied the bill, resulting in 320 hours of evidence in 70 – relatively relaxed and sympathetic – sittings. The biggest

Facing page: Building the elegant viaduct that takes the fast line over the Medway

3 The Ryrie Rules were in place from 1981, and can be said to be a key part of the Thatcherite approach. They stated that private money could only be used instead of public, not in addition to it. To be accepted by government, private proposals had to underbid the public alternative. The rules were relaxed in 1989, almost completely abandoned in 1992, and pressure on the Treasury from big contractors and banks helped to dislodge the last remnants in 1993.

4 The slower speed into London is constrained by the tighter radius of the route and by tunnel aerodynamics.

5 Stratford needed all the help it could get. Such was the run-down state of its town centre that the architect of the splendid new Jubilee tube station described it, after his first exploratory visit, as 'an abandoned city.'

'There are not, frankly, many Prime Ministers, or indeed many Ministers, that launch an infrastructure project or accepts its completion in front of the words on time and on budget'. Prime Minister Tony Blair opens CTRL Stage One in September 2003.

gainer from the process was Stratford, after the Select Committee had been taken to Holden Point, a tall block of flats near the station. The panorama from the top visibly demonstrated to the MPs just how close Stratford was to the City – as the picture on page 12, taken from the same point, graphically shows. The result was a recommendation by the Committee – accepted by the government – that would allow for both a domestic and an international station at Stratford in what became known as a 'long box'.

The parallel process, choosing the best group to build the CTRL, took from late 1993 to 29 February 1996. By April 1994 nine bidders had applied for what would be a design, build and operate contract, but their ranks had been been reduced to four[6] within a couple of months. Of the four, London & Continental Railways (LCR) was the only one which met the concept laid down by Colin Stannard in 1998–99, that it should not be led by a contractor.

LCR was put together by Arup's Mark Bostock and an unusual merchant banker, Nick Wakefield – a civil engineer by training who had been recruited in 1979 as a project financing specialist by SG Warburg. To provide vital experience in project management, Arup and Warburg immediately brought in Bechtel. London Electricity joined to supervise the complex electrical infrastructure. Revenue forecasts and commercial expertise came from National Express – a bus group that had flourished thanks to bus privatisation and which looked to its involvement with the CTRL to help it benefit from rail privatisation – and from Virgin, with its airline experience, which sold out its interest in 1998.

At the bidding stage SNCF/Systra, with their high speed railway expertise, were exclusive advisors to, and equity partners in, the LCR consortium. Halcrow, the specialist tunnelling engineers, were also invited to add their expertise in UK rail operations. Blue Circle initially became involved with the Consortium because of its enormous land holdings, amounting to 15,000 acres (6,000 hectares) in the form of

6 Eurorail, with BICC, HSBC, Natwest and Trafalgar House; Green Arrow, with Hochtief, Nishimatsu and Siemens; Union Link (with Lord Kingsdown, a Man of Kent and, as Robin Leigh-Pemberton a former Governor of the Bank of England as chairman, and Colin Stannard as managing director) with AEG, Holzmann, Mowlem and Taylor Woodrow; and finally London & Continental Railways.

disused chalk pits along the route in North Kent; they later decided to withdraw from the Consortium in order to concentrate on the associated property development opportunities.

In August 1994 the four finalists were asked to tender on three bases: no station at Stratford; a domestic station at Stratford; and both international and domestic stations at Stratford – in fact, seven separate bids were called for because the government had not yet made up its mind. By October Ebbsfleet, near Blue Circle's clay pits, had been chosen as the station site in North Kent; the following month Eurostar services began running into Waterloo on the improved Boat Train route chosen by BR in 1986.

Not surprisingly the French were amazed at the leisurely pace of the trains through Kent – the existence of at least one rural level crossing was a particular source of amusement – and were also struck by the fact that there was no evidence of a new line. What is more, the CTRL bill was delayed until the spring of 1997 because of parliamentary indigestion caused by the privatisation of Railtrack. Nevertheless the hope remained that the winning bidder, which would also enjoy the revenue from Eurostar, could be floated on the stock market in the course of 1997. The pressure was all the greater because the project accounted for over a third of the £5.6 billion total in the government's much-vaunted programme for Private Finance Initiatives.

LCR and the Trafalgar House-led Eurorail were chosen as finalists. On 29 February 1996 LCR was declared the winner: it had underbid Eurorail by approximately £400 million – partly because LCR's bid was based on more optimistic revenue forecasts, and partly because it had spotted in the fine print that, although the winner had to take on the useless, politically-driven Nightstar and provincial trains, they were not bound to run any services using them.

But within two years it had become clear that LCR's forecasts were as inaccurate as everyone else's, thus forcing a complete financial overhaul of the original bid. Luckily by then a Labour government had taken office and John Prescott was in charge of a super-ministry which included the Department of Transport. What a Tory tycoon had started, a Labour former trade unionist was to finish. When LCR had to ask for further government assistance Prescott, who had been transport spokesman in opposition during the dramas of 1988–91, was fully prepared. His solution was to get the government to guarantee LCR's debt, underwriting £3.7 billion of bond issues. This eliminated the need for expensive equity, and equally expensive and probably unfundable private debt, a combination that would claw back the £1.2 billion excess

1994

6 May

- Queen Elizabeth II and President François Mitterrand inaugurate the Channel Tunnel

2007

6 November

- High Speed 1 rail line is opened by Queen Elizabeth

THE FUTURE: COMMUTING TIMES FROM 2009

Times in minutes to London Terminus		
Station	**2007**	**2009**
Ebbsfleet	–	17
Gravesend	42	24
Medway towns	47	43
Sittingbourne	65	56
Ashford	83	37
Canterbury	102	61
Folkestone	98	63
Dover	112	74
Ramsgate	119	84
Margate	109	98

Above: from 2009 Kent commuting journeys will be markedly quicker, with wide implications for regeneration and growth

Facing page: the Right Line – HS1 as it now exists

which had arisen since the deal had been signed. Prescott managed to force the Treasury to agree because if the project had been aborted at this late stage the government would have been liable for very substantial sums in compensation.

POSTSCRIPT

The full story of the building of the two-stage rail link, the transformation at St Pancras and the wider achievements and implications for London, Kent, and Britain's future connections with the Continent – the turning of the dream into reality – would take another book. The project was divided into two stages. CTRL 1, the first 45 miles (72km) of a 68-mile (110km) route from the tunnel across Kent to Southfleet on the outskirts of London and then via existing routes to Waterloo, opened in 2003: thereby shaving twenty minutes off the journey from London to Paris. By 2006, with this new line eliminating many bottlenecks, over 90 per cent of the Eurostar trains were on time, and rail had taken over two-thirds of the London–Paris passenger traffic. In the 1998 settlement CTRL 2 (the far more expensive route from Southfleet to St Pancras, involving three new stations) had not been formally agreed, though it seems to have been assumed.

The nine years spent actually building the link were relatively uneventful. The principal roles were played through a partnership between Arup and Bechtel through Rail Link Engineering, which included Halcrow and Systra. Arup's considerable, but largely haphazard, growth over the years enabled it to supply most of the bewildering variety of services required. The whole programme, combined with the engineering excellence of its viaducts, tunnels and 'bunds', led the normally cynical SNCF to applaud CTRL1 as 'the best result ever achieved in Europe with the opening of a new high-speed line' – and to SNCF/French Ministry of Transport asking Arup, immediately after the route announcement, to advise on the planning of the TGV line through the Rhône valley.

The problems encountered on CTRL2 were far more complex, being mostly concerned with those involved in excavating sub-surface tunnels underneath the heart of one of the world's major capitals. Building a station at Stratford involved an enormous 'box' – a reinforced concrete structure a kilometre long, big enough to house three ships each the size of the Queen Mary 2. The close-packed approaches to St Pancras had to provide for Eurostar services; the commuter trains to run from 2009 on the new link; Thameslink services between Brighton and Bedford; Midland main line to Leicester, Nottingham and Sheffield; also links to the West Coast Main Line from Euston to the

THE RIGHT LINE – HIGH SPEED 1

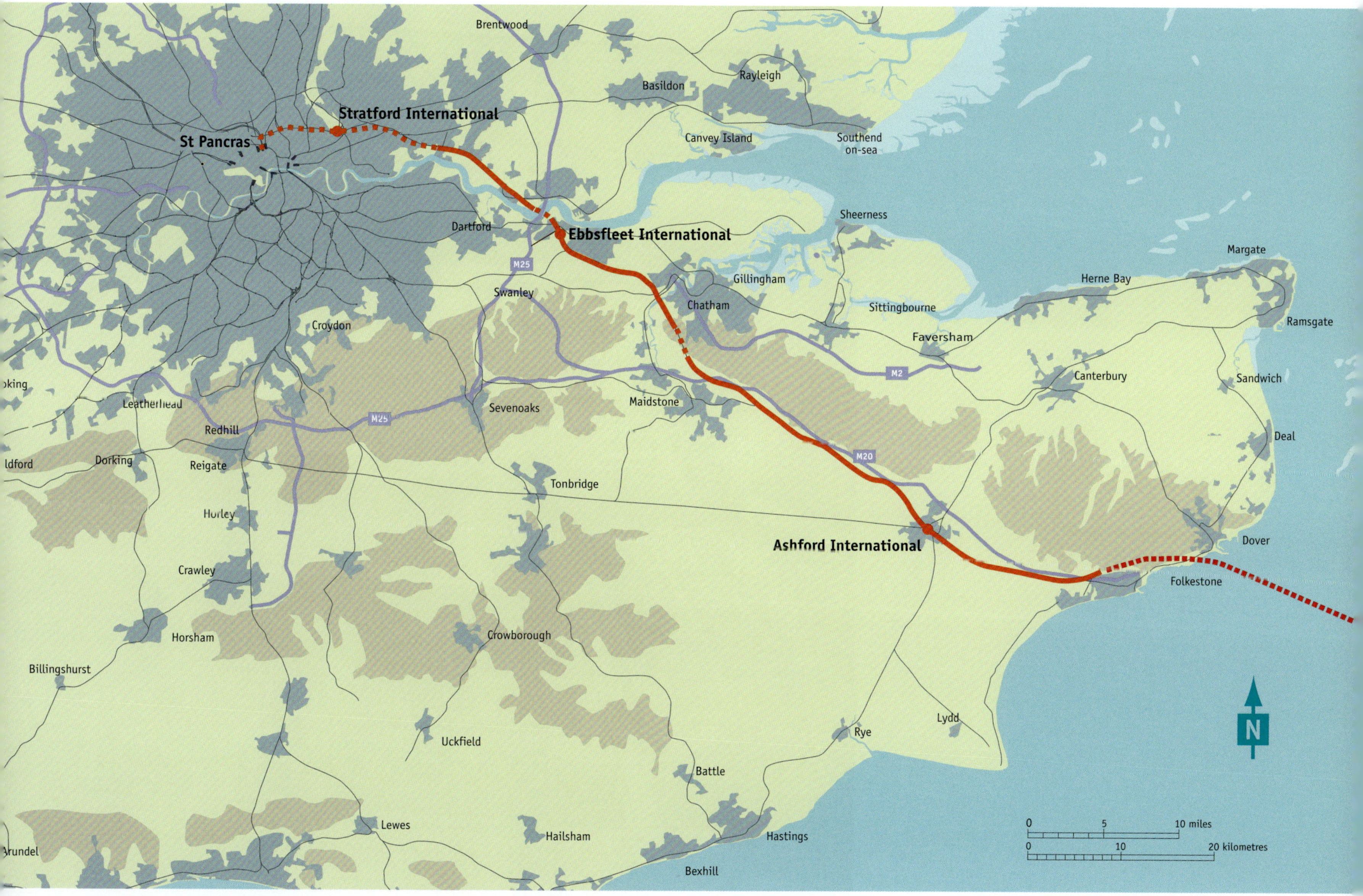

On the Right Line: the giant Stratford International station under construction in 2007. It lies at the centre of the vast area of reclaimed land being developed for the London 2012 Olympics. The River Lea, in the foreground, forms the spine of a regeneration zone which runs from the Thames up into North-East London.

north, and to the East Coast Main Line. All those as well as six Underground lines.

But these fiendish, three-dimensional-chess problems would only be apparent to the general public if they failed to work. The most outwardly obvious triumph of the project is the restoration of both halves of St Pancras: the famous Gothic hotel and the less famous, but equally magnificent, train shed which, when it was built in the 1860s, was the largest unsupported span in the world. Sir Gilbert Scott's magnificent hotel has been divided in two, with luxurious lofts atop the restored, sympathetically extended hotel. In Barlow's great 'train shed', the glazed area was restored to its original size. Although the architects Fosters provided a master plan, the actual design work was entrusted to a team, largely from Arup, headed by Alistair Lansley. Lansley had proved his abilities in the design and re-creation of stations at Ashford and, more triumphantly, at Liverpool Street. Exploiting the extraordinary strength of the Victorian building, his team, which included Mike Glover and Ian Gardner, both from Arup, has managed to open up for use the huge 'undercroft' beneath the platforms, built to store beer barrels brought by the Midland Railway from Burton-on-Trent. The overall result is the most splendid station in Europe.

Beyond the station, a new district, reclaimed from the dereliction of railway sidings and sheds, is emerging; King's Cross/St Pancras is – thanks in great part to the CTRL – a reborn quarter of London. Stratford, centred on its international station, is to be the hub of the 2012 Olympics, and then a site for new homes and a business and commercial district on a scale to rival Canary Wharf. Radiating out from Stratford and the Olympic sites are the tracts of long-blighted industrial dereliction of the lower Lea Valley, now the focus of a truly ambitious development scheme at the start of the Thames Gateway zone. Down-river, over in the abandoned chalk-pits of North Kent, Ebbsfleet station has sparked another development zone: 500 acres (200 hectares) of reclaimed land, the site for 3,000 homes, an enormous office complex – and car parking for Eurostar passengers close to the M25.

These are just the first, and quantifiable, benefits of the construction of the line on the route Arup identified back in 1989–90. Yet to come into focus are the scope of regional rail links to the Channel Tunnel, the pattern of European fast rail of which High Speed One is a part and the improvement to personal lives and business opportunities in Kent and East London triggered by the new commuter services.

Whatever happens, for reasons some of which we cannot yet imagine, I am sure that, within a decade, the CTRL will be taken for granted as a major contribution to British life, its absence as unthinkable as was its creation back in 1986.

MAPS

PICTURE CREDITS

Arup image library: 85 (Ove Arup), 87, 90, 98, 99. 101 (Ove Arup), 103, 127, 145, 156
Getty Images: 10, 21, 26 (Hulton Archive), 35, 122, 144, 153
James Harris: 12
Jason Hawkes Aerial Photo Library: 109, 147, 160
London Property Guide archive: 60, 119, 77, 142
Milepost 921/2: 19, 20, 40, 57, 72
PA Photos: 28, 32, 36, 66, 116, 130, 132, 141, 154
Science & Society Picture Library: 16 (Science Museum Pictorial), 17 (NRM–Pictorial Collection)
Caroline Simpson: 64, 77
Topham Picturepoint: 69, 80, 110, 132

INDEX